Adolescent Development
and Rapid Social Change

Adolescent Development and Rapid Social Change

Perspectives from Eastern Europe

Judith L. Van Hoorn,
Ákos Komlósi,
Elzbieta Suchar,
and Doreen A. Samelson

State University of New York Press

Published by
State University of New York Press, Albany

© 2000 State University of New York

For information, address State University of New York Press
State University Plaza, Albany, N.Y. 12246

Production by Diane Ganeles
Marketing by Patrick Durocher

Library of Congress Cataloging-in-Publication Data

Adolescent development and rapid social change : perspectives from
    Eastern Europe / Judith L. Van Hoorn . . . [et al.].
        p.   cm.
    Includes bibliographical references and index.
    ISBN 0-7914-4473-2 (hc. : alk. paper). — ISBN 0-7914-4474-0 (pbk.
  : alk. paper)
    1. Teenagers—Hungary. 2. Youth—Hungary—Social conditions.
  3. Hungary—Politics and government—1989– 4. Teenagers—Poland.
  5. Youth—Poland—Social conditions. 6. Poland—Politics and
  government—1989– 7. Political socialization—Europe, Eastern.
  8. Adolescent psychology—Europe, Eastern. 9. Social change—Europe,
  Eastern. I. Van Hoorn, Judith Lieberman.
  HQ799.H8A35   2000
  305.235′09439—dc21   99-39700
                                                             CIP

*To the students we interviewed
and their peers,
the omega-alpha generation*

Contents

Contents

Acknowledgments

We gratefully acknowledge our colleagues in Hungary, Poland, and the U.S. for their assistance, their critical ideas, and for the inspiration their own work provided. Many colleagues and friends graciously offered their expertise for many of the ten years we have collaborated on this project, offering their insights as to our findings, discussing their own work, and critically reviewing the manuscript.

We thank Sándor Komlósi for his wise counsel from the initial planning stage to the conclusion of this project. We gratefully acknowledge Dr. Iván Falus, Dr. Ibolya Vári-Szilágyi, Dr. Janus Reykowski, Dr. Anikó Bognár, Tünde Tamás, Phyllis La Farge, Dr. Sofia Słońska, Eve Lieberman, Dr. George Blum, Dr. James Derleth, Eric Oliver, Dr. Deidre McCloskey, and Dr. Barbara West. Their contributions have greatly enriched our work.

We received much help with the translation of needed materials. We thank Dr. Lázsló Imre Komlósi, Andrea Béres, Tünde Tamás, Susan Ralls, and Márk Sárváry for their tireless assistance. We thank Dr. Harvey Williams, Dr. István Horváth, Dr. Sándor Komlósi, Teréz Markó, Dr. Rachelle Hackett, and Peter Ács for contributing their expertise to our design and to analyses of the considerable data.

These interviews would not have been possible without ongoing cooperation from educators at the schools the students attended. In Budapest we thank Dr. Anikó Bognár, director of the Dual Language Section, Tünde Tamás, school librarian, and Sándor Hartai, school director at the Karinthy Gimnázium. In Pécs, we thank Dr. József Litkei, director of the Babits Mihály Gimnázium es Szakközépiskola, Jánosné Szolcsányi, director of the Leowey Klára Gimnázium, József Póla, director of the Nagy Lajos Gimnázium, Edit Rónaki, director of the Muvészeti Szakközépiskola, and Dr. Janos Hervert, director of the 500-as Szakmunkásképozo.

Special thanks to Piroska Komlósi for providing a decade of warm hospitality to our international group, to Susan Heath for her inspiring editorial support, and to Dr. John Livesey for his unflagging technical assistance.

We undertook this project nearly a decade ago and have received constant support and encouragement from the staff at State University of New York Press. We thank our editor Priscilla Ross and editorial assistant, Jennie Doling. We thank Diane Ganeles for guiding us through the production process with her patience. We thank Patrick Durocher for his marketing expertise. We publicly thank our anonymous reviewers for their comments and suggestions.

Adolescents at Historical Crossroads

CHAPTER ONE

The Omega-Alpha Generation

Studying Adolescent Development during Times of Rapid Social Change

Hungarian Election Set for March 25

The Washington Post, December 23, 1989

Hungary Seeks Withdrawal of Soviet Forces In Two Years

The New York Times, January 19, 1990

Walesa Takes Wide Lead in Presidential Voting

The New York Times, November 26, 1990

Polish Voters Buy Free Market Ideas

The Los Angeles Times, November 29, 1990

During the late 1980s and early 1990s great social, political, and economic changes occurred in central and eastern Europe. From a western perspective, as these headlines show, assumptions were made about the rapid pace and bright outcomes of these transitions. Eastern Europe seemed to be changing overnight. While the West was applauding, within these changing societies there was concern about the complex nature and unknown outcomes of these transitions.

In the years since the world watched countries such as Hungary and Poland undergo these changes, the preponderance of scholarly and popular writing on central and eastern Europe has focused on political and economic dimensions. Little has been written addressing the psychological consequences, particularly the consequences for young people coming of age during a time of such uncertainty. Yet these young people will be the next generation of adults who will continue to shape the outcomes for their countries.

The rapid social transitions that occurred in central and eastern European countries such as Poland and Hungary can provide a crucible for understanding the links between life and times. Adolescence may be a fruitful period to consider when exploring these links, a time when the influence of the environment on the integrated processes of cognitive, social, and emotional development is particularly apparent. It is often a time when young people develop dispositions to participate actively, or dispositions to withdraw from social and political engagement in their communities and nation (e.g., Jennings & Niemi 1981).

In times of dramatic social changes, it is particularly true that the adolescents are the last children of the old system and the first adults of the new. The Hungarian and Polish young people in this study can be considered the omega-alpha generation of these transitions. By listening to the voices of youth during transitions we can better understand their reactions to their changing societies, their engagement or apathy, their hopes, fears, and plans for the future.

Insight into young people's development is critical not only for understanding their present reactions, but for future understandings of this next generation of adults. Democracies are characterized by their involved citizenry. Whether or not the youth of Hungary and Poland will develop the values, knowledge, and abilities associated with democratic traditions—"democracy in the soul" (Csepeli 1993, p. 7)—has serious implications for the vitality of democracy and the future of their countries.

The study of adolescent development during periods of rapid social change can contribute to our theoretical understanding of general aspects of development as well as aspects related to development in specific places and times, in this case Hungary and Poland in the 1990s. Kéri (1993), a Hungarian political scientist, has pointed to the need to carry out "a vast number of case studies and descriptions of political sociography . . ." in order to understand young people's development of citizenship in all contexts ". . . where practicing and learning democracy go on every single day, and where the transformation of the dimension of participation continues as a matter of daily routine—though it may not even be called even politics or democracy . . ." (p. 35).

In addition to the interest research such as this has for developmental psychologists, political scientists, and sociologists, the results also have implications for practitioners who work with children, adolescents, and their families. For example, data regarding adolescents' knowledge, interests, and activities related to politics, the economy, and varied social structures can help inform educators facing the challenge of developing new curricula and teaching methodologies congruent with the goals of democratic citizenship so that students will develop the new competencies they need now as adolescents or, later, as adults. Similarly, studies carried out during rapid social changes provide information useful to mental health professionals trying to help students and their families cope with additional stressors.

The research presented in this book is among relatively few studies planned with the explicit purpose of examining the relationships between individuals' development, and the changing historical time and national context in which development occurs. Other psychologists and historians have noted the dearth of research that considers the social and historical contexts of development, particularly studies designed to examine development within the context of specific societal changes. In *Children in Time and Place*, Elder, Modell, and Parke (1993) point out that "the study of children in historical time and place identifies an important and neglected perspective in the ecology of human development" (p.vii). They emphasize that "(h)istorical and life transitions . . . represent strategic opportunities for understanding the link between lives and times" (p. 4). The intent of this book is to examine this "link between lives and times."

Part 1: Emergent Research

In 1990 and 1991 Komlósi, Suchar, and Van Hoorn, psychologists from Hungary, Poland, and the United States, discussed the practical and theoretical importance of studies that would examine the development of youth within the rapidly changing conditions in Hungary and Poland. From these initial meetings and subsequent conversations came the decision to conduct collaborative research on adolescents' sociopolitical identity development, i.e., their developing knowledge of and reactions to their country's changing social, political, and economic systems.

When discussing the possibility of collaborative research, we found that we shared a common theoretical perspective of psychological identity development as a holistic, systemic process that includes the changing environment. The challenge was to find a way to examine rapid individual development during a time of rapid social change. We attempted to develop a research design congruent with the fluidity and complexities of the processes of adolescent development and the fluid nature of the historical changes. After considering various models, we planned an exploratory, descriptive interview study. Our research took an ecological perspective of adolescents' views of what was happening in their country, communities, their homes, and their own lives.

In planning the research, we wished to examine how adolescents develop understandings of complex political constructs such as democracy and freedom, and how their understandings relate to their life experiences. Adolescents are typically involved in their own lives and not very politically active (e.g., Sigel & Hoskin 1981); yet at various historical junctures, youth have been leaders in demonstrations, revolutions, and wars. We wanted to find out what role, if any, they would play during the historical transitions occurring in Poland and Hungary. We also wondered whether social changes would result in life cycle changes, such as the age at which youth begin to work, their choices of occupations, time spent with peers vs. family, or their involvement in their communities.

Between 1991 and 1995, we conducted the three related interview studies described in this book. In the 222 interviews, we heard the voices of young people talking about growing up in changing times. As we shall describe, frequently we had a sense of déjà vu when students living miles apart and interviewed in different years responded in such similar ways.

> You become more of a person if you go through things that are really hard to deal with. It strengthens your personality. I think that many teenagers like me will be leaders. We are more optimistic people.
>
>   17-year-old student from Budapest, Hungary, 1991

> No one in our family has taken any part in politics, not even among my relatives. We are not interested in this . . . Life is important for us, we don't deal with politics . . . The changes have been basically bad for the people because they have no jobs. They have become poor . . . Ordinary people now do all they can at work just not to be dismissed. Everyone fears for his or her job. Due to inflation, everything is more and more expensive while wages do not change . . .
>
> The changes have no effects on my family. We notice inflation a bit. My parents are slightly more nervous now but there are no quarrels about money. Perhaps I get a bit less money from them. That's all. But we have as much as we need. Unemployment doesn't touch us, I am not interested . . . The changes have had no effects on my development.
>
> 17-year-old student from Pécs, Hungary, 1994

> The politicians were dogmatic. The policy of the government led to making the economic and social situation bad. The changes had to come. There was no alternative for them . . . We have democracy now . . . freedom of choice . . . of speech. The politicians are quarreling but, probably, it is the way of doing politics in a democratic country.
>
> The changes in Poland are very important for my generation. Although the political and economic situation is presently complicated, I believe it will improve. Maybe in five years . . .
>
> I am quite optimistic about the future if I finish my studies. I want to study economics. If I succeed, I perceive my future in bright colors.
>
> 17-year-old student from Gdańsk, Poland, 1992

That our research was planned and carried out during the transitions in Hungary and Poland was both a strength and a liability. Just as the topic of the study is that of adolescent development and rapid social change, so this research process, itself, has been an example of the challenge of conducting research during times of rapid social change. The study was designed in 1990 during the period of greatest upheaval in both countries, a virtual societal earthquake, and was carried out over an ensuing five year period of continual, though less dramatic change. Looking back, we view it as emergent research in which the design changed in response to the changing situation, the preliminary findings, and the lives of the researchers. Therefore, instead of a brief reference to the changes in the research design as well as in the lives of the researchers, we include more complete and personal descriptions of the studies.

Background of the Study

This research extends prior studies that have examined adolescents' reactions to social conditions. The general theoretical orientation of the study is based upon work that Van Hoorn conducted with Paula LeVeck and Perrin French on the effects of the nuclear threat on youth from 1983 through 1989 (e.g., French & Van Hoorn 1986; Van Hoorn & French 1988; Van Hoorn & LeVeck 1990; Van Hoorn, LeVeck, & French 1989). They found that little is known about how the political perspectives of ordinary people are influenced by their social contexts. Their research focused on the relationships between young adults' constructions of knowledge about the changing international political situation and the social environment of their everyday lives.

They first carried out a large survey study in 1983 in northern California. Follow-up, in-depth interview studies of a small sample of the 1983 participants were conducted in 1985 and 1988. The interviews focused on relationships between participants' understanding of the changing international political situation and their immediate, day-to-day lives.

Van Hoorn, LeVeck, and French (1989) found that when asked to discuss important world changes, young adults focused on issues at the macrosocial level that related to the aspects of their own lives that were of greatest personal affective and cognitive importance. For example, one young mother discussed state child care legislation; one Hispanic young man discussed the racial crises in South Africa (Van Hoorn & LeVeck 1990).

The present study employs the same psychosocial and ecological orientation and a similar design, with complementary use of qualitative and quantitative methodologies; a semistructured interview protocol was used, which included some of the items designed by Van Hoorn, LeVeck, and French. (See Appendix A.)

During the early 1980s, Eric Chivian, Jonathan Tudge, and John Robinson developed a survey instrument to examine adolescents' concerns about nuclear war and the future. The survey was used in a large cross-national survey study of adolescents in the U.S. and, with Soviet colleagues Nikolai Popov and Vladimir Andreyenkov, in the U.S.S.R. (1988). They reported, for example, that the Russian adolescents indicated considerably more optimism about the future than did their American peers. They also found that Russian adolescents' hopes and fears related more to social issues, compared with American adolescents' hopes and fears, which tended to be more personal in nature.

During the 1980s, researchers in several other countries also used this instrument to conduct large-scale surveys. In 1986, Susan Hollán, a Hungarian hematologist and public health physician, surveyed more than 1000 students from a representative sample of Hungarian secondary schools. Robinson and Van Hoorn assisted with the analysis of the data. In the spring of 1989, Van Hoorn traveled to Budapest to work on further interpretations of the data.

One of the Hungarians whom she met in Budapest was Tamás Simon, a professor of medicine. His immediate response to the findings was that it was imperative that a follow-up study be undertaken. He emphasized that the pace of social change, which had been increasing since the early 1980s, was proceeding at an unprecedented rate. Simon volunteered to conduct a replication of Hollan's 1986 survey, and this second national survey was completed in the fall of 1989.

The results of this follow-up study indicated that students were becoming more worried about their own health, suggesting changes in the stressors in their lives (Simon, Van Hoorn, Chivian, & Hollan 1990). In order to understand more fully the results of the second survey, Simon and Van Hoorn then interviewed a small sample of adolescents, with Simon conducting the interviews and serving as translator. These few interviews focused on the students' perceptions of and reactions to the rapid changes occurring in spring 1990. They clearly demonstrated students' interest in discussing these topics and indicated the particular insights that an interview study might provide. Some of the items in the present study are drawn from the 1990 survey questionnaire, and some questions from the informal interviews are also included. (See Appendix A.)

Research Challenges

Studying adolescent development during times of rapid social change posed numerous challenges to the development of a research design. Some problems relate to the nature of the changes themselves. First, little is known of the psychology of historical transitions, i.e., how people react to rapidly changing social conditions. Second, in 1990 there was considerable speculation about the outcomes of the rapid changes occurring in eastern Europe, but the outcomes were, of course, unknowable. Third, adults' contemporary perceptions about the transitions—their causes and effects—might differ from future historical accounts. Finally, adolescents' perceptions of and reactions to periods of transition might differ in significant ways from those of adults. Therefore, as researchers of one generation studying another, we were aware that we had an adult perspective on the important questions to ask. This perspective was based not only on our age but on our training, our personal views of the changes, and our speculations about the outcomes the changes would bring.

Many writers have discussed the necessity that all researchers become aware of the biases that result from their training and personal histories (e.g., Jansen & Peshkin 1992; Patton 1990). When conducting the interviews, analyzing the data, and discussing the results, Suchar and Komlósi observed that they, like all researchers in Poland and Hungary, faced their own personal responses as individuals "growing up in changing times," responses that affected their perspectives and insights. This realization was less obvious to Van Hoorn and Samelson who came from the U.S., a society that during the time of this research was changing more slowly. This multinational collaboration demonstrates the benefits of research on individual development and social transitions that includes researchers who provide the native (emic) perspective as well as others who provide the outsider (etic) perspective. Additional perspectives were provided as Komlósi and Suchar examined the similarities and differences in the Hungarian and Polish situations.

Our greatest challenge, however, was to develop a design that would examine development in changing social contexts. As we have emphasized, there has been little work in developmental psychology on the relationships between changing national, historical contexts and individuals' development. Some of the most extensive research has focused on development during particular historical times; however, most of this work has been retrospective so that researchers' questions were informed by a historical perspective. Other research has focused on current social problems, e.g., studies of adolescents' reactions to the threat of nuclear war, drug use, or HIV, but few of these studies consider historical processes.

We found no research design that addressed the features of the transitions we found most salient: the fluidity of the social contexts, the unknown outcome, the interplay of all processes of adolescents' development, and the activities of the adolescents within their social contexts. Simplifying the design by considering the social environment as static or by focusing on one domain of development such as cognition or affect would have avoided the crux of the problem.

A design that fostered a multidimensional perspective was critical. We viewed the encompassing perspective as the total global system in which these adolescents were developing. Therefore, the sociopolitical and economic changes that were occurring in Poland and Hungary were viewed as part of global systemic changes.

The metaphor of a split screen television image helps capture the multiple, dynamic processes of change we sought to capture (see Figure 1.1). The large screen shows the dynamic, global ecological system. Upon this full screen one can highlight particular aspects of the human social ecology; e.g., cultural, political, religious, and economic dimensions.

With the global view continually remaining on the screen, one can cut away to a more detailed picture of central and eastern Europe, including Poland and Hungary. One can then focus more specifically on a particular nation—e.g., Hungary, a particular city such as Budapest, a particular neighborhood and school, and, finally, a particular adolescent.

One can observe this adolescent as she interacts in her environment, in particular settings, her classroom, her family, her city. While viewing this close-up of the student participating in interactions within her environment, one can observe her simultaneously within the moving view of the Hungarian, European, and global environment.

Designing the Research

The designs of the initial and subsequent studies regarding sample size and composition were informed by both qualitative and

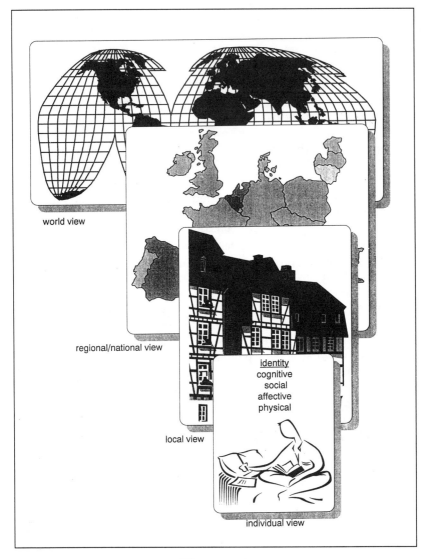

world view

regional/national view

local view

identity
cognitive
social
affective
physical

individual view

Figure 1.1
Viewing Adolescents in Their Environmental Contexts

quantitative research methods. Both approaches emphasize the importance of the trustworthiness of the data and the inferences that are drawn. Quantitative researchers are more likely to refer to the trustworthiness of data as validity. Creswell (1998), has suggested that terms other than validity be used in qualitative research to avoid qualitative versus quantitative debates. A number of alternative terms have been suggested including authenticity and trustworthiness (Le Compte 1992). In the discussions that follow, we use the term "trustworthiness."

In general, to achieve results that are trustworthy, quantitative researchers study relatively few variables across numerous cases whereas qualitative researchers examine numerous, often interrelated variables across relatively few cases (Creswell 1998). In interview studies employing qualitative methods, the emphasis is usually on conducting interviews until the researcher is satisfied that the latest interviews yield no new understandings, i.e., completion is achieved (Rubin & Rubin 1995). The present research design also used additional locales to examine similarities and differences among those interviewed.

The descriptive interview design that we developed allowed us to explore in considerable depth adolescents' perceptions of and responses to multiple social contexts over time. To avoid anticipating students' views or predicting the future course of the transitions, we intended the research to be exploratory in nature rather than hypothesis testing.

The qualitative methods we selected were well suited to these purposes. Creswell (1998) noted that qualitative approaches are "based on distinct methodological traditions of inquiry that explore a social or human problem" (p. 15). Patton (1990) emphasized that qualitative methods are "particularly oriented toward exploration, discovery, and inductive logic" (p. 44). He also noted that data from a relatively small sample of such interviews can contribute "depth, detail, and meaning at a very personal level" (p. 18) and that "greater attention can be given to nuance, settings, interdependence, complexities, idiosyncrasies, and context." (p. 51). It was within this methodological orientation that we designed, conducted, and analyzed our research.

We chose to use a semistructured process to interview the students in Poland and Hungary. Semistructured interviews are well suited to the qualitative method because of the breadth and depth of data they provide. This allows researchers to make sense of participants' experiences and cognitive-emotional processes. Lengthy interviews with open-ended questions and follow-up probes are useful when one's purpose is to understand how particular people comprehend the world in which they live and when the issues to be explored are novel, changing, and complex (e.g., Dekker & Meyenberg 1991; Haste & Torney-Purta 1992; Rubin & Rubin 1995).

In the summer and fall of 1990, Komlósi and Van Hoorn agreed on the design of the research. They completed the semistructured interview protocol and jointly conducted several pilot interviews.

Portraits

Our aim was to construct "portraits" of how particular groups of adolescents, living in a specific time and place, understood and responded to the changes occurring in that context. To achieve this aim, we decided to define a sample sufficiently complete to assure that we understood students' understandings of and responses to social transitions (Patton 1990; Rubin & Rubin 1995). It was not our intent to interview representative national or even citywide samples. Instead, we planned to discuss these portraits of adolescents from different nations, cities, and schools, both females and males, and their understanding of specific social contexts.

Consistent with our focus on adolescent development, we decided that the 1991–92 participants should be old enough so that they would have been young adolescents when the social changes became very rapid in 1987–1989. Accordingly, the 1991–92 interviewees were about sixteen, attending the second or third year of secondary school.

Gender was also an important consideration. Typically, more girls attend academic secondary schools and more boys, vocational schools. The relative proportions of girls and boys in vocational schools also differs with the vocational emphasis; e.g., fine arts vs. leather working. It was important to make sure that sufficient numbers of girls and boys from each type of school were interviewed so that appropriate qualitative and statistical analyses could be carried out.

The cities of Pécs, Gdańsk, and Budapest provided significant similarities and contrasts. Adolescents in Pécs, Hungary live in a medium-sized city, neither a national capital nor a village. Pécs is a provincial capital, known for its mixed economy based on mining, agriculture, and artisan industries. It is also a university city, with one of the oldest universities in Europe. In contrast, the adolescents in Budapest, the second site in Hungary, lived in a very different environment. Budapest is the national capital and home to twenty percent of Hungary's inhabitants. It is the center of commerce, industry, and most national institutions, and is definitely the vortex of political activity. Gdańsk, Poland provided a cross-national contrast to the two Hungarian sites. It is also similar to Pécs in that it, too, is a regional center with a major industrial base, its shipyards, the place where Solidarity began. Like Pécs and Budapest, Gdańsk is a city of historic importance. It has been a center of trade on the Baltic Sea since Hanseatic times and, as such, is an important center of science and the arts as well as commerce.

An Overview of the Three Studies

The following is an overview of the development of the three related studies that comprise this research project. The development of each study, the sample, and the time frame are described in much greater detail in the chapters that focus on Pécs, Budapest, and Gdańsk. To avoid confusion on the part of readers, throughout the book, we use the Americanized version of Hungarian names, with the family name last rather then first.

The Initial Studies: 1991–1992

The Pécs study. In order to gather responses from students with varying backgrounds and differing vocational aspirations, samples of students attending vocational, technical, and academic schools were included. Administrators in each of the participating schools were asked to select a sample of "typical" students that included both boys and girls. In the spring and fall of 1991, Komlósi and one of his research assistants completed interviews with a total of sixty-four secondary school students.

The Budapest study. As part of the review of the interview protocol and process, Van Hoorn began what was originally meant to be a brief pilot study with several students at the dual Hungarian-English language school in Budapest, an opportunity arranged by Simon. The director of the program, Dr. Anikó Bognár, was enthusiastic about the research and provided the opportunity for Van Hoorn to interview a greater number of students. Komlósi and Van Hoorn soon recognized that the interviews with the students at this special school in Budapest provided particularly useful data about the type and extent of variation in Hungarian adolescents' understandings and responses to the transitions. They therefore decided to expand the study. Van Hoorn conducted thirty interviews with students at the school during the winter of 1991, just as the study in Pécs was begun.

The Gdańsk study.   Suchar, a clinical psychologist at the University of Gdańsk, Poland, decided to join the project after hearing about the research at a conference in 1991. As a clinical psychologist, she was particularly interested in participating in a study involving in-depth interviews. In 1992 she conducted interviews with thirty-two students from a typical academic high school in Gdańsk.

The Moscow study.   In 1992, a fourth researcher, a social psychologist at Moscow State University, joined the research group and began a study of 250 students in Moscow. The economic changes in his country greatly affected his life. The following year he emigrated and did not continue the study.

Subsequent Studies

When we began the research, we planned one set of interviews for each site. A total of 126 participants were interviewed during 1991–92: thirty in Budapest, sixty-four in Pécs, and thirty-two in Gdańsk. During the period of most rapid change, from 1989 to 1991, most adults thought that political, economic, and social conditions would quickly stabilize. Particularly during the initial changes, there was widespread optimism that the transition to a more western-style democracy, and a healthy and wealthier market economy would be completed within a few years. However, as we analyzed and discussed the research findings in 1992 and 1993, it was becoming evident that the story wasn't over—that this would be a longer social, political, and economic transition than had been anticipated. We became curious about how Hungarian and Polish adolescents viewed their societies and their lives during this extended period, and we designed a series of follow-up studies. Thus, three complementary follow-up studies were conducted, with a total of 222 interviews conducted between 1991 and 1995.

The Pécs follow-up study. Komlósi conducted a follow-up study in Pécs in 1994. He first planned to find the students who participated in the initial interviews. It proved difficult to find the original sixty-four students, due in part to the historical transitions but due also to typical developmental changes such as moving away from home to find a job. He therefore decided to conduct the follow-up study with a sample that was generally comparable in terms of type of school, sex, and age (15–18 years old) to the sample interviewed at the time of the original study. Additional challenges had arisen due to changes in the educational system. Several public schools had become private; several vocational schools were combined with academic schools. These differences are explained later in more detail and implications discussed.

The Budapest follow-up studies. The Budapest data provided the opportunity to examine the views of adolescents living in the same country but in a different geographical area. As we discuss further in the section on Budapest, these students attended a specialized academic school and were atypical of the broad secondary student population, yet their views were often unexpectedly similar to those of the students in Pécs. The Budapest study also provided an opportunity to follow the same students over time. Van Hoorn conducted a second set of interviews in 1993 and supervised a third set of interviews in 1995.

The Gdańsk follow-up study. In 1992, Suchar interviewed thirty-two students in an academic secondary school. Her original intention was to interview at least thirty students in 1993 and 1994, thus providing the opportunity to make comparisons between years. Due to the transitions in Poland, Suchar's own life was also changing. In addition to her work at the university, she began in 1993 to work in a private enterprise she and her husband founded. This influenced the design of the follow-up Polish study. Suchar decreased the number of interviews as her other responsibilities grew. She interviewed sixteen students in 1993 and eleven students in 1994, all of the students attending the same academic secondary school as the 1992 interviews.

Part 2: Adolescents, Politics, and Everyday Life: Sociopolitical Identity Development

Our research provided an opportunity to examine the complementary processes by which particular social contexts influence adolescents' development as well as how adolescents influence their social contexts. We sought to understand these adolescents' views of their changing society and their reactions to these changes.

In this book, we consider sociopolitical development as the development of interest, knowledge, and activity related to the interrelated social, political, and economic spheres of society. This is consistent with the view that in participatory democracies "politics includes all social life and thus is not limited to formal government. . . . (Politics takes) place wherever conflicts happen, decisions are made, and power is involved" (Dekker 1997, p. 389.) Therefore, the study of adolescents' sociopolitical development includes many facets: their interests, knowledge, and social participation in local as well as national groups; their economic participation in everyday life; their preparation for future careers; their current political involvement, i.e., interests, knowledge, and activity; and their ideas about adult participation.

We view social and cognitive development as inseparable from emotional development. Adolescence is a time when emotions associated with ideas and ideals can be powerful. For example, adolescents frequently have strong feelings about a just government, about citizens' rights and governmental responsibilities, as the brief quotations cited earlier clearly illustrate.

Adolescence is also a particularly important time for sociopolitical identity development due to the interconnected social and cognitive development that occurs. During adolescence, young peoples' social radius widens. They become more competent in participating in diverse social groups beyond their families, particularly groups involving peers, schoolmates, teachers, and others in their communities. Experience and development are interrelated. Developing cognitive abilities leads to greater social competence as adolescents participate in diverse groups; conversely, social participation leads to the further development of social cognition.

Social cognition refers to one's understanding of the larger social structure. Adolescence is a time when young people become able to construct more abstract ideas about the structure of their society and how it functions. Social cognition refers to their understanding of the complex relationships involving themselves, their community, their country, and the world.

This area of research falls within the rubric of research on political socialization. Work in this field is carried out by psychologists, political scientists, and sociologists. As Dawson, Prewitt, & Dawson (1977) and Dekker (1991) point out, researchers from different academic areas typically ask different questions and approach these questions in different ways. Psychologists usually focus upon processes at the individual level, examining how individuals develop particular political orientations. Political scientists and sociologists usually focus on the macrosocial level, analyzing the ways in which social systems function to enculturate citizens to particular belief systems. Early on, however, these two seemingly distinct approaches were blurred as interdisciplinary fields such as political psychology emerged about 1960 and work by interdisciplinary teams proliferated. Indeed, in 1969 Langton pointed out that this distinction was artificial and, in *Children in the Political System*, also published in 1969, political scientists David Easton and Jack Dennis wrote pointedly that their definition of political socialization as a "developmental process through which orientations and patterns of behaviors are acquired" (p. 9) intentionally omitted presumptions as to whether children learn political orientations from others or develop them autonomously.

Today, both within and across disciplines, there is growing acknowledgment that individuals construct their understanding of the social world, including the political world, within their social context. Although theoretical differences still exist, most psychologists, political scientists, and sociologists working in this field share the basic orientation that meaning is constructed within a social context. This is certainly true of the Hungarian and Polish researchers—such as Boski, Csepeli, Erõs, Farkas, Fratczak-Rudnicka,

Kéri, Pataki, Reykowski, Skarzyńska, Stumph, Szabó, Vári-Szilágyi, and others cited throughout this book—who have carried out empirical studies during the transitions in their countries.

Developing Three Related Topics

As we discussed the issues surrounding adolescents' sociopolitical identity development, we found that our talk centered on three questions:

1. What were the relationships between more general aspects of psychosocial identity development and sociopolitical identity development?
2. How did young people understand what was happening in their society and, in particular, relationships between societal changes and their own lives?
3. What was young people's understanding of the sociopolitical concepts adults deemed important, such as democracy and free market economy?

Subsequently, these questions became the three main topics that the study addresses. The first question related to the topic we have called "Growing Up in Changing Times." The second question led us to the topic "Living History." The last question generated the topic we have called "Understanding Political Concepts." These three interrelated topics provided both a framework for development of the interview protocol and a lens through which we could view the data. Figure 1.2 shows the interrelated nature of these three topics.

Each of our three topics focuses on aspects of the political cognition and involvement of the adolescents we interviewed, such as their feelings about the transitions, their understanding of social changes, and their political behavior.

Growing Up in Changing Times includes more general aspects of psychosocial identity formation. *Living History* focuses on sociopolitical identity formation. We purposely include two meanings related to *Living History*: adolescents' understanding of contemporary history and their experiences of living in that particular time and place. Both meanings include a sense of being involved in history making. *Understanding Political Concepts* examines

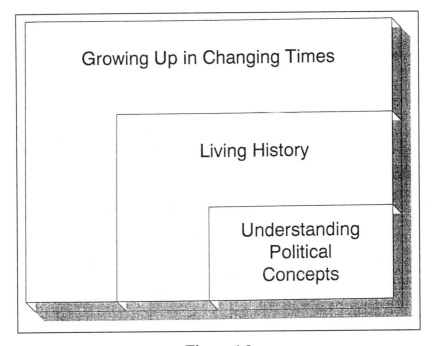

Figure 1.2
Sociopolitical Identity Development:
Three Interrelated Topics

adolescents' understanding of concepts frequently discussed by adults in discourse about "the transitions"—concepts such as democracy and a free market economy.

Growing Up in Changing Times

As we have discussed, one of our basic assumptions was that adolescents' perceptions of and reactions to changes and continuities, as well as the ways in which they understood sociopolitical concepts, were related to their overall developmental processes. These holistic processes included adolescents' developing relationships with the social world, their construction of meaning, and the relationships between these meanings and their feelings about the social context. Students' responses frequently illuminated how their construction of meaning was tied to issues of relationships, and demonstrated that both were central to issues of psychosocial identity. What they saw reflected the creative interplay of who they were and who they were becoming.

> I am a 17-year-old girl. I attend the Art School, I am in the third year. I have been playing the violin for more than 10 years. It is the most important school for me. I like music and art. Family, love, harmony, beauty, pureness, and faith are the most important values for me. I like living. I am basically even-tempered and I am able to be glad for little things. For example, for the sun shining or somebody talking to me nicely. The most important events in my life are connected to my study of music. The first when I got my first violin and then when I was accepted in this school. Of course, those events when my family goes to church on Sundays are important, too. . . . My family and my teachers give me what I need. I do not go to parties, only those that are held together with concerts.
>
> 17-year-old girl, vocational school, Pécs, Hungary, 1991

⬚

> I am a 17-year-old academic school student. My parents are employees. I have an older brother. He also attends the same school, and will have his final exam at the end of this year. He is a good student. I am not as good, but I do not have problems in studying. I am interested in everything. I like new technology, computers, videos. I have a guitar that I play at home. I usually go to play basketball with my friends. I am a person who is happy and likes to play. I have lots of pals. Briefly, I feel good. I am friendly and I have a sense of humor. I might take life easy, but that's me. I think love, friendship, honesty, and self-assurance are the most important values in a person's life. There were no essential, important events in my life, only that I was born.
>
> 17-year-old boy, academic school, Pécs, Hungary, 1994

Certain aspects of Erikson's psychosocial theory provided the overall theoretical framework for this research and, in particular, for this topic. In his work Erikson emphasized the social and cultural contexts as well as the historical moment, constructs central to our research questions (e.g., 1950/1985, 1964, 1968, 1986). Erikson also highlighted the importance of considering the relationships between individual development and historical, societal processes. For example, he discussed the mutually adaptive processes in the relationships between the development of adolescents' psychosocial identities, their families, their communities, their nation, and the global context. He also discussed the problems resulting from attempts to isolate individual and social processes.

Although many psychologists use the concept "psychosocial" in a narrow sense to refer to individuals' development in relation to interpersonal social settings, Erikson's own research consistently reflected a broader, holistic perspective that included the historical time and the broader culture as well as more proximal settings such as home or school. From his early historical, biographical work on Hitler and Gorky, to his extensive biographies of Luther and Gandhi, to his later work on elderly residents of California, Erikson focused on the connections between individuals' lives, their culture, and the historical period in which they lived.

Erikson (1986) pointed to the ways in which the developing person and the social context simultaneously influence each other: "... the eight stages of psychosocial development ... produce the strengths for mutual involvement in an ever-increasing social radius, from infancy through adulthood and into old age" (p. 33). Mutual involvement refers to the influences of the individual upon the environment as well as the environment upon the individual, to "being alive, by stimulating the 'environment' as it stimulates us; for as we become vitally involved, we are also challenging the environment to involve us in its convincing ways" (p. 33).

In his extensive writings on adolescent psychosocial development, Erikson addressed five facets that we draw upon in the present study: (1) the relationship between a culture at a given historical moment and identity development in adolescence; (2) the relationship between thought and identity development in adolescence; (3) the description of the central tasks of adolescence; (4) the emphasis of the continual reintegration of the central crises of previous stages during adolescence; (5) the importance of adolescents' contributions to their society.

In order to understand how a student comprehends particular changes—e.g., why a student identified a given change and discussed that change in a particular way—and to understand that student's discussion of political concepts, we needed to construct a more complete portrait of the student. To do so, it was critical to augment the demographic information typically collected such as age, sex, type of school, grade, and parents' occupation with more comprehensive information about the students' life events, their hopes for the future, their wishes, fears, and values.

Living History

> I cannot decide if it's good or bad. It's democracy right now. People are free. But the economy is getting worse. Life is harder and harder. The mines have been closed. The workers have been kicked out. It's good that the Russian soldiers left, but we don't really feel they have.
>
> 16-year-old academic high school girl, Pécs, Hungary, 1991

The topic *Living History* focuses on adolescents' understandings of the historical changes: their nature, causes, and effects. Erikson linked the formation of psychosocial identity to adolescents' growing sense of themselves as living in a place that has a past and a future and being someone who, likewise, has a past and a future. He described how adolescents construct their identities in relation to their historical, societal context:

> True identity . . . depends on the support which the young individual receives from the collective sense of identity characterizing the social groups significant to him: his class, his nation, his culture.
>
> (Erikson 1964, p. 93)

He wrote that the true formation of a psychosocial identity is not possible before the "fully developed mind begins to envisage a historical perspective . . ." (Erikson in S. Schlein 1987, p. 676). Thus, a fully developed identity includes a "fully developed mind." This means that adolescents have a growing capacity to extend their perspective and participate in their broader society.

According to Erikson, the timing of psychosocial identity formation in adolescence is dependent on the nature of adolescent thought as well as on the social roles of young people. The adolescent mind begins to grasp abstractions such as the philosophical world of ideas and, more specifically, the ideologies available at that time and in that culture: "It is an ideological mind, and indeed, it is the ideological outlook of a society that speaks most clearly to the adolescent . . ." (Erikson 1950, p. 263).

To explore students' understanding of the abstract "philosophical world of ideas" and their "historical perspective," we needed to develop items that gave them the chance to discuss the continuities and changes in their world, at the national level, at the city and neighborhood levels, in their families, and in their own lives. Because our inquiry included these multiple social contexts, we needed a conceptual framework for describing and differentiating among different contexts as well as different times.

We turned to Bronfenbrenner's ecological perspective (e.g., 1979, 1988, 1989, 1993). Like Erikson, Bronfenbrenner (1993) emphasizes that the study of development is the study of processes occurring over time and across space. Drawing upon Einstein's well-known metaphor, Bronfenbrenner wrote:

> ... development takes place in a moving train, and that train is what we may call the "moving macrosystem."
>
> If there are two trajectories, one embedded within the other, what is the relationship between them? Is the individual simply caught in the current of history, or does he exhibit a momentum of his own? ...
>
> (1979, p. 265)

Bronfenbrenner described development as taking place within a complex social system with subsystems, or levels, that nest one within the next. We found this model useful in distinguishing the different relationships between adolescents and the different aspects of their social context. (Social ecological systems are discussed in more detail in chapter 2.) The macrosystem, the inclusive, supraordinate system, refers to the comprehensive patterns of relational systems that characterize a culture, e.g., the economic and political systems, the educational and occupational opportunities, the roles of adolescents and adults, and the roles of females and males. Exosystems nest within macrosystems. Exosystems contain at least one setting that does not include but influences the individual. For example, for these adolescents, events occuring in their parents' workplaces such as changes in pay affect not only their parents but them as well. Mesosystems, the next level of subsystems, refer to conceptual links among microsystems. Microsystems are those systems in which the person is actively involved. Important microsystems in adolescents' lives include their home and school. If we explore links among microsystems, we may find, for example, that it is more likely that a given student will develop an interest in politics if political conversations occur in both the student's home and their school.

Bronfenbrenner (1979) also stated that the processes of macrosystem development set in motion changes throughout the subordinate systems right down to the individual level. "Thus the members of a changing society necessarily experience developmental change at every psychic level—intellectual, emotional, and social" (1979, p. 265).

Bronfenbrenner's social ecological perspective was useful in developing a systematic series of items that addressed students' perceptions of continuities and changes from the national level to their own individual level. All participants responded to the same series of questions. For example, in order to investigate students' understanding of continuities and changes, we asked them to talk about the ways in which their personal lives were the same before the changes began; the ways in which their family life remained the same; the ways in which their neighborhood and city were unchanged; and finally, the ways in which their country was the same. Following this, students were asked to speak at length about the changes that they perceived as occurring at these levels; and to discuss their perceptions of "the most important changes." They then described in detail how the most important changes were affecting their country, their city, their neighborhood, their family, and themselves. For example:

> The same number of my friends think the changes are good as those that think they are bad. We talk a lot about it. We usually agree that the change itself is not bad, but that how it is going to be (after the change), that is the problem.
>
> 17-year-old academic school boy, Pécs, Hungary, 1994

✴

> There was a time when everyone was very excited. We used to watch Parliament. We wanted to know the up-to-date political situation. It's all over. I'm disappointed. I wanted to see more change. Now the original impulse is over.

Many people became unemployed. People are more nervous. Un-
educated people got into a very hard situation. But I like the
changes.

> 17-year-old boy, academic school girl, Pécs, Hungary, 1994

Understanding Political Concepts

As we have noted, Erikson emphasized that adolescence is a
pivotal time for the development of political cognition. In adolescence, people begin to develop an abstract understanding of the
political concepts central to the ideologies of their time. Erikson
explained that as individuals mature, they become better able to
understand their world. He pointed to the "verifying power of cognitive growth as it refines and expands with each (psychosocial)
stage the capacity for accurate and conceptual interplay with the
factual world" (1982, p. 72).

> I think that everything has changed. Perhaps the thing which is
> not as good as it should be is the political situation. I'd better try
> not to be interested in politics or I'd become neurotic. I think that
> on this level there is no justice. I don't accept the situation that
> there are people who have billions and then some who don't have
> enough to buy bread. And I think that everyone feels the same. So
> many Polish people, including my family, are ashamed of our
> government . . .

> At school we have no freedom because if you try then the teachers
> will remember you . . . so freedom at school is only a theory and
> the practice is completely different.

> 18-year-old academic school girl, Gdańsk, Poland

Sigel and Hoskin's (1981) conceptualizations of adolescent
political involvement and cognition, as well as their empirical study
of U.S. adolescents, helped us develop this third topic. They describe
political involvement as the overarching concept that includes cognition, affect, and political behaviors. Their conceptualization of
adolescents' political involvement is consistent with Erikson's comprehensive view of adolescents' psychosocial identity development.
We included some of their items in the protocol used in the present
study. (Used with permission. See Appendix A.)

As we developed this topic, we focused on specific social, economic and political terms frequently heard in public discourse such

as freedom, democracy, government, free market economy, and nationalism. We sought to elicit adolescents' explanations of these terms as well as related examples from their daily lives.

> (Freedom means)... that you can say what you think, that you can do what you want, and ... you feel secure, safe in your country. In school, of course, we have the right to express our opinions but the consequences may be terrible.

> And free market economy means that we can sell everything wherever we want—you can sell any goods and everybody can start his own business.

> (The purpose of a government)... first of all the government should take care of the unemployed people who are not able to (manage) financially....

Sigel and Hoskin's inclusive view of political understanding incorporates both *Living History* as well as *Understanding Political Concepts*. And both topics are included in the overarching framework, *Growing Up in Changing Times*. In the following chapter we describe the interview procedure and protocol. An illustrative interview is developed that demonstrates how the three topics are intertwined.

CHAPTER TWO

The Interview

This chapter provides a more comprehensive description of the interview protocol and process. The lengthy interview protocol was planned to allow the students the opportunity to use their own words to inform us, a process that promoted rich, holistic descriptions. To illustrate the richness of this process, we have used excerpts from a 1994 interview that Komlósi conducted with Márk, a student attending an academic secondary school in Pécs. The first section of this chapter introduces 17-year-old Márk. The second section reviews the interview process. The third section describes the development of the protocol items and analysis, and is organized according to the three interrelated topics: *Growing Up in Changing Times*, *Living History*, and *Understanding Political Concepts*. Márk's responses underscore the holistic processes of adolescent development and the interrelations among these three topics.

Introducing Márk

At the time of the interview, Márk was one year away from his final exams. His school program emphasized mathematics and computer science. Before the Second World War, Márk's school was run by the Roman Catholic Cistercian order. After 1990 the new government returned many former parochial schools to their original churches. Márk's school was returned to the Cistercians, after almost fifty years under state control.

Márk's father, who worked as a manager in a cooperative, had completed a specialized academic high school as well as a technical school. Márk's mother, who also had an academic high school diploma, worked in a solicitor's office as a secretary. His brother was sixteen and a second year student at an agricultural secondary school.

Márk's parents had been divorced for two years. The brothers lived with their father next door to their grandparents in a small village about thirteen miles from Pécs. Their house was about two-hundred square meters. The grandparents had been employed as agricultural workers and now worked a farm of their own, about fifteen acres, with the help of the boys and their father.

According to Márk, most of his family's income came from his father's wages of 30,000 Forint. (At the time, this was about $250 a month and above the national average.) Additionally, the family had income from selling the produce from their farm. When necessary, Márk's grandparents contributed to his family's expenses from their retirement pay.

The Interview Process

To understand adolescents' perceptions of and reactions to the transitions, it was important to listen to them discuss the changes and continuities, and the interview process was designed to encourage this discussion. The semistructured interview protocol included probing questions to elicit more complete responses and enable interviewers to ask follow-up questions. These strategies allowed students numerous opportunities to elaborate upon their initial answers. Furthermore, the use of multiple questions about each topic was a method that enhanced the trustworthiness of the data and analyses (Berg 1995). Like most students, Márk appeared comfortable expressing his opinions and concerns.

Interviews were conducted with individual students in private, quiet rooms with few distractions, where they could not be overheard. The interviewers used several strategies to build rapport with the students. In contrast to interview processes in which the interviewer limits all feedback, the interviewers encouraged the students' ease and talk with smiles, nods, and affirmative murmurs—affirming the response itself, rather than the content of the response. Thus, whether or not the students responded with answers that the interviewer agreed with, the interviewer gave a neutral but encouraging indication to continue. Patton (1990) describes these interview techniques as support and recognition responses, and considers the relationships they engender, "empathetic neutrality." Rapport and empathy involve respect for the individual being interviewed, a critical dimension of the interviewer's sensibility. The distinction between support or recognition and neutrality of opinion was an important one for us to consider.

Neutrality refers to the interviewers' position regarding the content of the responses. Interviewers' opinions often differed from students' opinions due to the nature of the changes and the wide range of people's responses to them. Thus while interviewers gave support and recognition responses, they refrained from reinforcing particular opinions. It was also important that nonverbal as well as verbal cues were culturally-appropriate indications to students that they speak as much, but not more, than they wished, and not an indication that the interviewer agreed with their statements. For example, in his interview, Márk talked about his distrust of the old regime as well as both the first and second elected governments. The interviewer was careful not to let Márk know if the interviewer agreed with Márk's appraisal of the situation but to encourage Márk to explain more if he wished.

We were also aware that the school setting could have a strong influence on students. School is a place where students are judged by their answers, where students show competence by means of their abilities to respond verbally to questions of the adult authority's choosing. For good students such as Márk, this has been a positive experience; for others, a negative one. Typically, students in academic secondary schools with highly competitive entrance exams view the school setting as one that enhances their feelings of confidence. In contrast, other students may have had negative experiences with adults in school contexts. During the interviews such students might have assumed that they did not know the answer to a question or, if they did, might not have responded. In this way adolescents might be playing out their perceptions of the role of the "good student" or the "poor student" within their interviews with us.

In many cases, students like Márk who attended academic schools gave answers that were more complete and complex than those in vocational schools. It may be that the students in vocational schools knew far more than their responses indicate, but the characteristics of the setting, including interactions with the interviewer, may have limited their responses. Conversely, students who viewed themselves as "good students" might have felt compelled to answer more completely or even to invent, in order to demonstrate that they were articulate, knowledgeable, and had good ideas. It was important to take all these issues into account when examining the responses.

The order of the interview items also contributes to the sense of rapport between interviewer and participant (Patton 1990). In a further effort to help students feel more comfortable, we ordered the items so that the first questions focused students' attention on a topic they knew about, themselves. In these initial open-ended items, students were asked to describe themselves and talk about their interests. Some students were talkative and very self-disclosing. Others were more reserved. But all students seemed interested and more self-assured when talking about themselves. We thought that students would not be as comfortable or assured when trying to provide details about historical events and social changes or more abstract political and economic concepts. Therefore, these items were placed later in the interview.

Finally, the last item in the protocol asked students to discuss their vision of a "good life in twenty years." This item was placed last in order to help students who struggled to answer items about political concepts end the interview on a comfortable note. Márk's positive answer was typical of most students in the study: "Happiness and love will be in our family."

The Interview Protocol and Analysis

We developed the protocol to examine participants' historical perspective and their perceptions of their "involvement in an ever-increasing social radius." Figure 2.1 illustrates the model we used. The horizontal axis represents the social context, space, the continuum from the self to family to friends to the global context. The vertical axis represents the historical context, time, from the present moment back in time in the life of the self, of family members, and then to distant history, as well as forward to the future of the self, e.g., work and children, and then to the distant future. Throughout this chapter, we elaborate upon this initial rendering.

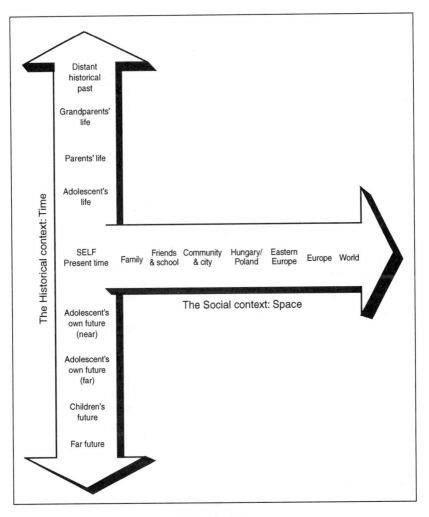

Figure 2.1
Studying Adolescents' Development within
Changing Social Contexts

We designed a wide range of items. The items in the interview protocol exemplify each category of questions that Patton (1990) describes: experience questions; opinion and value questions; feeling questions; knowledge questions; sensory questions, including questions about what people have seen or heard; and time frame questions, i.e., any of the above questions asked about the past, present, or future; and demographic questions.

The following profile of Márk is organized following the three topics introduced in chapter 1. Márk's responses illustrate how all the dimensions of adolescents' sociopolitical identity formation are related. Thus, although we discuss particular items in relation to a specific topic, most items relate to two or all three topics.

In keeping with research that is primarily qualitative in nature, most of the items were open ended. For example, each participant was asked to identify the changes he or she deemed important, and discuss the reasons each change took place, the effects of the changes on their lives, the lives of family members, as well as the effects on their neighborhood, city, and country.

Based on the narrative data from interviews, we constructed an elaborate coding method for thematic and concept analyses as well as the construction of the individual portraits. Each response was first coded using a different category for each separate answer. For example, when responding to the question about the most important changes, a student's responses might include "free elections," "more goods in the stores," "freedom of speech," and "anyone can start a business." All would be coded separately. Then, in subsequent analyses, the separate categories could be recoded, e.g., to find out the frequency with which students focused on more inclusive topical themes and concepts such as democracy or a free market economy, or to see how many students cited improved living vs. worsening living conditions, etc. (e.g., Berg 1995; Patton 1990; Rubin & Rubin 1995).

To provide additional information about students' reasoning and the trustworthiness of analyses, open-ended items that generated qualitative data were frequently complemented by forced-choice items which used ordinal scales. Such use of complementary qualitative and quantitative analyses is becoming more common in research of this type (Berg 1995). For example, students were asked: "On a scale of 1 to 7, . . . how do you feel about the change you just discussed?" Several such items employed Likert-type scales, e.g., "When you think about the future, do you feel very pessimistic/ pessimistic/ sometimes pessimistic and sometimes optimistic/ optimistic/ very optimistic?"

This research is related to and draws upon other interview and survey research in the field of political cognition and socialization. A number of items from related studies were included so that the results could be examined and discussed in relation to previous findings (see Appendix A).

Growing Up in Changing Times

The items that develop the topic *Growing Up in Changing Times* are typical of those in much of the research on identity formation, research that focuses more narrowly upon individual adolescents, their families, and friends. These protocol items are the ones that most people relate to Erikson's psychosocial theory. However, as we have shown in our discussion of Erikson's work, all protocol items relate to the encompassing subject of psychosocial identity formation.

Particular identity types are available in particular social contexts, defined by place and time. Individual variations and adaptations are, likewise, framed by particular social contexts. By definition, this time of change in Hungary and Poland was marked by a changing sense of identity related to the level of the macrosystems, including class, nation, and culture. The questions that interested us were those which explored how these particular adolescents' identities were related to their changing societies. For example: how would changes in lifestyles and living standards affect the identities that these young people were developing?

In exploring students' psychosocial identity formation, a major focus was their own view of their involvement in their society. When formulating the items for the protocol and analyzing the interview data, we examined aspects of adolescents' psychosocial identity formation along the continuum from the more personal to the more social.

The initial item in the interview was intended to elicit students' spontaneous self-descriptions: "First, would you please tell me about yourself?" We found that the students were relaxed in talking about themselves, frequently giving many descriptors. Subsequent items, though open ended, asked students to talk more specifically about their interests, the important groups in their lives, their hopes, worries, and values. Numerous items focused on their views of their future, their hopes and plans for adulthood, and their levels of optimism/pessimism. Responses were analyzed to find patterns by type of school, by age, sex, and year the interview took place.

At the time that we developed the protocol and through the ensuing years of the research, there were discussions in the national and international media and among some citizen groups as to whether nationalism was increasing in eastern and central Europe, including Hungary and Poland. Several items elicited information about the students' national identity. For example: "How do these changes influence how you think about Hungary/Poland and being Hungarian/Polish?" "What are the things that make you proud to be a Hungarian/Pole?" "What are the things that make you not so proud?" "What country do you see as a model for the kind of society you would like to have in Hungary/Poland? Why?" "If you imagine Hungary/Poland in ten years as a 'good place to live,' describe what the living style would be."

Another series of items related to students' plans for their future and their sense of hope. In order to understand how these students saw their future unfolding, we asked related groups of items. Students were asked to indicate how optimistic or pessimistic they felt on an item that used a Likert-type scale. In a second related item, they were asked to describe their degree of optimism/pessimism when they thought about the future. A third item asked whether they thought that, assuming they had children, their children's lives would be better, worse, or the same as their own (or whether they didn't know). Fourth, students were asked to compare their lives with their parents' lives. In order to see how they perceived their lives within the context of the wider national and international context, they were also asked to rate their level of satisfaction with themselves, their city, their nation, Europe, and the world at three points in time: before the changes, at the present moment, and ten years in the future. To understand more about students' life goals, we asked students to pretend that we were interviewing them twenty years in the future and to tell us what their life was like.

Many items asked students to reflect on their own developmental processes. For example:

"You've been talking about a lot of changes. How does living in this time of change affect your development as a person? When you are five years older (__years old) and look back on this time, how do you think you will think that it has affected your development as a person?"

The following excerpts from Márk's interview illustrate how the students' responses to these protocol items provide a more complete picture of their developing identity. When Márk was asked to describe himself, he responded:

> I am a bit light-minded. I often feel that I could do something but that I don't put enough energy into it, but, in the end, it turns out that I'm not that good at that thing. In addition, I am reliable and hard working in studying and working in the family enterprise. I do anything left for me to do and I carry out whatever I decide to realize. But I am not self-willed. I am friendly and I love my relatives. I very much like to be with my parents, grandparents, my uncle's family, my girlfriend's parents and her relatives as well.

In this initial description of himself, Márk introduced a theme that he echoed throughout the interview, the theme of the importance of love and relationships. He emphasized his love for his family, mentioning his grandparents, girlfriend, and uncle's family in addition to his parents and brother. When asked about the important groups in his life, Márk again emphasized family and friends. The only group outside of family and close friends that Márk mentioned is his school choir. In addition, he spontaneously included the importance of his national identity.

Márk sees himself as a person with a wide range of interests:

> Besides studying, as a pastime, I am interested in running a farm. But the most important thing for me is computer technology. I have a fairly good computer at home with which I "work" quite a lot. I am actually interested in everything. I go hunting, fishing, or take trips for pleasure. Of course, what I like best is being together with my girlfriend.

Márk's thoughtful responses to the items about wishes and fears also center on the theme of the importance of family. Although his answers included an international aspect, war and peace, and suggested a developing social awareness, he related both his hopes and fears to his personal desire for a peaceful life with his family. He named his three wishes as:

> 1) A peaceful and happy life with my present and future family. I want to create the conditions of living for my family. 2) To get

a university degree with my girlfriend. I think a university degree gives you a kind of security in life. You can deal with problems on a higher level then. 3) To have peace in the world, mainly in Europe, and in our environment. . . . Not to have to be afraid of war, destruction.

Márk was well aware that in Pécs he was living in close proximity to the war in Croatia: "You can get a shocking experience day by day hearing about the mass slaughtering 100–200 kilometers far from here. . . . And you can do nothing about it."

His anxiety about war was also reflected in his answer to the question about fears: "I am afraid of war because there are war actions very close to us. I am not afraid of anything else. I am only afraid of senseless destruction. I am not afraid of AIDS or any other diseases."

When Márk was asked about the values he considered "most important" he again emphasized loving, harmonious relationships:

A deep, intense link to one person is important for me. Happiness is important, by which I mean that there are no conflicts either in the family or in the everyday relationships. Love and appreciation are important. Success is important for me . . . when I can see that something I have started has results.

Not surprisingly Márk talked a great deal about his parents. He also pointed to his friends, saying that although he did not have a wide group of friends, their values were similar to his. His response suggests that he thinks a great deal about his relationships with important people in his life:

My father's life is very edifying for me. Or, the way my father solved his life problems is important to me. I couldn't and still can't agree with the way my mother solved her problems, so that's just a lesson for me. My values are very different from my mother's values. I have always been closer to my father. My link to him has always been stronger. So it's clear that I have accepted his system of values. I have more goals regarding some things though, like studying, schooling, in which he was not successful.

Throughout the interview, in his self-description, his wishes, and responses to numerous items, Márk emphasized the importance of education in achieving his goals. One of Márk's wishes was to obtain a university degree. When Márk discussed his school performance he indicated his strengths but also his concern that he did not work hard enough:

> For me, studying is the most important thing in my life now. I'd like to get into the university. The entrance exam is known to be very hard. So I take studying very seriously. I regard myself as an intelligent student, but I am not satisfied with my diligence. I study easily, especially the things I am interested in. I am up on quite a lot of things.

Márk's desire to get an education was related to both his feeling about the lack of opportunity his parents had and the obligation that he felt towards his family, as well as his general orientation toward the future:

> In my opinion, my life is easier than my father's life was. His family had to work harder for a living. As a child, his help was also needed. Today we have more luxury articles which have become natural parts of our life . . . a car, computer, a comfortable apartment. When my father was growing up, a holiday abroad was unimaginable. One was happy if he could go somewhere within the country.
>
> What I just said referring to my father is relevant to the comparison with my mother's life as well. But it was even worse for her because when she was a young girl she lost her mother. She and her elder brother were brought up by their grandmother. They lived under even worse financial conditions.
>
> My father also wanted to study in a university but he didn't manage it. I am now the focus of the family. Having a university degree, I will be able to create a stable life for myself, I think.

In response to the item on the important groups in his life, Márk spontaneously discussed the importance of being a Hungarian. Later in the interview, he was asked related questions about his national identity, e.g., what made him "proud" and "not so proud" to be Hungarian, as well as questions about nationalism. Although Márk included his nationality in his initial description of himself, none of his responses to the follow-up items conveyed a chauvinistic quality:

> Sports results make me proud. A lot of Hungarian scientists are acknowledged all over the world for their inventions. We have world famous composers and historical figures. And today there are still plenty of intelligent Hungarians in many parts of the world. We are considered a good labor force in the West. In any field.

> I'm not proud that we have a lot of negligent and uncultured fellow-countrymen who litter the streets, throw the rubbish out of cars. They're noisy. They don't take the other person's wishes into consideration.

In discussing the future, Márk once again emphasized his desire to have a happy, stable life, and, particularly, a loving relationship. For Márk, striving toward a happy and prosperous future necessitated preparing for a good career as well as having the ability to maintain a loving family. Indeed, Márk's desire that he and his girlfriend obtain university degrees related not only to their future careers but also to his wish to be able to "deal with problems at a higher level." When thinking about the future, he was also aware that his wish for a good life could be threatened, particularly by war. Márk clearly felt he had little control over the war saying ". . . you can do nothing about it."

Overall, however, Márk was optimistic about the future. He had a great deal of trust in his father's optimistic appraisal of the situation in Hungary, saying, "I am not really an optimist, but optimism describes me rather than pessimism. I trust in the future and I trust in myself, that I will be able to assure a living for myself and my family, just like my father assured it for us."

In numerous publications, Erikson wrote of the choices and challenges of adolescence, including the emergence of a consistent sense of self, one that includes both "identity" and "identity confusion." For example:

> There follows adolescence, with its basic tensions between the development of a sense of psychosocial identity and its interplay with an unavoidable identity confusion. As this tension gets resolved, a sense of fidelity emerges both toward one's own accruing

identity and toward some overall orientation that helps unify one's
identity with an existing or emerging ideological world image.
(1986, p. 35)

Márk's responses illustrate that he is, indeed, developing a
sense of who he is and what he hopes to become. His developing
sense of self is relatively consistent. He thinks of himself as family-
centered, friendly, and generally responsible. He has made rather
definite plans for his future. He has a serious, permanent relationship with his girlfriend and is preparing for a career in teaching,
a field he considers both stable and interesting.

Living History

The research was designed during a period marked by major
changes at the national levels in both Hungary and Poland. Within
an interval of two years, multiparty national elections were held,
the large numbers of Soviet soldiers left both countries, many
national enterprises were privatized and other businesses started.
These changes that affected national institutions and international
relations were generally the most visible and were the focus of
stories in the Western media. We wanted to find out not only
whether and how students perceived changes at the national level,
but also their understanding as to how these changes were affecting their lives, their families, and the lives of others they knew.

Although in national and local media, as well as in everyday
conversations between adults, there was a great emphasis on the
changes taking place in Poland and Hungary, little attention was
being paid to continuities. In order to understand students' views
of societal processes, we needed to explore their perceptions of what
had remained the same as well as what had changed. To make
sure that all students addressed the same dimensions of their social contexts we developed a series of items that followed the same
pattern in each interview. While the initial items focused on the
student, subsequent items focused on the student's family, then
friends, then "people you know," then their neighborhood, then
city, and finally their nation.

We used Bronfenbrenner's ecological model as a conceptual
guide in the development of items related to *Living History* and in

analyses of the data. In developing his model, Bronfenbrenner first focused on delineating the relationships of the levels or subsystems. In 1990, when we developed the protocol and in 1991 when we began the interviews, our thinking was informed by his earlier work (e.g., 1979, 1988, 1989), referred to as the social ecological model. Bronfenbrenner's subsequent development of this perspective (e.g., 1993, 1995) emphasizes the importance of developmental processes occurring over time, the process—person—context—time (PPCT) model. This changing emphasis is also reflected by referring to the perspective as bioecological rather than social ecological (e.g., Bronfenbrenner 1995).

From the beginning, our study emphasized change and time—developmental processes occurring over time. As the following examples of Márk's responses illustrate, Bronfenbrenner's perspective (1979, 1988, 1989) was useful in informing us as to how students themselves might perceive the links between their lives and the historical time. The following is an introduction to the four ecological subsystems Bronfenbrenner describes: the microsystem, the mesosystem, the exosystem, and the macrosystem.

The Microsystem

> A microsystem is a pattern of activities, roles, and interpersonal relations experienced by the developing person in a given face-to-face setting with particular physical, and material features, and containing other persons with distinctive characteristics of temperament, personality, and systems of belief.
>
> Bronfenbrenner 1989, p. 227

The microsystems of the students in this study included their families, peer group, and school settings. Márk had moved from Pécs to a nearby a village with his father and brother, next door to his grandparents, and he also spent considerable time with his girlfriend and her family. He continued to go to the same academic secondary school in Pécs. These are microsystems central to Márk's life. We designed items that systematically examined the students' understandings of, and responses to, continuities and changes in the microsystems typically important for adolescents. We also designed items that asked students to assess how others in these microsystems thought and felt about changes. For example, when

Márk identified "the operation of private enterprise" as an important change, he was asked how his father, mother, and his friends had felt about this particular change.

The Mesosystem

> The mesosystem comprises the linkages and processes taking place between two or more settings containing the developing person (e.g., the relationships between home and school, school and workplace, etc.). In other words, a mesosystem is a system of microsystems.
>
> Bronfenbrenner 1989, p.227

An example of a mesosystem is the linkage between school and home. Márk and his girlfriend had a serious relationship that had been developing over the time they spent with each other in choir, at school, and on vacations with their families. According to psychosocial theory, the defining crisis of early adulthood is that of intimacy and isolation. These mesosystem linkages promoted Márk's developing ability to sustain a loving relationship as an adolescent as well as in the future as an adult. This was one of his primary life goals.

A second life goal that was supported in his home as well as in school was Márk's interest in pursuing a university degree related to science and math. Márk discussed studying diligently. He had the support of his family in his desire to continue his studies. This support—and the connection between school and home—was also evidenced in the family's purchase of a computer, which Márk identified as a luxury item for his family, but one that was important for his school studies and future career.

The Exosystem

> The exosystem encompasses the linkages and processes taking place between two or more settings, at least one of which does not ordinarily contain the developing person, but in which events occur that indirectly influence processes within the immediate setting that does contain that person (e.g., for a child, the relationship between the home and the parents' workplace; for a parent, the relation between the school and the neighborhood group).
>
> Bronfenbrenner 1989, p. 227

Throughout the interviews there were numerous examples of settings that did not contain the student but influenced the student's development. Changes at the national level resulted in the Catholic Church reclaiming schools that had been run by the state. There were changes as well in many of the other schools in Pécs as some technical and academic schools were combined. (In fact, this change influenced the course of this study since some of the technical and academic schools that had been part of the 1991 study were combined with other schools in 1993–94.) Likewise, changes in the national economic structure resulted in personal changes in Márk's family's financial outlook.

The Macrosystem

> The macrosystem consists of the overarching pattern of micro-, meso-, and exosystems characteristic of a given culture, subculture, or other broader social context, with particular reference to the developing investigative belief systems, resources, hazards, life styles, opportunity structures, life course options, and patterns of social interchange that are embedded in these systems. The macrosystem may be thought of as the social blueprint for a particular culture, subculture, or other broader social context.
>
> Bronfenbrenner 1989, p. 228

Márk listed the establishment of private enterprises, the opening of borders and free trade, and economic reforms as the changes in the national system that he considered most important. Indeed, this transitional period was characterized by changes in the macrosystem, including a change of regime, a process of democratization, the introduction of a free market economy, and changing relationships with other countries.

Figure 2.2 illustrates how Bronfenbrenner's (1989) constructs of the levels of the social ecology helped us develop a series of items that examined adolescents' perceptions of Living *History*. These items focused on the continuities and changes at the different levels of the ecological system. We developed numerous protocol items in which students were asked to talk about their understandings of continuities with the past, the historical nature of the transitions, important changes, their causes and effects.

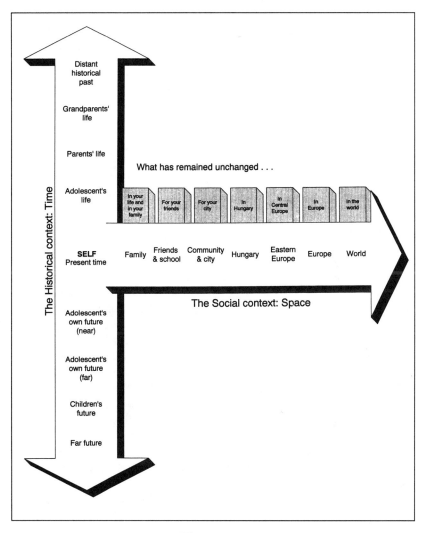

Figure 2.2
Living History: **Continuities and Changes**

Students were asked to construct a comprehensive overview of their perspective of major events in the form of a timeline of the historical events. Márk recalled more events than most of his peers, showing that he was relatively aware of news relating to the macrosystem, at the national and international levels:

> 1989, the Berlin Wall was demolished . . . the first signs that the power of the Soviet Union had weakened . . . revolution in Romania . . . the development of the multi-party system . . . demonstrations and the re-burial of the 1956 revolutionaries in Hungary . . . the first free election . . . forming a coalition government . . . the Soviet army left Hungary . . . the Southern Slav crisis (i.e., in Croatia, Serbia, Bosnia)—a war that has an effect on us as well . . . the general (Hungarian national) elections for the second time, the victory of the socialists, efforts to join NATO. I don't really remember the exact dates.

Since *Living History* is a process, not merely a recounting of events, the focus of most items was on students' perceptions and reactions to continuities and changes. They were asked numerous questions relating to the specific continuities and changes they identified. Items focused on specific dimensions of the social ecological system. Students were asked to think about the past three to four years and describe what had remained unchanged in their own lives and in the lives of their families. Parallel items focused on what had remained unchanged in their neighborhood, their country, "this region in Europe," Europe, and the world.

Consistent with his discussions about his identity, Márk's responses regarding continuities in his own life focused on the caring relationships in his family: "Nothing has changed in my life . . . .Human relationships have not changed in my family. We're together now just like before. We had whatever we needed and it's the same today."

In contrast, when he talked about other villagers, Hungarians, and Europeans, he emphasized people's lack of harmony.

> In the life of our village, differences between people concerning their way of thinking and also concerning financial issues have become more pronounced. People remain envious. Many can't bear it if someone has something. They, of course, don't think about the hard work it took that person to get that thing.

> The mentality and the way of thinking of the people has not changed in Hungary. People expected a sudden rise in the stan-

dard of life as a result of the changes. They wanted suddenly to have an easier life. But they don't want to do anything, just like before. Unfortunately, they don't understand the features, the characteristics, the essence and the process of a political-economic change . . . just like they didn't understand it before the changes.

The majority of items related to the theme *Living History* focused on students' perceptions of and reactions to the changes. When asked about his general opinions of the changes, Márk indicated that he didn't think that the political changes going on in Hungary had a significant impact on him personally: "The change of the system did not really touch us directly. But what we perceived was that we could feel ourselves more free. The borders opened towards the West, too." He gave the example of spending a holiday in Spain with his family and his girlfriend's family.

Márk did, however, perceive that the changes had affected Hungary as a whole: "The changes had a negative effect on the economy. Or at least here in Hungary. Prices were suddenly increased while wages just stayed the same."

When asked to name the most important changes, Márk named changes in the macrosystem and again emphasized that the changes did not affect his family. He did not discuss his family's move to the village nor his school's change to a parochial school. He explained that his generation was so young when the changes started that they were not aware of the early changes. He pointed out that his parents did not discuss the changes with him, that he felt only a vague sense of dissatisfaction.

In his response to the item about the most important changes, Márk pointed to the differences between the way a child and an adolescent understand their societies. This is a key distinction that Erikson also made.

We didn't really feel the changes because we were primary school pupils at that time. We could only feel something through our parents. But they discussed these matters just between themselves rather than with us. This is why I can't really mention a particular example. Nothing has changed in my life. I only remember the dissatisfaction in my environment. Earlier, people were dissatisfied about some things. Now they're dissatisfied about other things. Yet they wanted this change. (At the time) I couldn't intervene in anything. I couldn't vote.

After naming what they perceived to be the most important two or three changes, students were asked to describe numerous aspects of each change. These items included:

> When did this change begin? Tell me what was it like before this change? How are things now? Did this change happen slowly or quickly? What were the reasons that this change happened?

> (If appropriate) Did ordinary citizens/people have any influence in making this change? How? Did your parents? People your family knows? You? Your classmates? Other young people?

> Does this change affect everyone equally? For example: People in the cities/ people in farm areas; workers, middle class, intelligentsia, minority groups? Who in Hungary/Poland favors the change most? Who favors this change least?

Márk focused largely on economic changes, listing private enterprise, open borders, free trade, and economic reform.

In addition, students were asked to rate their feelings about the specific changes they had described on a scale of 1 (positive) to 7 (negative). They were also asked to estimate the rating of their mother's feelings, their father's feelings, "most of their friends'" feelings, and most Hungarian/Poles' feelings.

In elaborating on each of the major changes he identified, Márk mentioned both positive and negative consequences. He focused on changes, like private enterprise, that were part of his microsystem as well.

> The changes started in 1989–1990 when I was twelve years old. I was in the sixth grade of primary school. Before that, private enterprises had been rare. Trade had been a privilege of the State and it was oriented to the Eastern Market. Our economy was of the Soviet type. Private property was not characteristic, and therefore the people did not feel that the State's business was theirs.

> Today anyone may establish a private enterprise. And you can even get credit. The interest rates are high though. Free trade has come to life, but there are a lot of quality problems. There is a lot of confusion in the economy which hinders development. The pace of the changes was very quick except for the reforms in the economy.

Márk was asked a parallel series of questions about the effects of these specific changes on himself, his family, his community, and Hungary. Once again he reiterated that the changes had not greatly affected his family. He did notice changes in his environment, particularly people's livelihood and the area's infrastructure. It appeared, however, that he had little opportunity to discuss these changes. Just as he did not discuss these issues with family, he did not discuss these issues with friends, even though he did mention that his friends had the same values.

No substantial change took place in the life of my parents.

These changes changed the lives of many people in our environment. A lot of them could re-claim their old properties and started to run businesses. Some of them have opened shops. In my area, no one's situation has gotten considerably worse. . . .

I don't really talk about these issues with my friends from class. Several of their families have opened shops, I know. I can't see any changes when I think about other youngsters, unless I think of the luxury articles some of them have. They go around in luxury cars at a young age and they have first class clothes, too. At the same time, others remain on the same level.

These changes should have led to the greater development of Hungary, but the "clever" people still seem to come off well, just like earlier, in contrast to the "fair (honest) workers."

In my area, in the village, the development of the telephone network, the gas and water conduits are the results of the changes. The infra-structure has developed. The system of supply has improved. You can buy more things in the shops.

The changes had very similar impacts on my neighbors and friends compared with me and my parents. Actually, we can feel the changes only in an indirect way.

Compared to his peers, Márk was fairly knowledgeable and perceptive. It appears that he obtained information through the media, school, or through direct observation of changes in his environment. However, he reported few discussions about these changes with the people he identified as important in his life, his family, his girlfriend, and his friends. Although Márk was developing a growing understanding of the relationships between the changes and their varied effects, he emphasized that the changes did not greatly affect himself or his family. There is a distance between his perception of the changes that happen in the macrosystem and the microsystem.

Understanding Political Concepts

Adolescents begin to develop the abstract understandings of political concepts central to the ideologies of their time. In public and private conversations as well as in the media, adults were talking about democracy, freedom, free market economies, nationalism, and other political, economic, and social concepts. As we have previously mentioned, Sigel and Hoskin (1981) described political involvement as the overarching concept that includes political cognition, affect, and behaviors. Their conceptualization of adolescents' political involvement is consistent with Erikson's comprehensive view of adolescents' psychosocial identity development. They describe political cognition as involving one's factual knowledge, one's awareness of the important current socio-political issues, and one's comprehension of key constructs of one's political system, e.g., democracy. In responding to the items related to these themes, students like Márk demonstrated their factual knowledge, awareness, and understanding of political concepts.

In a series of items related to *Understanding Political Concepts* students were first asked to define the concepts, such as democracy and freedom. Follow-up items generally asked students to provide more details or asked that they relate the abstract concept to concrete situations. For example, students were asked to define freedom. In follow-up items, they were asked to discuss whether they thought that they had freedom to disagree in school, both at present and before the changes. Similarly, the open-ended item "What do you see as the key features that any country has to have to be a democracy?" was followed by items in which students were asked to identify possible features as essential or nonessential, e.g., trial by jury, right to hold private property, free elections, a good standard of living, a written constitution. Examples of other abstract concepts they were asked to define are free market economy, the purpose of a government, and the meaning of a good citizen (see Figure 2.3).

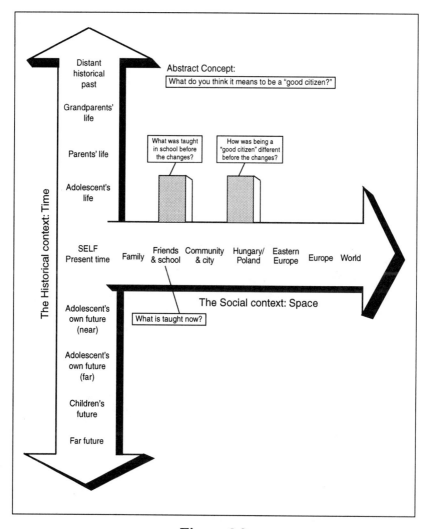

Figure 2.3
Developing Political Understandings:
Abstract Concepts and "Real Life" Applications

Márk gave comparatively detailed answers to the items about political concepts. His definition of democracy emphasized equality: "For me, democracy means that all are treated equal, all have rights in the same way. The people live in freedom."

Márk's definition of freedom was similar to his definition of democracy, and again emphasized equality:

> Laws concern all (people) in the same way. And all can express his or her opinion . . . no one is penalized for it. This is then freedom of speech. No differences are made among people, for example, freedom of religion.

After explaining what he thought freedom meant, Márk spontaneously added: "Freedom of speech is guaranteed at our school. We have a student government. We may intervene in the way things are going. I, of course, don't know how it was in the past. High school was always different (from primary school)."

In this response Márk relates an abstract concept to his experiences at school. During the interview, many students related abstract concepts such as "freedom" to their own experiences in their microsystems. In addition, many of the more abstract protocol items were followed by items that related to students' experiences.

Although he was relatively knowledgeable compared to his peers, Márk's responses to the items addressing satisfaction with the political situation revealed that he had low levels of trust and satisfaction in the present as well as the former elected governments, as well as in the past regime. Sigel and Hoskin (1981) described political affect as a complex feeling state that includes aspects of trust. Political trust includes the dimension of confidence. A second dimension of affect is satisfaction, which also includes the cognitive judgment of "goodness," e.g., of governments or their policies. Márk was not trustful that people had equal economic opportunities, pointing out that only a small group of Hungarians was able to take advantage of these changes. In his discussion, he did not include an example from his own microsystem, but presented a general indictment of the national situation:

> The changes have touched upon fundamental matters that concern the life of the country. They resulted in a lot of contradictions. For example, extremists appeared, and social differences among people sharpened. The changes were favorable to the clever people. You can't get better by honest work, not even today.

When asked to elaborate on how the "clever people" were able to take advantage of the changes, Márk responded:

> Those who started their businesses in time or those who were "close to the fire"—close to power—or they themselves were leaders in the previous system.

Another series of items focused more on the political involvement of the students themselves, their families, and friends. Students were asked open-ended questions about citizenship and citizenship education, for example, "What do you think it means to be a 'good citizen?" "Was it different before the changes?" They were asked whether there was a citizenship education program in the schools prior to the changes, and, if so, what was taught, as well as whether there was a current program and what was being taught. Students were asked for their opinions regarding what should be the role of the school in "preparing you and other students to be citizens? What would you like to learn about citizenship in school?" These open-ended questions allowed students to discuss both psychological and legal aspects of citizenship (Dekker 1997). This differentiation is particularly important in many countries in Europe, such as Hungary and Poland, in which citizenship and nationality are not synonymous.

Márk thought that a good citizen was someone who "takes advantage of having the right to vote, doesn't deny being Hungarian, and tolerates the decision of the majority." He went on to explain that, "earlier, this concept had another meaning. Loyalty to the Communist Party was more important than devotion to the nation."

Márk was one of the few students in the study who said that he had studied citizenship education in school, though he found it rather useless:

> Civic knowledge was taught within history in the schools. But it was just like mentioning facts. We didn't learn anything about it in detail. We still don't study anything special in this topic. Matters of study have not changed since then. . . . I think the schools' role is important. They should have a serious role in teaching history in a true way to students so that students could worthily declare themselves Hungarians, being proud of that. We should study more about Hungarian history, traditions, and culture.

Numerous items addressed political involvement as it relates to the community and nation. Students were asked whether they, their family, or friends had been involved in politics before the changes and then asked whether they would be more or less likely to be involved at present. Later, they were asked whether they supported any political program or party and why, and then asked, if they were old enough to vote, whether they would vote and for which party.

Márk discussed politics as if the term referred only to national or international affairs. He underscored his distrust of politics and explained that he and his family were never interested in politics. He did not relate his apparent interest in the student government at his school to anything that was "political." In response to questions about knowing people who had taken part in the changes or in politics, Márk replied: "No one in my family or anyone of my acquaintance took part in political life earlier. I didn't like politics, and still I don't, because as a child I couldn't say anything about it."

Not only did Márk stress that he did not know anyone involved with politics, like most of his peers, he said he was not the least involved: "I don't support a political program of any kind and I am so very much uninterested in it that I haven't even thought about which party's program I could accept. Actually none of them. They can only promise."

We also noted that Márk's responses focus on changes at the national level and the level of his family. He does not focus on intermediate levels such as the political situation in Pécs or his school. This pattern of concern was common to many of the other students we interviewed and is discussed in greater detail in the conclusions.

Adolescents' Contributions to Their Societies

Erikson is one of few theorists who acknowledged and discussed adolescents' contribution to their societies, writing that, just as historical processes affect adolescents, so societal, historical processes are affected by them:

Historical processes in turn seem vitally related to the demand for identity in each new generation; for to remain vital, societies must have at their disposal the energies and loyalties that emerge from the adolescent process. (Erikson in Schlein, 1987, p. 676)

Young people like Márk are challenged to take the changing roles expected of them in their society, in Poland and in Hungary, and to come to a new psychosocial equilibrium with societal forces. We were interested in exploring how these young people's "energies and loyalties" related to the needs of their societies and how they were meeting these challenges. For example, while new possibilities had opened to be entrepreneurs, industrial workers were generally suffering lowered status and wages.

When asked about how his life might be if we were to meet him in twenty years and find him happy with his life, many of the issues and feelings that Márk discussed throughout the interview were reflected in his optimistic response. His answer showed him to be concerned about the wider society, including issues such as war and peace. However, the social changes in Hungary did not seem to influence his plans. This appears consistent with his distrust of national governments and "clever people" who exploit situations for their own advancement. It is also consistent with his focus on the microsystem of the family serving as a place of refuge and protection against what he perceived as the negative changes in the macrosystem.

His response focused on his desire for a happy family and a fulfilling job, consistent themes throughout his interview. Márk chose the path of aspiring to be a teacher, a path that was relatively safe and without the challenge of finding a new soical equilbrium. Yet it is one that will allow him to contribute his energy and vitality to the larger society through his work with youth and his interest in new technologies.

I'd be thirty-seven. I'll have had a family by then. I hope to have my own family house as well. My job is also important.

Wars will have been forgotten by then. There will be peace everywhere. And the world will be unified, both economically and politically. Borders will only be of a symbolic meaning. Or at least in Europe.

I'll be a teacher of math and physics and perhaps computers. I'll teach in a high school. I'll love my job.

I hope I'll have some free time, too. I'll go hunting and fishing with my two children. My wife will be a teacher as well. We'll have all we need. I'll be a good father of my children. Happiness and love will be in our family.

An Introduction to the Sections on Hungary and Poland

An ecological approach involves examining how historical changes in the macrosystem affect people's daily lives. Therefore, we begin the sections on Hungary and Poland with introductions to the complex histories of these countries followed by summaries of the origins and trajectories of the transitions. The first part of these accounts presents geographic and demographic information. The second part provides a brief historical overview for readers unfamiliar with Hungarian or Polish history. Because all historical accounts have biases we have relied upon the work of a number of well-known scholars. The reader should keep in mind that at the time of the writing of this book Hungarian and Polish history was being widely re-examined. This was not the first time the histories of these countries had under gone re-evaluation. Nevertheless, we hope that the historical context we provide will help readers understand how students' knowledge of their history contributed to their sense of being Hungarian or Polish and provided a lens through which they viewed current events. The third part of these accounts summarizes the origins and some major events of the transitions during the period in which the interviews were conducted so that readers will be oriented to the specific events and changes that the students discussed.

PART TWO

Hungary

CHAPTER THREE

An Introduction to Hungarian History and an Orientation to the Pécs and Budapest Studies

In school, at home, and through the media, Hungarian students are taught a view of history that emphasizes macrosocial transitions, periods of upheaval and hardships at the national as well as personal level. Hungary's location, a landlocked country in the heart of Europe, at the crossroads of eastern and western Europe as well as central and southern Europe, has made it an area that has experienced frequent sociopolitical changes. As of 1996, Hungary occupied 93,033 square kilometers and shared borders with Austria, Slovakia, Slovenia, Croatia, Serbia, Romania, and the Ukraine (Schöpflin 1996).

Although the average family income of the students in this study was low relative to the average family income in western Europe or the United States, it was high relative to that of other former socialist countries in the region. At the time of the last interviews with the students in Budapest, 1995, the mean household income for an average family of 2.8 people was $5,900 U.S. (Encyclopedia Britannica 1996). During this time, about 90% of households had televisions, washing machines, and refrigerators (Economist Intelligence Unit 1996). Hungary had a large industrial base, with 35% of its labor force working in industry. Agriculture and tourism were also vital to Hungary's economy. However, despite the increase in consumerism, by 1995 unemployment, which had been negligible during the communist regime (though hidden unemployment prevailed), had risen to 11.5%. Inflation rose dramatically to 30.5%, impacting national policy and the lives of most Hungarians.

In 1993, Hungary's population was approximately 10.2 million. The population for the two cities in our research was 2.1 million in Budapest and 183,000 in Pécs (Encyclopedia Britannica 1996). Children under the age of 15 constituted 18.6% of the population. Youth and young adults, 15–29 years, constituted 22.0%. The age range of the students in the study crosses these two demographic groups.

As of 1990, 29.2% of the population had attended secondary school and 10.1% had attained higher education. Therefore, the students in Pécs and the students in Budapest who wished to attend university were atypical of adolescents as a population since less than 12% attended university.

The Distant Past

Both Hungary's central location and its generally level terrain have made it an ancient crossroads of traders as well as a fertile plain enticing to conquerors and settlers of different ethnic origins. Two thousand years ago various ethnic groups, particularly Slavs, lived in the area of modern Hungary. In 35 B.C. Roman legions conquered the area west of the Danube (Transdanubia). This became Pannonia, a province of the Roman Empire.

In 896 the Magyars arrived, probably from the area between the upper Volga River and the Ural Mountains. More than 90% of all Hungarians acknowledge the Magyars as their ancestors. Led by Chief Árpád, the Magyars subjugated the various peoples living in the Carpathian Basin. In elementary school, Hungarian children learn this history, as well as its linguistic implications. Theirs is a language that sets them apart from their Slavic and Germanic neighbors.

The 900s were an important transitional period. Within one century the Magyars consolidated their control and, by 1000, the most powerful noble established the kingdom of Hungary, and converted himself and his subjects to Christianity. King István (1000–1038) became a historical figure of mythic proportions. In becoming a Christian kingdom, Hungary experienced yet another transition. Hungarians considered themselves and were considered more a part of the western European domains. This preference for identification with western Europe has continued throughout ensuing centuries.

Hungarian students learn that the twelfth century was a golden period. Hungary was a very large and well-populated European state. Béla III (1172–1192) was one of the richest sovereigns in Europe. Raised in Constantinople, he symbolized the strengths of the cultural synthesis of east and west (Okey 1986).

Transitions with historic importance for all of Europe also occurred during the thirteenth century. In 1222, the lower aristocracy revolted against the mismanagement and extravagance of the barons and King Andrew II. Andrew was forced to accept The Golden Bull which limited the king's power and assured the nobility certain privileges. Although the Golden Bull pertained solely to males of noble birth, Hungary's charter was among the first European charter of political rights, after the Magna Carta.

In elementary school and throughout their later history courses, Hungarian students learn of the critical and symbolically important transitions of the sixteenth century that posed questions of ethnic and national identity. In 1526, the Hungarian king was killed in a battle with the Ottoman Turks. Independent Hungary was then partitioned among its three neighbors: the Ottoman Empire, the Hapsburg Empire, and the principality of Transylvania (Rady 1992).

The next century saw yet another major transition in the macrosystem. After more than a century of multiple foreign rulers, the Hungarians fought with Hapsburg forces to drive out the Ottoman rulers. Areas in Transylvania were also reclaimed by this new alliance. Unfortunately, following the repressive Ottoman domination, Hungary became largely subject to Hapsburg rule. Hapsburg policies further served to separate Hungary from the social changes occurring in western European countries (Okey 1986). Hungary's emerging renaissance towns, with their developing merchant class, became devitalized and rural feudal domains with powerful lords became stronger. In reaction to the harsh Hapsburg rule, and coinciding with the first stirrings of nationalism occurring throughout Europe, the Hungarian nobleman Ferenc Rákóczi led an uprising in 1703 but failed to alter Austrian domination. Here one sees how nationalism, democracy, and patriotism combine in the history of the Hungarian people.

In Hungary, the age of enlightenment took the form of enlightened despotism, with the Hapsburg rulers and landed Hungarian nobility in control (Okey 1986). It was a time of periods of progress toward enlightenment, followed by periods of repression. In school, students learn of the notable Hungarians who led independence movements. Indeed, István Széchenyi, Sándor Petőfi, Lajos Kossoth, Ferenc Deák, József Eötvös and others represent part of widespread European national, independence movements that were occurring in many parts of Europe during the mid-1800s. These efforts failed. Neither democratization nor independence occurred in Hungary which was cruelly punished by the Hapsburgs. However, since the Austrian monarchy was impoverished due to its military defeats with Italy, France, and Prussia, a group of nobles, led by Deák, were able to force a "Compromise" with Emperor Francis Joseph of Austria in 1867 that resulted in the formation of the dual Austro-Hungarian Monarchy.

Recent History

In the late nineteenth and early twentieth centuries, the Hungarian government actively supported the growth of industry, mainly in Budapest. This period was a time of great social transitions for many of the great-great-grandparents of the adolescents in this study. Budapest became the center of trade and industry. Its population grew to approximately 800,000 in 1900 as many families moved from traditional villages to this burgeoning urban hub, among them many Jews. A new elite bourgeoisie developed. Transportation was modernized. Budapest's elegant subway was the first built on the continent. In keeping with a long Hungarian tradition, the arts flourished. And then the First World War broke out.

In 1918, after the defeat of the Austro-Hungarian Monarchy, Hungary officially became an independent republic and Mihály Károlyi became its president. He soon resigned in protest of the Allies' demands, at the armistice negotiations held at Trianon, that Hungary surrender most of the land that had historically constituted Hungary.

The Treaty of Trianon resulted in major life changes for the majority of the Hungarian population. It formally ceded two-thirds of Hungarian territory and three-fifths of its population to its neighbors (Rady, 1992). Large numbers of ethnic Hungarians remained in large areas of previously Hungarian land that now became part of Austria, Romania, and the newly created states of Czechoslovakia and Yugoslavia. Today, many Hungarians have relatives who live in the neighboring countries and consider themselves ethnic Hungarians. This may be particularly true of the students living in Pécs, a city less than 50 miles from Croatia. From 1920 until the end of World War II, much of Hungarian politics focused on regaining ethnic Hungarians and "amputated" lands.

Soon after Karolyi's resignation, in March 1919, Béla Kun formed a coalition but predominantly communist government, the second in Europe. Kun, too, worked to regain parts of lost Hungarian territory. Hungarian incursions into its former territory that had just become part of Slovakia and Transylvania, as well as capitalists' fears of Kun's communist rule, led to a coup by Admiral Miklós Horthy, a Hungarian supported by western powers. A brief invasion of Hungary by Romanian and Czechoslovakian forces followed, including the siege and brief occupation of Budapest. Kun quickly resigned. Admiral Horty restored the Hungarian monarchy, declared the throne "vacant" and named himself Regent.

Between 1919 and 1945 Hungary made numerous appeals to international bodies as well as individual nations for the restoration of land. Nazi Germany's support of the restoration of the land Hungary considered within its traditional borders, as well as traditionally close historical ties between Hungary, Austria, and Germany, were important factors in Hungary's wartime alliance with Germany. The growing national and worldwide depression also contributed to the rise of right wing pro-fascist groups in Hungary. In 1932, Horthy appointed Gyula Gömbös, the leader of the Right Radicals as prime minister.

In 1937, Hungary joined Germany and Italy in the Anti-Comintern Pact. A year later, Nazi Germany officially supported Hungary's claim to parts of Czechoslovakia, Romania, and Yugoslavia. In the 1939 elections, the fascist Arrow Cross received 25% of the vote in the Hungarian elections.

The lives of the grandparents of the adolescents in this study were changed forever by World War II. By 1940 German troops were allowed to pass through Hungary to invade Yugoslavia, and Hungary fought in the war as an ally of Germany. Horthy remained in power until 1944 when Germany offically occupied

Hungary and installed Ferencz Szálasi, the leader of the Hungarian fascist Arrow Cross. The Allies, mostly Soviet, invaded Hungary in 1944. On January 20, 1945, Hungary's provisional government signed an armistice ending the war.

At the close of the war, Hungarians experienced a series of rapid transitions. In the first post-war elections, a coalition of several parties was established with support for democratization, modernization, and land reform. In this election, the three major winners were the Smallholders who received 57% of the vote; the Social Democrats, 17.4%; and Communists, 17.0% (Okey 1986). Despite this poor showing, by 1947 the Communists had become the predominant party. In May 1949, the Communists presented a single slate of candidates for the election. In August, a Communist Peoples' Republic was proclaimed with Mátyás Rákosi as party leader and premier. Hungary was now within the Soviet sphere of influence.

The parents as well as grandparents of the present generation of adolescents continued to experience political and social upheavals throughout the 1950s, with periods of relative relaxation followed by periods of relative repression. During the early 1950s, Hungary's economic policy mandated rapid industrialization, particularly the development of heavy industry. The collectivization of agriculture meant nationalization of large estates as well as smaller holdings. This process not only affected owners, but in many cases resulted in mandated relocation of peasants to areas such as Budapest and Pécs that were being industrialized.

The purges of the early 1950s were changes that resulted from efforts from within the Hungarian communist party to consolidate power from particular factions and were influenced by Stalin's purges in the U.S.S.R. The year of Stalin's death, 1953, brought relative political relaxation, including Imre Nagy's rise to power. Within two years, however, changes in the U.S.S.R. as well as Hungarian politics resulted in Nagy's forced resignation and the renewal of Rákosi's power. But the political winds soon changed once more. Resulting in part from Khrushchev's reforms, Rákosi was forced to resign and Erno Gerő became prime minister. The apparent political thaw gave hope to reformists within the Communist party as well as to opponents from the broad political spectrum. Resistance in Hungary coincided and was associated with resistance to Soviet domination elsewhere, notably Poland.

On October 23, 1956, resistance began after university students demonstrated in support of reformers in Poland and demanded that Nagy be reinstated as prime minister. Soviet troops already stationed in Hungary acted to stop demonstrations. By October 30, Nagy established a multiple party coalition, was made head of the government, and declared Hungary a neutral country in the East-West alignment. He requested assistance from the United Nations but received no answer. A deployment of 200,000 Soviet troops invaded Hungary. Nagy was overthrown, and János Kádár became premier. An estimated 200,000 Hungarians fled the country. Kádár's government arrested and jailed participants in the uprising. Nagy and other leaders of the reform movement were executed.

By the beginning of the 1960s, the moderate wing of the Party began to gain more power. Kádár was becoming known, both in the East and the West, for moderate policies, exemplified in his well-known conciliatory statement of 1961 that "He who is not against us is for us" (The Economist Intelligence Unit 1996). His government instituted largely successful economic reform. In 1968, during a period of relative relaxation, the Kádár government introduced a new economic plan, the "new economic mechanism" (NEM), a plan for "market socialism." The NEM provided the state-owned operations with some autonomy and also provided a legal mechanism whereby workers were permitted some private sector work. Additional reforms in educational, social, and political reforms were instituted.

The Transitions

The generally strong European economy of that time, Hungary's NEM plan, and large western loans, greatly improved Hungarian's living standards during the late 1960s and early 1970s. But by the mid-1970s the relatively strong economic situation had began to worsen and by the mid-1980s, when many of these adolescents interviewed began school, Hungary was in a severe economic recession. Nascent political changes were already beginning to occur. Open criticism of the government increased as did more subtle forms of criticism. For example, by the mid-1980s membership in the Communist youth organization had declined by 20%. Underground, *samizdat* publications such as *Beszelö* appeared.

The changes in the Soviet Union also influenced the incipient transitions in Hungary. During this period, Gorbachev's rise to power took place amid deteriorating economic and social conditions in the Soviet Union. In 1986, Gorbachev proposed *perestroika* and *glasnost*. These reforms within the Soviet Union also provided the basis for the hopes of reformers within Hungary and other Warsaw Pact nations as it became evident that leaders such as Kádár did not have the support of the Soviet leader (Rady 1992).

In March 1987 public demonstrations took place in Budapest, with demands for increased liberalization. Although Kádár remained party leader, Károly Grósz gained power and became Chairman of the Council of Ministers. Although his promotion was not viewed as a victory for the reform wing, Grósz was widely viewed as pragmatic rather than rigid.

During 1987 members in the reform wing of the Communist part became increasingly outspoken in their criticism of government policy (Rady 1992), often working through an umbrella organization, the Patriotic Peoples Front. A leader of the group, Imre Pozsgay, promoted radical reforms in economic policies. Independent organizations could not yet be established; yet with Pozsgay's important sponsorship and leadership, the Hungarian Democratic Forum was founded (Rady 1992). By May 1987, the government's tight control was on the wane.

The pace of changes that had quickened in 1987 became more and more tumultuous in the succeeding three years with major events occurring weekly, a veritable social earthquake. It was during this time that many of the participants in these studies became adolescents.

Many of the prominent critics of the government were members of the Communist Party. By 1988 criticism within the Party leadership became more open and direct, and attempts at discipline became less effective. Party membership fell. Demonstrations continued. In an effort to regain both the allegiance of members as well as authority, numerous changes were made during the special Party conference of May 1988. After thirty years, Kádár was ousted from his position as General Secretary as well as from his membership in the Politboro; Grósz was appointed General Secretary and retained his current position as Chairman of Council of Ministers; and party reformers such as Pozsgay were appointed to the Politboro (Bruszt and Stark 1992).

In events that symbolized the passing of an era and sociopolitical transformation, Imre Nagy was rehabilitated and reburied in June. And in July, Kádár died. By November, Communist party leaders considered Grósz "too conservative" regarding change and forced him to resign. Miklós Németh replaced him as Chairman of the Council of Ministers. Reformers were also appointed to head several key ministries (Rady 1992). In December the National Assembly voted to allow the establishment of independent political organizations as well as the right to demonstrate, thus legalizing parties that already existed and the pattern of demonstrations that had already emerged.

During 1989 the structural change to multiparty democracy and a market economy occurred. In February 1989, the Central Committee of the Communist Party agreed to support the transition to a multiparty democratic structure. Public opinion polls in the late spring of 1989 showed that the Communists would win if elections were held at that point. Reform communists such as Pozsgay thought that the Communist Party could "seize the high ground as champions of democracy and use their superior resources, organization and well known candidates" (Bruszt and Stark 1992, p. 43). When, during the Round Table negotiations with opposition groups held during the summer of 1989, the united Hungarian opposition insisted that the goal of any agreement was free and open elections, the Communists agreed. In hindsight, according to Bruszt and Stark (1992), the outcome seems surprising when one considers that it was the very weakness of this opposition that led it to adopt this uncompromising stand. As Ash (1992) wrote in comparing the Hungarian situation with that in Poland: "These negotiations might loosely be compared with the Polish Round Table. But whereas the Polish Party negotiated with Solidarity *at* a Round Table, the Hungarian Party was negotiating *with* a Round Table" (Ash 1992, pp. 440–441). In Hungary, the transition to democracy occurred with no deaths, no violence, and few mass demonstrations.

An official agreement was signed in September and elections scheduled for November. Hungary was proclaimed a democratic republic on October 23, 1989, an event widely cited by the students in their interviews.

There were many important historical events and many critical decisions made during this time. For example, one outcome of the negotiations between the Hungarian Socialist Workers Party and the Hungarian Socialist Party was that Pozsgay was the only presidential candidate acceptable to both. But should the president be elected prior to the national elections for the legislators? At the suggestion of the Alliance of Free Democrats, Premier Miklós Németh agreed to have a national referendum on the issue of whether the president should be elected prior to the legislative election, or elected after this election which was scheduled for spring 1990. In this first referendum, voters chose to postpone the election of the president.

In March, the National Assembly altered the constitution so that the president would be elected directly. Also that month, an official agreement with the Soviet Union was signed regarding the withdrawal of troops and the withdrawal began. Parliamentary elections were held in March and April with sixty parties participating, including ten major parties. Indeed, many students mentioned the difficulty of knowing which party to support. The Hungarian Democratic Forum won 165 of the 386 parliamentary seats; the Alliance of Free Democrats, 92 seats; the Independent Smallholders Party, 43 seats; the Socialist Party, 33 seats; the Federation of Young Democrats (often called FIDESZ), 21 seats; and the Christian Democrats, 21 seats (Economist Intelligence Unit 1996.)

József Antall was chosen prime minister. As one of the first acts of this new democratic process, Antall came to a special agreement with the Free Democrats. As a result he gained their support for impending legislation and gave his support for their nominee, Árpád Göncz, to become president.

The numerous challenges this govenment faced would have been difficult for any stable, experienced democracy. They were particularly problematic for a flegling democracy which lacked an involved civil society and had limited experience with a market economy. At that time Hungary's economic problems were severe. Hungary had Europe's highest per capita debt and a 20% inflation rate, leading to rapidly decreasing living standards (Echikson 1992). Hungarians were inventing what democracy and a market economy would mean in their society. The new government was committed to a market economy including the privatization of national industries. As of 1990, only 10% of workers were listed as working in the private sector (Hungarian Statistical Yearbook, cited in Economist Intelligence Unit 1996). Policies of privatizing industries and com-

pensating former landholders had social costs such as unemployment. Similarly, deregulating prices resulted in inflated food and
energy costs. In their interviews, several students point to the
October 1990 strike by taxi drivers in response to the rise in gaso-
line prices and to the protests by university students.

The Economist Intelligence Unit (1996) reported that during
this time most Hungarians were under "severe economic and social
pressure." Many needed a second or third job to make ends meet.
This, too, is evident in some of the interviews with the Hungarian
students. Indeed, there was increased incidence of stress-related
illness such as alcoholism.

The first sets of interviews were carried out in Budapest and
Pécs in spring 1991. By that time the pace of change had slowed.
The new government was installed but the actual changes in laws
and regulations governing the economy, politics, foreign relations,
and other spheres needed to be hammered out. People expected
swift change. "The political process was characterized by a growing
malaise" (Schöpflin 1992, p. 430). Inflation reached 30%. The official unemployment rate reached 5%, high relative to previous official rates. In the 1991 interviews, many students pointed to these
national problems.

The following year, 1992, was also a year of continued political debates regarding policies that attempted to "reconstruct society in a new image" (Schöpflin 1993). The state of the economy was
a center of attention: problems with privatization remained to be
resolved, the standard of living continued to decrease, inflation
continued, and the number of unemployed grew, although the rate
of foreign investment remained strong.

The political situation became even more complex with numerous political splits. The by-elections of 1992 were marked by
low voter turnout and voter apathy (Schöpflin 1993). At the same
time, there was a heated national debate, which some students
discussed, regarding the issue of who controlled the media that
was symbolic of clashes in which people saw democracy under seige
in this case the right to information.

> Viewed from the inside, Hungary appeared to be highly turbulent
> during 1993, but viewed from the outside matters seemed rela-
> tively stable.
>
> Schöpflin 1994, p. 439

The second set of interviews were carried out in Budapest in the winter of 1993; and in Pécs in the winter of 1993–94. The beginning of 1993 saw the continuation of the political and economic issues of 1992. The Hungarian Democratic Forum resolved its problems with the militant politician István Csurka by forcing him and the other right wing radicals out of the Forum, after which they formed their own group, Hungarian Truth and Justice Party. The government coalition was successful in forcing their media policies through financial controls.

The economy continued its poor performance. According to official figures, exports fell 17%; inflation rose 20%; the deficit remained among the highest per capita in Europe; and the currency was devalued for the fifth time (Griffin 1994). It also remained difficult to obtain realistic measures of the economy since a sizable proportion of the new market economy was the growth of the "gray economy," i.e., the unreported sale of goods or rendering of services.

Months after the follow-up interviews in Pécs, in May 1994, voters supported the Hungarian Socialist Party, thus returning many from the old Communist Party to power. Voters were concerned about proposed cuts in social spending and, perhaps, some were nostalgic for what seemed a more secure time prior to the transitions. The Socialist Party won 209 of the 387 seats in Parliament. They selected Gyula Horn as prime minister and formed a coalition with the Alliance of Free Democrats.

By 1994 the private sector of the economy had grown from 10% in 1990 to more than 50%. Trade was another bright spot, with a 20% rise in exports. The debt, however, remained staggering. In response, the new government proposed an austerity budget in the fall of 1994. In order to reduce the deficit, they planned to reduce social programs, raise energy prices, and institute other cuts in spending. This was contrary to many people's expectations of the Socialists. Their popularity soon plummeted, partly because they did little to explain the reasons for the policy to the voters or, indeed, to the Free Democrats (Griffin 1996).

In March of 1995, Lajos Bokros became finance Minister and put through a program that included spending cuts as well as new fees for services, including the university fees the Budapest students mention in their 1995 interviews. Cuts in social programs were unacceptable to others in the Socialist Party as well, and several ministers resigned. The Constitutional Court struck down parts of the program as unconstitutional. Such austerity measures to address the national debt were extremely unpopular with voters—and many students. The economy was not improving quickly. In 1995 the forint was again devalued and inflation rose over 25%. This was the economic context the students in Budapest discussed during the third set of interviews that were conducted in the fall of 1995.

Introduction to the Hungarian Studies

Three important differences are apparent in a comparison of the Budapest and Pécs samples. First, the Budapest sample is a longitudinal sample, that is, the same students were interviewed at different times, whereas the Pécs sample is cross sectional, that is, similar samples were interviewed at different times. The responses of the Budapest students provide an opportunity to examine the same young people's development in a particular context during the specific historical period of the early to mid-1990s. Alternatively, the Pécs sample provides insight into how 15–18 year-olds viewed the social and political situation in 1991 and, again, in 1993–94. Thus, we obtain different historical perspectives from these two samples of young people.

Secondly, the students from Budapest were from a much more metropolitan and political community than the Pécs students. For American readers, the differences between these cities might parallel the difference between Washington, D.C. and Raleigh, the capital of nearby North Carolina. The students from Budapest were geographically closer to the political changes that were taking place in Hungary. Lastly, as previously mentioned, the school in Budapest was an innovative academic school that was not representative of academic high schools in Hungary. The students in Pécs attended schools that more closely represented the types of educational experiences most students in Hungary were receiving during the time of the study.

Despite the differences in these two samples, the 1991 responses of the Budapest students were similar in many ways to those of the students in Pécs who were also interviewed that year. As we discuss in the two chapters on the studies as well as in the concluding chapter, the extent of the similarities in responses across these two groups of adolescents suggests that the political transformation of their country affected Hungarian adolescents in ways that often transcended more specific environmental settings.

CHAPTER FOUR

The Pécs Study

Portraits of Two Students in Pécs: Csaba and Mária

Csaba (interviewed by Komlósi in 1994)

Seventeen-year-old Csaba lives at home with his parents and a younger sister and is studying carpentry and scaffolding in a vocational school. He has an elder married brother who works as a mason. The family currently lives in a rural area outside of Pécs. Csaba appears to have a quiet, calm nature. He speaks slowly when answering Komlósi's questions.

Growing Up in Changing Times

Csaba explains that his mother completed eight years of primary school. She is 37 years old and works in a kindergarten program as a nurse. His father, also 37, was a miner and is now a disabled pensioner. The income from his mining job was good enough to allow the family to get a flat when Csaba was young. Csaba explains that during the changes in the economic system many mines were closed and the staff reduction was "easy to carry out" since it could be stated that mining work was dangerous for miners' health. After working for twenty years in the mines, Csaba's father was declared disabled.

During his interview, Csaba spends considerable time discussing the details of his family finances, obviously a topic of personal as well as family interest. He explains that his father's retirement pay is 32,000 forint a month (the same, for example, as a Hungarian university tutor's salary and less than $300 U.S.). His

73

mother's monthly salary is 12,000 forint. They also receive a family allowance of 6,000 forint. His father's mother, who lives with them, receives retirement pay of 14,000 forint. According to Csaba, this combined income allows his family to have a comfortable lifestyle.

A year before his interview the family moved from Pécs to a little village, seventeen kilometers away. Csaba explains that it is easier to manage living in a village since needed "vegetables, potatoes, fruits, etc." can be grown in the garden. Csaba's family bought a three room house that is 150 square meters, large enough to give the family "a satisfactory degree of comfort." The family has an 11,000 square meter field where they grow wheat and corn for sale, in addition to vegetables for their kitchen. Csaba is aware that the changes resulted in the loss of his father's job but he says that with the move to the village his family is coping well with their economic situation.

Csaba emphasizes that his family enjoyed the change of environment, but he misses his friends from Pécs. Because he still attends school in Pécs, he is able to spend time with many of his friends from his home city. Csaba talks at length about his 16-year-old girlfriend with whom he has a "serious relationship." His girlfriend's family lives in Pécs. Her father is also a disabled pensioner and her mother is a cashier in a big department store.

When Csaba talks about school, he mentions that his family does not really encourage him to study, aside from rather formal statements about the importance of being motivated. His grades in primary school were poor and he had to repeat a grade. Now that he is at the vocational school, his grades are better. Csaba explains, "I was not a diligent student. I didn't like studying. Now I am more interested in school. And, I am a better student. I have a good grade-point-average." He points out that he has even decided to spend an extra year in school in order to study German. He explains that he wants to speak German well enough to get a job in Germany or Austria. According to Csaba, before the changes in Hungary, jobs abroad were very rare but now an increasing number of young workers are trying to go abroad. In thinking about the future, Csaba hopes to take advantage of the new opportunities that the political and economic transitions have brought.

When he is asked to discuss his personal qualities Csaba presents a dichotomy, first discussing his independence and then his willingness to meet the expectations of others:

Generally speaking, I am self-willed. I do what I want. I get what I want to get. I fight for it until I get it. I save money if necessary, for example, for a nice pair of shoes. When I'm working on something I work until things become just like I want them to be.

My other feature is that I'm yielding. Both in the family and with my friends. I do what they say, if I can. Sometimes I am lazy . . . Or . . . almost always. When I'm in my bed it's difficult for me to get up and go.

Csaba's self-description also indicates that he focuses on the problems and events of the present. He does not mention liking his future trade or talk about what he would like to achieve professionally. Football is mentioned as a favorite pastime, but he explains that he does not regularly attend training, and has no future plans to play on a team. His activities focus on the satisfaction of present social needs such as spending time with his friends and girlfriend. On weekends, he and his friends like to go to discos to dance. Sometimes he stays at his girlfriend's home for the night. Sometimes, she stays at Csaba's home.

Like his peers Csaba mentions his family first when discussing the important groups in his life. Csaba reports that there are currently no quarrels or serious conflicts in his family. There used to be a lot of quarrels because he would come home late, but there are no problems now. He says he is "almost" treated as an adult. Csaba reports that the group that is next in importance to him is his group of friends, adding, "having fun with the guys is important."

When talking about his values, Csaba mentions, "being sure of myself . . . the most important thing is to know what I am doing." The second value he considers to be important is knowing what he wants to do in life. The next value on his list is "happiness." Money and material resources are also important to Csaba. He describes his family as relatively well-off financially and he gets quite a lot of money to spend as he wishes.

Csaba considers his family of primary importance in the development of his value system. He considers his father's impact to be the strongest, but he also mentions the influence of his friends.

My system of values is very similar to my father's. I am just like him. It's slightly different from my mother's system of values, but we can discuss everything. No conflict results from this. She is more yielding. My friends' way of thinking is similar to mine, but many of them are not as persistent as me. I have more of a sense of responsibility. I have more initiative as well.

Csaba's values are reflected in his wishes:

Let me have so much money that I'll have no problems any more.

Let me live in happiness because it's better than unhappiness.

Let me have an understanding wife so as not to have quarrels.

When first asked about his fears, Csaba first says he has none, but then, "perhaps it's the war that I am afraid of because I may lose my family then." He lives only ten kilometers from Croatia which is at war at the time of this interview. Despite the close proximity to tragic war activity, Csaba feels protected among his friends and with his family.

Living History

Csaba shows far less enthusiasm when talking about politics than when discussing his family and friends. When asked about the changes that have been occurring in his part of the world, Csaba does not relate any of them to his personal life. He states quite emphatically:

My family and my group of friends have not changed. I am not interested in the rest. My father is a disabled pensioner and since he has some extra jobs our financial situation has improved. My close environment has completely changed due to the move. However, I don't know what has changed and what remained unchanged in Hungary. Of course, there were changes in Europe. The war in Yugoslavia broke out. There were some changes in Romania as well, but I don't know what. Almost everything has changed in the world. But I couldn't say anything in particular.

Csaba's answers to specific questions about what has changed focus on the Hungary's financial well-being, particularly the changing job market. He speaks with strong emotion, describing the hardships many people face:

The communist system is over. As communism came to an end, the number of the unemployed started to increase. No unemployment had been there before. Everyone had jobs ... [Now] the worth of the forint is becoming worse and worse and the debt of the country is increasing. . . .

Unemployment and money devaluation appeared only recently, after the fall of the communist system. [But] the country's running into debt started after WW II. Today, people have no jobs. They can't produce. They're poor. Due to inflation and the debt, the economy has gotten worse . . .

. . . The changes have been basically bad for the people since they have no jobs. They've become poor. Now ordinary people do everything they can at their places of work just not to be dismissed. Everyone fears for his or her job. Due to inflation, everything is more and more expensive, while wages do not change. People don't feel that the debt of the country is increasing.

When asked to comment on how others around him perceive the changes Csaba becomes less talkative; not only does he indicate his own dislike for discussing this topic, he suggests that this is a topic that his friends also do not discuss:

I don't know how my parents and their acquaintances perceive the changes. I don't perceive them, I can only see that I can't remember the prices in the shop because of the rise in prices. I don't know if my friends or other youngsters can perceive anything of it. But I am not interested in this anyway. We don't talk about things like this. . . . The changes have no effects on my family. We can perceive the inflation a bit. My parents are slightly more nervous now but there are no quarrels about money. Perhaps I get a bit less money from them. That's all. But we have as much as we need. Unemployment doesn't touch us. I am not interested in it.

Despite his father's forced retirement and his family's move to the village, Csaba does not view the changes as having important effects on his family. Nor does Csaba perceive that the changes have had much of an effect on his development into adulthood. Csaba first says definitively, "the changes have had no effects on my development." Despite this position, later in the interview Csaba says, "I think the changes touch all people in the same way. There are no differences between village and city people . . . But the people oppose any changes."

When asked if there had been anybody either in his family or in his environment who took some role in politics either before or after the changes, Csaba replies:

> Life is important for us. We don't deal with politics . . . don't sympathize with any of the parties. I don't know what they are doing. I don't know whom I'd vote for if I had to.

Understanding Political Concepts

Not surprisingly, Csaba is not very interested in talking about political concepts such as citizenship or citizenship education in school:

> I've never encountered such questions at school, neither in the primary school or vocational school. I don't even know what belongs to this topic (civics or citizenship education) and what the study of civics is about. I don't know if the school should have any role in bringing up people to be good citizens.

When talking about what it takes to be a good citizen, Csaba focuses on workers doing their work properly, "I think a good citizen is one who goes to work every day. He does all that he has to do. It never meant anything else." His understanding of freedom underscores a strong sense of personal freedom, "for me, freedom is that nobody interferes in my business. I do whatever I want. . . . For a country, it means that it is not dependent upon other countries."

Commentary

Csaba appears content with his life and presents himself as a family-centered, calm adolescent who values harmonious relationships. When he talks about the changes in Hungary and their effects, he speaks with concern and emotion about the negative impact the changes have had on people's lives.

Yet Csaba says that he does not think that he or his family have been substantially affected and is without negative emotions when talking about his family's situation. From the way that he focuses on his family's financial well being and living conditions, it is clear that he and his family feel that their lives are presently quite comfortable and happy. Overall, Csaba is oriented to the present moment, but he has changed his incipient plans for his future in response to the changing opportunities. He envisions working abroad as a way to financially improve his life rather then expand his horizons. His increased diligence in studying may also be related to the increased possibilities he sees, as well as his increased maturity, both combining synergistically. Csaba's emphatic statement that he and his family are uninterested in politics, that "life is important for us. We don't deal with politics," seems a succinct summary of his experience of growing up in changing times.

Mária (interviewed by Komlósi in 1994)

Mária is a 17-year-old girl who attends a vocational school, where she studies the piano. Mária's father finished secondary school and is currently employed as a manager in the food industry. A year before her interview Mária's father became unemployed for a period of time when the state factory where he was employed became privatized. Mária's mother has a university degree and is an English teacher at a secondary school. The family lives with Mária's grandmother outside Pécs.

Growing Up in Changing Times

Mária describes herself as "impatient, a little bit untidy, but I like giving my best." She thinks of herself as a loving person and reflects, "I can love. If I love someone I love them very much. Of course, I try to accommodate to everyone else."

Mária says that besides her family, music and her Catholic religion are the most important things in her life. When discussing the events that have had the biggest impact on her, Mária mentions her grandfather's death as the most difficult event, followed by the challenging entrance examination for her secondary school with its music program.

Mária names reading as a favorite pastime. Her favorite books are romance novels. She explains, "maybe this type of novel fits my music interest the best." She also enjoys ballet and art, but comments that she does not "do sports" though she likes to play basketball "just for fun."

Mária's responses to the question about the groups that are important to her are consistent with the elements she mentions in her self-description. After her family, Mária says that the Catholic community is most important group in her life. Her peers at school are also important to her, and she adds that, "I have good relationships with my classmates."

Mária perceives herself as "sometimes a pessimist and sometimes an optimist." Overall she feels that her life is better than her parents' lives were when they were her age, and she greatly appreciates how they have tried to make this so:

> My life is totally different from theirs . . . I get everything from my parents. They work hard so that it will be good for me.

In her self-description Mária emphasizes her ability to love. When asked about values that are important to her, she says that most important value is "love." The value she identifies as the second most important, "caring for others," is also related to love:

> I got these values from my family . . . My values are very close to my parents, particularly my father's. The relationships and love I have from them [are important].

Mária also mentions her grandmother's Christian beliefs and her primary school music teacher as being important influences on her values. In talking about her music teacher, Mária points to the critical importance of timing, "her attention was important [to me] and she started me on the right path with music."

Mária's three wishes reflect her loving and caring nature as well as her sense of adventure:

> The first would be having a lot of money. I would love to travel to see the world. My parent's income is low and we can't afford to travel. My second wish would be peace for the world. I did not think about this before when the war was far away from us, but now people are killing each other in the next country. People are evacuating because of the war [in the former Yugoslavia] and [refugees are] coming to Hungary, so I want peace for the world!

The third wish is that I would like to live a happy life and make my family happy too.

Mária's fear is that she will lose someone she loves:

To lose a member of the family is the most terrible thing to me. I realized this when I lost my grandfather. I didn't have this fear before.

Mária sees the fear she has about losing a member of her family as "connected to the Yugoslavian war and the Chernobyl atomic disaster. I am afraid of war."

Asked for her picture of what a good life twenty years in the future would be like, Mária sees a relationship between her own life and the situation in Hungary:

I haven't ever thought about that. I would like to have a family. Maybe the condition of the country will be better, so my conditions will be better because of that. I'd like to work. I'd like to be a good mother and a good wife. I'd like to do my job as well as possible and enjoy what I do.

Living History

When asked to list the most important changes that have occurred in Hungary, Mária focuses on the change in the national mood rather than the events themselves:

The most important event was the Proclamation of the Republic on the 23rd of October, 1989. First everyone was very enthusiastic, everyone expected a lot from the new government. They trusted in the new government. [Later] the mood became bad and everyone was embittered. . . . Nowadays people . . . don't live well, except for the people who became rich taking part in privatization.

Mária notes that the political and economic changes seemed to happen very quickly, before people were ready for them, and mentions the establishment of the multiparty system as one of the two most important changes. When discussing the politics of the new system, Mária criticizes the way the public was informed about what was happening in their country saying, "the Free Democratic opposition handled the media. It's so easy to manipulate the people this way." Despite her criticism, overall Mária supports the change to democracy and declares, "I think everyone considers the change [to democracy] to be very positive."

Mária mentions privatization of the economic system as the other important change. She is critical of the results, saying that "the shelves are full of products, there is a big variety, but the quality is often not good."

Indeed, Mária explains that her family attempted to take advantage of some of the changes in the early 1990s. Her father was involved in a brief private business venture but the company soon closed. She jokes that when privatization was first introduced, "private ventures started to grow as fast as mushrooms." Given the fact that Mária's father lost his job as a result of the political changes in Hungary, it is interesting that she says, "the changes didn't make a big difference in my family's life." She goes on to explain:

> A lot of people complain a lot. Mostly, unemployment causes problems for a lot of people . . . My parents and others in my environment talk much more about politics. They follow the political changes. . . . But I don't think too much about this topic. So our life has not changed very much. We don't have more or less money. We live like before.

Understanding Political Concepts

Mária seems engaged in the discussion when talking about political concepts but ambivalent in her responses to political activity. However, when asked what she thinks are the key features of a democracy, Mária names quite a few and includes several details. In addition, like many of her peers interviewed in 1994, she acknowledges that she sees her own freedom in relationship to the freedom of others:

> The important parts of democracy are the multiparty system, the shared power between the judicial and the executive branches, free elections, that everyone can advise the government [free speech], and a written constitution . . .

> There is a strong relation between democracy and freedom. For me, freedom means that I can do what I want to do. I do what I decided to do, but in a way that is not injurious [to others].

Mária perceives that in the past she and her family were really not interested in politics, and even though her past membership in the Young Pioneers might have been viewed as political involvement she considers it forced participation:

> We've never been part of the political life. I was a member of the youth organization, the Pioneers, but that doesn't mean anything, because we were forced to do that. No one paid attention to it, so it was not a serious political thing.

In response to items about voting preferences, she says that her parents always vote. Whereas she had previously said that "I don't think too much about this topic" (political changes), her answers to items about voting reflect a different picture:

> I'm really interested in the recent political events. The Christian Democratic Party is the most appealing to me. They are the most normal and they have good leaders . . . If I had voted [in the last election] I would have voted [for them].

She says that citizenship education was "not important in Hungary" before the changes although she had heard about what she called "internationalism" in school. Commenting on citizenship education after the changes, Mária points to a critical problem:

> These days they talk about citizenship, the good habits of the citizen. They [the teachers] never had to think about this, so they are not comfortable with this topic.

During her discussion about the curriculum of the school, Mária mentions casually that she is a member of the school council. Of all the students interviewed in Pécs, she was the only student who talked about being a school council representative. However, she named this as she would membership in any school group. Marta did not seem to perceive her role in the school council as part of a change of system or as political involvement, nor did she draw any parallels to her previous membership in the Pioneers.

Commentary

Mária portrays herself as someone who is a loving daughter, a religious person, and a serious student of music. Although she has not yet thought a great deal about plans for her future, her initial vision is in keeping with her other responses, to be a good wife and mother, to enjoy her job and do it well. Mária connects her future situation with the "conditions of the country." Mária talks seriously about her views of the social changes. She expresses definite opinions, but appears to have relatively little factual knowledge, naming relatively few changes and focusing on people's emotional responses. Mária talks about the effects of the changes on Hungary, particularly the economic impacts on other people, but emphasizes that she and her family have remained relatively unaffected. This contradicts other information she provides about her family such as her father's failure in a new private enterprise and her family's low income. How can this lack of logical conclusions be explained? Perhaps her sense that little has changed for her family is related to her own feeling that, "I get everything from my parents. They work hard so that it will be good for me."

Mária's answers about her own and her family's political involvement suggest that she has limited, prescribed ideas about what constitutes involvement. Mária evidences identity confusion related to her own political involvement. On the one hand, she is active in school leadership, identifies her interests with that of one of the political parties, and plans to vote. Although she is not able to talk about the changes in her society in detail, she can list quite a few characteristics of the new democratic government and shows considerable concern for the welfare of other Hungarians. Despite this, she does not see herself as someone who is politically involved, nor does she define citizenship in this way.

The Pécs Study

Pécs is considered one of Hungary's most beautiful cities and is a popular tourist destination because of its historical architecture and museums as well as the bountiful gardens growing in its gentle Mediterranean subclimate. The architecture of Pécs reflects its location at the crossroads of trade as well as invasion, with buildings from Roman, medieval, Turkish, and Hapsburg times, as well as Stalinist-type block high-rise apartment buildings from the post-World War II era, and newly constructed modern buildings. Throughout history, the buildings have changed to reflect changing times. The foundation of St. Bartholomew's church, built on the ancient market square and still at the hub of modern Pécs, became the foundation for the Turkish mosque of Pasha Kasaim Gasi. After the defeat of the Turks when it again became a Catholic church, the minarets were removed and it was renovated in the contemporary Baroque style. The students interviewed in Pécs walk along streets lined with buildings constructed in past centuries. Adaptations of old buildings to new times have occurred during the contemporary transitions as well, with high tech stores opening in centuries-old buildings and billboard advertisements juxtaposed against stately mansions.

These students attend schools in a city that is also rich in educational history. Schools were established in Pécs in the eleventh century and a university was founded there in the fourteenth century, one of the first in Europe.

Pécs Sample Demographics

Interviews were conducted with sixty-four high school students during spring 1991 and sixty-eight students during winter 1993–94. The interviews were conducted in Hungarian with individual students in a private setting at the schools. Komlósi was assisted by several graduate students in the 1991 interviews and personally interviewed all the students in 1993–94.

Table 4.1 presents demographic information for both samples. In 1991, females were represented to a greater degree because of the higher representation of females at several schools. As can be seen from Table 4.1, fewer technical school students were interviewed in 1993–94. During the intervening years, changes had been made in the Hungarian educational system, and some academic and technical schools were combined. The thirty-six students identified as attending academic schools included students in technical programs who attended these combined schools.

Table 4.1
Pécs Sample Demographics

	1991	1993–94
Academic	19	36*
Vocational	21	23
Technical	24	9
Male	24	38
Female	40	30
Ages: 15	3	12
16	21	18
17	38	26
18	2	12
Mean age	16.6	16.6
Total	64	68

*Combined numbers of academic and technical students

Growing Up in Changing Times:
In the Circle of My Family

I am very family-centered. I spend all my spare time with my parents and my little sister. I cannot imagine my life without them. Family gives you peace in your soul and harmony.

The development of psychosocial identity involves increasing coherence in the growing sense of self. The students in Pécs consistently discussed themselves in the context of family relationships. They emphasized their closeness to their families, particularly their parents. Although they enjoyed the company of friends, they perceived their family as the people from whom they sought support and with whom they talked when facing important issues in their lives. Quite a few also talked about the importance of girlfriends or boyfriends. Their sense of their future was rather vague, but generally optimistic. Overall, although some pointed to the ways in which their development as a person might change as a result of social, economic or political changes, few had strong opinions or discussed issues in detail.

What they did not mention is also worth pointing out. In these open-ended discussions, few made any reference to political, economic, and social changes at the national and local level, or how these changes affected their lives. In discussing relationships within important microsystems, relatively few talked about the microsystems of the school, club, or church that would have connected them to exosystems in the broader community.

Comparisons of the responses of students from the three types of high schools, of males and females, and between the students interviewed in 1991 and 1993–94, indicated homogeneity among the samples and across time. Some of the 1993–94 data also suggest incipient changes in the role of adolescents from the time of the first interviews.

The following are typical excerpts from the initial, open-ended self descriptions of a student from a vocational school and a student from an academic school interviewed in 1991. These excerpts illustrate the importance of family for these adolescents. They also illustrate typical characteristics of these adolescents' development: the importance of peers, the development of personal interests, and their perception of the role of school in developing their career goals.

> I am a 16-year-old girl. I attend a vocational school. I live with my parents. I was born in Pécs. My parents are skilled workers. I have a younger brother. He's in the 7th grade. I don't really like studying. I am not interested in anything besides music. I also like dancing and going to discos with my pals. There were no big

events in my life. What is important for me? Well, love. I feel good
with my family and my friends. I am a joyful, nice, friendly girl.
I am just nervous sometimes . . . then it is better if they don't talk
to me.

16-year-old girl, vocational school, 1991

※

I am a 17-year-old academic school student. My parents are employees. I have an older brother. He also attends the same school,
and will have his final exam at the end of this year. He is a good
student, I am not as good, but I do not have problems in studying.
I am interested in everything. I like new technology, computers,
videos. I have a guitar that I play at home. I usually go to play
basketball with my friends. I am a person who is happy and likes
to play. I have lots of pals. Briefly, I feel good. I am friendly and
I have a sense of humor. I might take life easy, but that's me. I
think love, friendship, honesty, and self-assurance are the most
important values in a person's life. There were no essential, important events in my life, only that I was born.

17-year-old boy, academic school, 1994

Students spontaneously talked about important groups in their
lives. When asked to describe themselves, these adolescents responded
with descriptions that emphasized their important primary relationships rather than ones that focused on more individual characteristics such as "happy," or membership in more inclusive groups
representing association with macrosystem groups such as "Hungarian," "Catholic," "Protestant." Most students' self-descriptions focused
on the here and now. Few students spontaneously spoke in detail
about future career plans, although many named getting into their
secondary school as an important life event.

As a way of further checking the trustworthiness of students'
emphasis on the importance of family, we followed items about self-
descriptions with an item asking them to name the groups they
thought were most important in their lives. Some aspect of family
life was emphasized by more than 80% of the students, e.g., having
a "happy family." This suggests that their family was not only the
most important relationship, but that they viewed their relationship
to their family as central to their understanding of themselves.

The group affiliation of secondary importance was peer groups
(friends, social clubs, sports), followed by school, and only then,

identification with groups that related to the macrosystem such as religion and nation. (See Appendix B, Table 1.) These findings are consistent with those Pataki (1991) reported in a major empirical study with a large sample carried out prior to our first interviews in Pécs. Pataki found the ties between Hungarian secondary school students and their parents were strong, that parents were very important role models and, indeed, that students' family orientation was stronger than the researchers had expected.

Although the initial items gave students the opportunity to talk about the impact of social changes on their lives, only several did so, e.g., mentioning a parent who had lost a job. Likewise, only a handful discussed thinking about career plans in relation to changing employment opportunities. The student quoted below was one of the few:

> I am 16 years old. I attend a vocational school . . . I like studying, but I am afraid of not getting a job after finishing school. Maybe I will have to learn another profession. My father says that a man's value depends on the number of professions he is good at, so I am not really frightened. I get every support from [my family].
>
> 16-year-old boy, vocational school, 1994

Across all school types there was great homogeneity in students' descriptions of themselves. There was also great consistency in students' self-descriptions in 1991 and 1993–94 with emphases on family, peers, etc.

Some statistically significant differences did emerge, suggesting that the 1993–94 sample was an evolving new cohort. In 1993–94 we found still small but growing proportions of students who mentioned working, being helpful at home, and speaking their opinions, although none made an explicit connection between changes in their home or school (microsystem) and those at the national level (macrosystem). In 1991, only one student said he was working. In contrast, by 1993–94 about one-tenth of the students mentioned that they worked. Since working during adolescence had not been a common activity for young people in Hungary, this small but statistically significant change is notable.

There was also a difference in the proportion of students who described themselves as helpful when asked to name their personal characteristics, both "positive and negative." In 1991, the most common responses were "lazy," "happy," "changeable moods," and "sometimes irritable." In 1993–94, "lazy" was still the most common response, but one-fourth of the students used "helpful" when describing themselves, a term used infrequently in 1991. For example: "I am helpful at home, too." Indeed, such responses may reflect the students' desire to be more useful at a time when their parents were often working longer hours, as many were. If this is the case, it illustrates once again that many adolescents described their personal characteristics, their sense of self, within the broader framework of relationships with family and friends. It may also be suggestive of a change in the roles of adolescents in the context of the social changes that were taking place in Hungary at that time.

Other responses that occurred with greater frequency in 1993–94 may also reflect relationships between changing social conditions and changes in development, particularly the emphasis on democratization, and the roles of adolescents. For example, "I give my own opinion" was named by 12% of the students in 1993–94 and suggests that students perceived themselves able to communicate more freely. One 16-year-old female academic school student put it this way:

> I feel that our class is more open, more honest than, for example, my brother's. Our teachers often tell us that we can always give our opinion . . . Yes, I always say if I do not like something. I am not an arguing-type, I would rather call myself open. They accept my being this kind of person. I always tell my opinion. We argue in a good way.

At the same time, the 1993–94 participants seemed more apathetic. In 1991, students seemed to have interests such as sports and music, each mentioned by more than a third of the students. Interest in the opposite sex, and thinking about one's future were named by about a quarter of the students. In contrast, in 1993–94 the most common response was either to say that "nothing interests me" or else not answer the question. Although "music" and "friends" were still relatively common responses, their frequency also diminished.

Being Hungarian

During the course of our research, wars were being fought among the newly declared nations of the former Yugoslavia and the fighting in Croatia could be heard in Pécs. These conflicts were associated with militant or nationalistic groups that had emerged in some countries in central and eastern Europe. In Hungary, the issue of national consciousness has been a long-standing subject of popular as well as academic discussion, given the historical frequency of shifting borders which resulted in people who regarded themselves as ethnic Hungarians living in neighboring countries during some periods, and large numbers of people who regarded themselves as "not Hungarian" living in Hungarian territory during other periods. Szábo (1992) discusses several studies that focused on this issue. For example, he cites a survey carried out in the late 1970s in which respondents were asked the question: "Who am I?" Ninety percent responded "Hungarian;" 70% responded "a white person;" and 53% responded "European." During that same period, a survey of students showed that 95% responded that being Hungarian was "something to be proud of."

When asked what made them "proud" and "not so proud" to be Hungarians, the responses of the students we interviewed showed that they appear comfortable with their Hungarian identity but did not judge themselves superior to others:

> I was very proud of being Hungarian during the Olympic games. The successes of our athletes made me proud. But I am not proud of some tourists' actions abroad. The way they behave is uncivilized.
>
> 16-year-old girl, academic school, 1991

> I am proud that Hungary gave many clever people to the world. Our best scientists could profit by their knowledge in wealthier countries. There are many world-famous Hungarian people. But I am not proud of the low living standards in this country and, because of it, other countries look down upon us.
>
> 17-year-old boy, technical school, 1994

Most students responded to these questions with answers such these. In 1991 the most frequent answer contained pride concerning the social and political changes but this response was given by fewer than 12% of the students. By 1993–94 no student gave this response. When asked to comment on what made them "not so proud to be Hungarian" the most popular answer in both years was the behavior of Hungarian tourists abroad, named by about 20% in 1991 and about 10% in 1994.

Facing the Future

A critical aspect of psychosocial identity development is the development of a sense of self that includes past, present, and future. Young people's orientation toward the future is particularly important during times of historic change. Several of our interview items explored students' views of their future, their hopefulness, and their plans. We asked students to name three wishes and three fears for their future, to assess their level of optimism/pessimism, and to describe what "a good life" twenty years in the future would be like. We also asked them to discuss how they thought that living through this time of social change might affect their "development as a person."

In 1991 students were more optimistic about the future of Hungary than in 1993-94. At the same time, more students expressed wishes and fears related to economic concerns in 1991 than in 1993–94. There was a trend toward being more optimistic about their own future than the future of their city or country in both years.

Wishes and fears.   Questions about wishes and fears have been included in more than a dozen previous international studies of adolescent populations. Researchers have discussed the results of this item in terms of emphasis on personal concerns vs. societal concerns about the environment (e.g., Chivian et al., 1988).

The students in Pécs emphasized more personal aspects of wishes and fears such as health or financial welfare rather than social ones.

> If I had three wishes, my first would be to have lots of money. I am bored without having money for anything and having to ask my parents for it all the time. Though it is said that money will not make you happy, it is very hard to be happy without money. My second wish is to be educated and clever. I could manage my life better in the world. The third is to be beautiful. It is easier to reach your goals if you are.

> But I have fears about war. It is going on only some kilometers away from here. Sometimes they shoot over [the border from

Croatia to Hungary]. And I am also afraid of death. I am afraid of living in vain, that nobody will remember me. My third fear is disappointment. I am afraid of being cheated, of being used although I give my love.

17-year-old girl, technical school, 1991

※

[If] I had three wishes, the first would be to have peace for sure. We cannot live in restlessness, in war. The second would be a happy family, because it is the most important for everybody. The third is to have understanding among people, to have peace on this Earth, finally. War, an economic crash, and the growth of inflation are my fears. You would not be able to live happily without money.

17-year-old girl, vocational school, 1991

※

If I had three wishes, I would wish for the economic welfare of the country, health, and a successful life and career for me. [My fears] are poverty, illness, and war.

17-year-old boy, academic school, 1994

When we examined the respondents' three wishes to determine the proportion that were social rather than personal, we found that in both 1991 and 1993–94, more than 60% of the students named wishes that were all personal. The important exception to this pattern was peace and war. It should be remembered that by 1993–94 these students had been hearing the sounds of explosions often less than fifty miles away and seeing many refugees. In addition, Pécs was serving as a strategical center for UN peacekeeping personnel.

Between 1991 and 1993–94 there was a statistically significant change in the way that the students focused on financial well-being. In 1993–94 fewer students mentioned a wish about financial welfare, a good job, or fear of poverty. Instead, they named increasing inflation and the rise of unemployment more frequently than in 1991. Perhaps these findings can be understood when one considers that the early years of the transition were marked by greater uncertainty, including the spectre of bad times. By 1993–94 there was greater inflation and unemployment, but, as we shall see, many students perceived themselves as relatively unaffected, and, therefore, might have been less fearful. (See Appendix B, Table 2 for a summary of students' most frequent wishes and fears.)

Measures of Optimism and Pessimism

We examined the student's responses to forced choice, Likert-type items about their own future and their children's future across years. A comparison of means (student's t-test) revealed that students' optimism regarding the future rose significantly between 1991 and 1993–94. This pattern was true for students from all three school types, vocational, technical, and academic, as well as for females and males. In 1993–94, 56% of all students responded that they felt optimistic or very optimistic; 38% responded sometimes optimistic and sometimes pessimistic; and 6% responded pessimistic or very pessimistic. Most students also explained that their life was better than the lives of their parents. For example, Mária underscored that her "life is totally different from theirs. . . . I get everything from my parents. They work hard so that it will be good for me."

Many surveys of Hungarian adults conducted since 1990 have also included items regarding levels of optimism. We found overall parallels between results from these surveys and the data from the students in Pécs, although a higher proportion of the adults sampled were slightly more pessimistic. For example, in a national poll conducted July 8–12, 1994, adults were asked, "About your future, would you say you are. . . ." Forty-four percent of the participants responded generally optimistic; 14% responded generally pessimistic; and 39% responded that they were uncertain (Gallup 1994).

A Good Life in Twenty Years

When asked to describe themselves in twenty years and to assume that they would be happy with their life at that time, few students in either year talked about expanded possibilities for their future because of the changes. This is consistent with their sense of themselves as members of a family that can take care of one another and that mistrusts the outside world. Students expressed visions of a happy family, their own home, and often an interesting, well-paying job. Their responses to this question related to their self-description, their values, and wishes. The results were consistent over the two interview periods. Mária's response was typical. She spoke about hoping to be a good mother and wife who enjoyed her job and did it well. Two other students replied:

> In twenty years our lives will be nice. I will have a husband. We live a happy family life. We will have kids. We will be a nice family. We will buy our own house with a garden and swimming pool. I am optimistic.
>
> 16-year-old girl, vocational school, 1991

※

> I am optimistic. I think the country will have been out of the crisis by then. The signs of a better standard of living will be visible. I will have a house of my own. I will live there in happiness with my family, my wife, and my kids. We will love each other. My wife will care for them and study with them. We will have a good place of work. Both of us will have interesting jobs.
>
> 17-year-old boy, academic school, 1994

As the above examples illustrate, students provided few details about their lives. Vári-Szilágyi (1992) studied the future orientations of Hungarian students, young intellectuals, and professionals. She explored the differences of their future orientations and categorized them according to their planning behavior in a first set of studies and according to the proportion of hopes and fears in a second set of studies.

Types of future orientation were obtained and characterized along two criteria: whether or not the participant had one or more goals in the future field of work-activity, and whether this goal or goals were elaborated, i.e., firm or definite. This appeared, in effect, a combination of hopes and wishes. She identified one group of planners who had goals in the sphere of work that were firm and definite. She identified quasi-planners as those who had goals but whose goals were weak and indefinite, more like hopes, dreams, or wishes. There was a group, "family planners," who did not have goals in the sphere of work but who had firm goals with respect to their future families. The fourth group were non-planners, those with no firm goals in any sphere of life.

Vári-Szilágyi reports that the message of the first study is that the planner-types were the most mature type since, in general, they had developed definite goals not only regarding work, but in other spheres of life as well. They were more sure in their subjective probability that they would reach their goals. This was true even though they had more fears with regard to the obstacles in their field of work at the time of the previous regime. Those who had more fears, who had definite plans in spite of the difficulties, and who were more creative, were more inner-controlled and more optimistic.

The students in Pécs who were most specific about their jobs were those attending vocational and technical schools who were training for specific professions. Even they, however, did not discuss specific employment opportunities relating to these vocations. These results also point to the importance of considering the transitional nature of the time the Pécs study was conducted. It is easier to plan for a future that one sees as a road that continues smoothly from the present than for an unpredictable future at the end of a road that cannot be mapped.

Students' Views on How Growing Up during Transitions may Influence Their Individual Development

> When you are five years older . . . and look back on this time, how do you think that it will have affected your development as a person?

During the first interviews in 1991, more students talked about being optimistic, but also about their worsening financial situation. In 1991 slightly more than 20% of the students said that growing up in a rapidly changing time made them more optimistic, as illustrated in the following example:

> I can't feel what these changes in the country mean in my life but I think I can get more possibilities to study, to have scholarships abroad, to travel. I'm optimistic about the effects of the changes. I already feel I approach problems in a different way. When I decide upon an opinion, I take more points of view into consideration. I like to discuss and reason, to prove. Maybe I can pay much more attention to someone else also. These changes result from my chance to hear and read a lot of opinions. I didn't experience things like these before.
>
> 17-year-old academic high school girl, 1991

By 1993–94, the percentage saying they were optimistic had dropped to less than 10%.

In 1991, when talking about how their development might be affected by the changes, 12% of the students called attention to their worsening financial situation, as the following example illustrates:

> My parents' increasing financial problems affect my life. Now we need more money for life in high school. I can't go to the cinema or to the disco with my friends because I have no money. I don't get enough from home. I'm sure it affects my development. It makes my group of friends smaller and I can't pay enough attention to the events in the world.
>
> 16-year-old academic school boy, 1994

But here, too, by 1993-94 fewer students discussed financial problems.

In 1991 about 40% of the students we interviewed said they were unaffected by the changes.

> There are not any effects on my development because of the changes. I depend on my family and I get the same quality of life that I expect. My school didn't change anything. I get the same things there as before. Sometimes we are happier or more nervous, but it doesn't mean anything. So my development is just going on like before. There is no contact with the conditions of the country.
>
> 16-year-old vocational school boy, 1991

By 1993–94, however, only about 25% said they were unaffected and a majority could discuss some personal impact of the changes. For most, however, this impact was minimal. This statistically significant difference is consistent with the findings we will discuss under *Living History*. In 1991 most of these young people believed that the changes were having significant effects on the country. But they did not believe that the changes had any significant effects on themselves or their own family. Csaba's response was typical when he said that, "politics has changed a lot, but I don't know too much about it because I'm not interested." Another student replied:

> I can tell you sincerely I cannot decide which things influenced my development. I think the changes didn't influence me in any

way. Teenagers didn't change anything. The topics are the same for us. We don't care about politics. We are not interested in politics. We live life like before. I don't feel and I don't expect change. It's possible a lot of things changed for the country but it doesn't mean anything in my personal life.

15-year-old boy, vocational school, 1993

There was also a great rise in the percentage of students who gave no answer, from 0% in 1991 to about 25% in 1993–94. Giving no answer could be interpreted as an equivalent response to the "unaffected" answer. Another interpretation is that these students do not perceive any changes. This too suggests the development of cohort differences between the 1991 and 1993–94 participants.

Students interviewed in 1993–94 experienced the social conditions during the previous regime and the period of most rapid changes as children rather than as adolescents. As the years pass, children developing into adolescents may be increasingly unable to conceptualize how their development may have changed because they were not adolescents at the time of the most rapid changes. As changes become institutionalized and the pace of change slows, students remain aware that they are "growing up," but are no longer aware that they are "growing up in changing times."

Commentary

Overall, these adolescents were more likely to note changes in the macrosystem than in their microsystems. Although the adolescents we interviewed in Pécs in both years felt there had been significant changes in Hungary, in general they did not feel that the changes greatly affected their own lives. Few students in either year felt they had more possibilities for their lives because of the changes, although some acknowledged the effect of increased freedom of speech, particularly the right to express their own opinions. In general, students either declared that the changes did not affect their development into adulthood or were undecided.

In both years, students felt their families were their most important reference group. As we have discussed, Erikson (1986) described fidelity as central to the emerging sense of psychosocial identity:

It [fidelity] is the cornerstone of identity and receives inspiration from confirming ideologies and affirming companionship. (p. 35)

Throughout their interviews, the adolescents in Pécs affirmed the centrality of their relationship with their family, sometimes a boyfriend or girlfriend that had been accepted into the family, and also their friends. They had developed a sense of trust within their families. However, as they extended themselves beyond the radius of the family, their levels of trust in the social system decreased. If these family patterns are firmly entrenched, and have existed for decades and possibly centuries, they may be difficult to change within one generation. A central unanswered question is whether families can remain supportive of their members, protective of their children, and yet open to the wider world.

Living History:
Families as Filters

I feel good about [the changes]. There is freedom. I feel free. A lot of people complain that it's hard to live because there aren't enough jobs. I haven't noticed that. In my family everything is O.K. I have what I need, enough money.

Vocational secondary school boy, 1991

I have good feelings about the changes. I feel much more free. Maybe it's just my personal feeling, but we always hear that "we became free," so people get this feeling. It's true that this change is not so easy. We have hard financial conditions. It means that the government starts to use the people's money. Life becomes very hard for a lot of people. We can hear a lot about the lowest salary levels and people's decreased social levels. But it seems that a lot of people got rich. We are not changed by this situation. Our life is just going on.

Academic secondary school boy, 1991

My parents and their friends think the same way. They criticize this situation and the government. I'm fed up with their "friendly conversations." I'd rather go to my room and listen to music very loudly.

Vocational secondary school girl, 1991

As we have stated earlier, the study began in 1991 and the first interviews took place after the first wave of major changes in Hungary—such as the fall of the Kádár government, the establishment of a new form of government with a multiparty system, and after the first national elections—yet during a time when major changes were still occurring frequently. Inflation had reached 30% and unemployment 5%. The second series of interviews in Pécs were conducted in 1993–94 prior to the spring elections in which the Socialist Party gained 32.9% of the vote and the next most popular party, the Free Democrats, only 19.6%. By 1994 the private sector of the economy had grown to 50%. The national debt remained very high and the government had introduced a new austerity budget.

During both sets of interviews we explored what these adolescents thought were the key events that had occurred in Hungary and their ideas about the most important changes. Numerous items asked students to describe transitions in terms of the continuities and the changes at the national macrosystem level. They were asked to discuss the effects of the changes on themselves, their family, their neighborhood, and their city.

Parallel items asked them to talk about their feelings about these changes as well as how they thought others felt, e.g., their parents, friends, and "other Hungarians." In general, the data suggest that in 1991, at the beginning of the changes, these young people expected more from the changes, like the Hungarian population at large (Bruszt and Simon 1991).

We also wanted to discover students' perceptions of their own interest in politics. In the preceding section we discussed the interests that students named. None mentioned politics. Had we not asked these questions it is probable that most students would have never spontaneously discussed politics.

As we discuss throughout this section, students' responses to these items show striking patterns of consistencies. Individual student's responses showed a great deal of repetition and redundancy, contributing to our confidence in the trustworthiness of these results.

The students rarely mentioned changes in their city or neighborhood, instead they reported changes within their families. Data from the items related to *Living History* illustrate once again that these students' psychosocial identity was defined primarily within the circle of the family and secondly, their friends. Far fewer discussed participating in organized clubs or groups. This points to the relative absence of levels of community or civil space between students' personal lives and national politics.

Changes in the macrosystem affected their families in differing ways, and at different times and rates. The students' responses reflected these differences. Many responses were also marked by incongruities and inconsistencies, e.g., students who talked about their family's financial hardships but also about their family's new car or house. The students' responses also illustrated the ways in which their families isolated and protected these adolescents from the insecurities of the changing social, economic, and political context, and instilled a mistrust in national politics. There was little evidence that many students felt involved as active participants in the processes of change. Rather they saw themselves and their families as passive recipients of the changes. This was true of students attending all three different types of high schools, vocational, technical, and academic, of males and females, and in both the 1991 and 1993–94 interviews.

Few discussed the effects of social changes on their peers, their schools, or on their activities in social groups. They paid little attention to the effects of changes on their city or neighborhood. Students were aware, albeit in a general and sometimes vague way, of the changes at the level of the national macrosystem. In contrast, they focused primarily on their families. Changes that affected their families were the most salient. Furthermore, they rarely associated the changes within their families with changes in the macrosystem, for example, privatization.

Students' responses in 1991 and 1993–94 indicated some important differences. For example, in 1991 the students were confused about what had changed and unsure of their opinions about the changes. By 1993–94, more spoke about particular changes and their effects.

Interest in Politics

In both years, the largest group comprised those students who said they didn't care about politics, about 40%. Like Csaba and Mária, they were often the students who stressed throughout their interviews that neither they nor their families were interested in politics, that "politics doesn't interest us," that they "lived their own lives."

In comparing the adolescents interviewed in 1991 to those interviewed in 1993–94, we found suggestions of incipient but possibly growing political interest and activity. In 1993–94 there was a small, non-significant increase in the number of students who responded that they liked "dealing with politics" (25% vs. 20%).

> Politics is interesting. I do not say I am not interested in what is happening to us in the country and in the world, but I cannot recall what is happening. Everybody tells his or her version, but we cannot say who was right. However, we argue a lot in the class. It is interesting to know other people's perspectives. There was somebody whom I liked before, but he has strange ideas. He is not my friend anymore.
>
> 16-year-old, technical school, 1994

In 1993–94, six students reported that they had been involved in politics. While low, this number is still noteworthy since in 1991 not one student said they were involved. Similarly, in 1993–94 some students mentioned having friends who were active in politics, while none said this in 1991.

A number of related items assessed students' level of interest in the news as well as how they obtained news that would include political information. Students were asked how often they watched or listened to the news, or read the newspapers. Few indicated an active interest in the news. Also, in 1991 none of the students mentioned having read *samizdat* materials, the alternative underground materials often published by university students and others that carried dissenting positions prior to the change of regime.

Students Construct a Timeline

We wondered what a contemporaneous timeline would look like through students' eyes, given that they frequently heard that they lived in a "historic time." Secondary school history texts, written by adults, often depict important historical events on a timeline and all the students understood this item. The great majority of students included just two or three events in their timeline of "the most important events," reflecting their relative lack of interest and knowledge relating to their national macrosystem. A few included personal happenings, particularly events in the microsystem of their family.

The major events young people identified differed in 1991 and 1993–94. Even though there was a brief period of two years between the interviews, the major events and changes of 1989–91 were talked about in more general terms as they became more remote for the students in 1993–94. In 1991 there was a greater emphasis on Hungarian national events and the four most frequently cited events were the fall of the Kádár regime, the proclamation of the republic, the establishment of the multiparty system, and the first parliamentary elections. In 1993–94, students included more changes in their own personal lives, but also identified more international events, especially the war in the countries of the former Yugoslavia. The four most frequently cited events were the first free parliamentary elections, the war in Yugoslavia, the proclamation of the Hungarian Republic, and changes in their own personal life such as beginning a new school, love, or friendship.

Identifying Continuities and Changes

Ambiguous perceptions and ambivalent feelings predominated during the interviews as students attempted to make sense of the transitions. However, even when students' responses showed depth, they frequently reflected a lack of interest and involvement. There were numerous differences in the students' responses in 1991 and 1993–94 that once again suggested that the age of the students during the height of the transitions was an important variable as was the length of time a particular change had been occurring. Few differences were found among students interviewed at vocational, technical, and academic schools, or between girls and boys.

The two illustrations that follow present Éva's and László's responses to key items in the long series of questions. Their responses exemplify relationships among the students' perceptions of continuities and changes at all subsystems of their social ecology and reflect the consistencies of an individual student's responses to different items. Éva's and László's responses show the pattern common to many students, that they have developed a sense of their identity as people who are close to their families and distrustful of national and global macrosystems.

Éva, a 16-year-old girl interviewed in 1991, attended a technical school for the arts. She talked about the continuity of family members helping each other, but revealed that the situation had changed in her own family, that it was now her parents who helped her grandparents. Despite these statements, Éva also viewed her environment as unchanged. Her responses reflected pessimistic perceptions of the Hungarian and European macrosystems but suggested some engagement:

> Everything changed. Nothing is fixed. The whole world! War . . . peace . . . compromises. Nothing really happens at all. But everything is changed. This is the world today!

> I think people should help each other. Not only half of them. The whole world! Maybe this way anything could happen. We have to destroy [these differences and] make everyone equal. We can't have these social contrasts—rich and poor, happy and unhappy.

> In my life only learning and love are unchanged. Everything else changed. Everything changed in my family, too. A couple of years ago my grandparents helped us. Now we help them. In any case we help each other.

> In my environment everything stayed the same. In the city where I live too. The economy is still in the same trouble in Hungary also. Nothing changed in Europe. We get only "words," but we cannot see the results.

László, a 15-year-old boy from an academic high school, was interviewed in 1993. When describing himself, he said that his personality was changing and mentioned his sense of frustration that his parents didn't understand that he was growing up. He also talked about his efforts to correct "mistakes." Like others in our sample, László felt that his family's financial situation had worsened but, like some others as well, he provided incongruous information when he said, "we built a . . . . [new] house." Like most students in both years, László expressed a sense of detachment and passivity about the situation in Hungary and Europe.

The tone of the following excerpts from László's interview reflects his involvement in his family as well as his emotional detachment from the wider social context, including his political passivity:

Since I started to go to high school, my group of friends changed. But I stayed the same.

Nothing changed in my family. The relationship between me and my parents is the same as before. We argue with my sister, like before. But if we need each other, we help each other. My grandma helps us solve problems just like before.

In my environment, nothing changed. I have almost the same friends.

Nothing changed in Hungary. The politicians argue about every small thing instead of doing something. In neighboring countries nothing changed. The standard of living is low like before.

Everything stayed the same in Europe, too. Smaller states had to do what they were forced to do to get loans from the West. That's why we are in such bad conditions. Today it's the same.

Nothing changed in the world. The big countries [and] the monopolist firms tell us what to do. They don't care about protecting the environment so that they can make a bigger profit.

Other researchers have reported similar findings. Szábo's (1991) overview of the processes of political socialization in Hungary prior to 1988 is consistent with our findings. He reported that, at that time, anti-political views were widespread, and that most families had negative attitudes toward the state and most were in favor of economic reforms that would result in privatization. According to Szábo these attitudes fostered children's development of political passivity.

When discussing their own lives, students tended to focus on positive aspects of stable conditions. As a group, they seemed generally content with their personal lives, commenting on their close relationships to their family and their friends, and often talking about a significant girlfriend or boyfriend.

In contrast, they were often critical when focusing on aspects of national continuity, e.g., "people's ways of thinking" were viewed as contributing to the continuing problems of the nation. Regarding change or continuity at the macrosystem level in Hungary, in middle Europe, the rest of Europe, and in the world, we found that many students had no opinion. Particularly in 1991, most answered: "I cannot decide." And even when they expressed different opinions, they didn't appear to have a comprehensive worldview. Most telling, they did not reflect on the disintegration of the Soviet Union and what that meant for Hungary and other nations in eastern and central Europe as well as throughout the world. In 1993–94, fewer responded: "I can't decide." Students gave more opinions about their national macrosystem as well as the macrosystems of Europe and the world.

The students were then asked to name key changes, to identify "the two or three most important changes," to describe how the change took place, and to discuss the effects of the changes upon themselves, their family, their neighborhood, their city, and Hungary. As part of this discussion, we asked them to evaluate their own feelings toward the changes and to estimate the feelings of parents, their friends and their parents' friends, and "most Hungarians." Students were first asked to list the changes they considered most important. On average they listed two or three; some listing as many as seven or as few as one. When coding the data for the following analyses, a maximum of five responses were coded. Next, after they had listed the changes they thought were important, students were asked to select the most important two or three changes and answer a series of more than a dozen items about each particular change.

In 1991, many of the students did not express a clear view of the changes nor what form of society was going to exist, as the following example illustrates:

> I cannot decide if it's good or bad. It's democracy right now. People are free. But the economy is getting worse. Life is harder and harder. The mines have been closed. The workers have been kicked out. It's good that the Russian soldiers left, but we don't really feel they have.
>
> 16-year-old academic high school girl, 1991

In 1991, the students were generally positive when they talked about political changes. There were more total responses related to democracy than in 1993–94. When they talked about several changes, topics related to democracy tended to be the first. The most frequently identified "important" change was the multiparty system, named by 48% of the students. Similar responses, "the change in the political system" and "becoming democratized" were mentioned by 38% and 29% of the students respectively. Twenty-three percent of the students mentioned increasing inflation and 19% identified unemployment.

Among those interviewed in 1993–94, there was less specific emphasis on the transition to democracy, although the responses regarding political changes were still generally positive. Instead, students emphasized those changes related to a worsening economy. In these cases, most said that they and their family were basically unaffected but many pointed to national financial hardships, and 30% specified unemployment.

We carried out the following analysis to determine whether there were differences between 1991 and 1993–94 in the themes as well as the order of the responses. A maximum of three responses were included for each participant. The responses were first weighted so that a student's first response would receive more weight than that student's third response. For example, "free speech (3 points), inflation (2 points), free press (1 point)." The responses were then categorized according to their thematic content, e.g., positive views of democracy, negative views of democracy, or, for another analysis, positive views of the economy, negative views of the economy. This analysis demonstrated that by 1993–94, compared with 1991, not only was there a decrease in the total responses related to democracy, but that there was also a change in the order in which students listed democracy-related changes.

This finding suggests that students were starting to think that democracy was becoming less salient as a topic of discussion. Perhaps they began to think of the new governmental structure as a normal state of affairs. During the earlier years of the transitions, the old regime had disintegrated and the multiparty system was instituted. There was a lot of discussion in the media about arguments among the political parties and about aggressive political speeches of members of several parties. Political commentators compared the activities of the previous communist government and the new government. In 1991 these were the changes most students discussed.

At the time of the 1993–94 interviews, the multiparty system and the end of the communist dictatorship were not major themes to the degree that they were in the first interviews. Some students had begun to recognize that democracy and freedom were not instantaneous changes. They became aware that the growth of democracy and freedom was related to other factors as well. However, students still thought about elections because a soon-to-be-held national election was being discussed in the news. In 1993–94 Hungarians heard more about unemployment and privatization in the media. In talking about privatization, Mária used a memorable phrase she probably heard, "private ventures started to grow as fast as mushrooms." The increased focus on unemployment and privatization also indicated that students were focusing on issues that dominated the current news, as well as on events like the proclamation of the republic that were being discussed as "historic."

We carried out the same analysis for responses related to the economy, weighting the order of the responses and categorizing them into positive versus negative opinions about the economy. By 1993–94 students were more apt to mention more changes relating to a poorer economy but this increase was relatively small. The majority of changes related to the economy were negative. This was particularly true if the first change a student named was an economic one. As one would expect, it was also typical of students who had experienced changes within their own families. For example, both Csaba's and Mária's fathers had lost their jobs and both were among the students who pointed to the problem of unemployment.

Overall, our students' generally low level of concern about the economy contrasted with the national poll results at the time which showed that Hungarian adults had significant concerns about the economy (Gallup 1994). This suggests that the adolescents we interviewed were less interested in financial matters than adults, and gives further weight to the hypothesis that these young people were insulated from the effects of the changes by their families.

Students' Perceptions of the Effects of the Changes

After students identified the two or three important changes that they wanted to talk about, we continued with a series of items that focused on their perceptions of the effects of the changes on themselves, their family, their neighborhood, their city, and Hungary. In 1991, "democracy" and "people became free" were the most popular changes that students discussed. In 1993–94 no students mentioned "democracy" as the first change they talked about.

An examination of all the responses to this item indicates that more than 70% of the students in both 1991 and 1993–94 felt that the changes had at least one positive outcome for their lives. Despite this, a sizable group responded that their lives had become harder and referred to their increased financial problems. They now had to make more serious decisions about how to spend their money.

> The strongest effect I feel is the rising prices. This influences my life so much. I can't handle my life as easily as before. I don't feel as carefree as before. I'm always a bit nervous because of the future.
>
> 17-year-old girl, vocational school

In their discussions of the effects of each of the two to three "most important changes" almost half the students in 1991 and 1993–94 said they couldn't really notice the effects of the specific changes they mentioned on themselves personally. As we have indicated, this was true for some of the students like Csaba and Mária who had talked about parents losing jobs or placed on some form of government disability. Once again, their responses show the students living their lives within their family and at school where their interpersonal relationships remained more or less the same. Indeed, 38% of the students emphasized that their lives went on as before.

> There is a good and a bad side of the change too. My circumstances have not become worse. I feel good. I have a lot of friends. I have everything I need. I understand that my parents have no money for luxury stuff. I think it's going to change soon . . . around ten more years.
>
> 16-year-old girl, academic school

Students' discussions of the effects on their family showed a similar picture. They talked about both positive and negative effects on their family, yet most students' answers did not reflect adverse feelings. Like the student in the example above, many students consistently emphasized the continuity of family life, e.g., "There is no perceptible (visible) change;" "I don't see any change."

Although some students did not mention any financial changes when specifically asked about changes, they did mention financial issues in subsequent discussions. These students then talked openly about changes in their family's life, but did not appear to associate these family events with changes at the national level. Some were major such as a family's building a new house or a parent losing a job because of the closing of a mine.

In the context of the wider environment, students usually expressed ignorance about how other people in the wider environment of their neighborhood and city felt about the changes. The most typical response appeared to be, "I have no idea how much it impresses them. We don't talk about this. I don't hear anything about it." Even when the students tried to estimate how their friends felt, many said that they didn't know. When they did make an estimation, the ratio of the negative to positive feelings was about the same as that they gave for their family. Some students expressed open disinterest in the opinions of others:

> I'm not really interested in anyone else's opinion. We can hear it in the bus station. People talk about everything. I don't pay attention. When something is really going to really happen, then I will pay attention.
>
> 16-year-old boy vocational school student, 1991

During the interviews students were asked to discuss the effects of the changes on other Hungarians.

> Everyone feels the changes. It was very good for some people. But there are people who think the whole thing is very bad. A lot of people, of course, cannot understand what is happening around us. It seems that they change their opinion every day.
>
> 16-year-old academic high school student, 1991

※

> The changes are going on smoothly. Everyone has to recognize it whether they say it or not. The changes are very good for some people. They drive brand new types of cars like Mercedes, but at the tax office they say they have a minimum-level salary. There are a lot of those people . . . They just figure out how many "small doors" we have for people who are skillful [in finding loopholes] in Hungarian laws—and how much money we don't get to handle social problems. Some people get unemployment aid payments who really don't need it. Then there are people who don't get anything who do need it to live. So this is my impression of how this whole thing is for people.
>
> 17-year-old girl, academic high school, 1994

The students displayed little knowledge of how the changes had affected the general populace. Even when they mentioned the financial hardships felt by their own families, they did not necessarily relate those hardships to the situation in the country at large. It is therefore not surprising that they displayed a lack of strong feelings about the changes.

Feelings about the Changes

In 1991, many of the students seemed uncertain as to what, if anything, had really changed and seemed ambivalent about their feelings. Almost a quarter of the students said that they "couldn't decide" how they felt about one of the changes they discussed.

> I don't feel what's changed exactly. They talk a lot about this, about that, but I don't really recognize any changes. My opinion is that nothing is better—nothing is worse. But I cannot really tell you what I feel about it.
>
> 15-year-old girl, academic school, 1991

Often, their perceived lack of feeling was accompanied by a sense of apathy about politics.

> I don't feel bad. I feel the same as I did before. I can't really decide if there is a serious change or not. Of course the TV is full of everything. Someone thanks God for the changes. Someone is crying because of them. It's the same with the government. A lot of people are criticizing them. There was a demonstration against them. I don't care. I'm OK.
>
> 16-year-old-girl, academic school, 1991

Most students gave at least one response that was generally positive, usually in relation to political situations, such as this student who spoke about the changes with hope:

> I feel our world is much better than before. So much is happening around us. We don't know where to look. We can hear about everything, of course. The newspapers write about those things we didn't know anything about before. A lot of bad things have been discovered. Maybe after that they [politicians] are going to pay much more attention to what they dare to do. I'm optimistic about the changes.
>
> 17-year-old girl, academic school, 1991

Approximately a fifth of the students, however, revealed negative or pessimistic feelings.

> I don't feel that anything is better. It's worse for me. You can see
> all over that everything is full of problems. My parents argue
> much more also. I have to think about what I'll spend my money
> on much more. Until this time I always had money in my pocket.
> Now it's often empty. Anyway, I always try to find a way to feel
> good.
>
>   17-year-old boy, vocational school, 1991

Overall, in 1991, these young peoples' reactions were uncertain, changeable, and involved both negative and positive feelings.
Indeed, their feelings were similar to the majority of Hungarian
adults at that time. Many people felt confused and insecure, undecided about exactly what was happening or whether the changes
were good or not. Great expectations for rapid changes often led to
rapid and great disappointments. For example, throughout 1990,
Bruszt and Simon (1991) carried out a series of public opinion polls
before and after the parliamentary and local elections. Within this
one year, public opinion about political and economic issues changed
substantially. Prior to the 1990 parliamentary elections the majority of respondents were generally optimistic, with sixty percent
agreeing with the statement that "a new era would begin after the
elections." Vastly different results emerged in follow-up surveys
conducted only six months later, with only five percent replying
that their expectations regarding multiparty democracy had been
fulfilled and 71% replying that they and their families were somewhat worse or much worse off economically than they had been the
previous year.

In 1993, Kéri, a Hungarian sociologist who has written exten-
sively about political socialization, noted that the political and social
transitions that were occurring in Hungary were marked by unemployment and crime:

> We may be in the worst part of the transition already: the ex-
> pected crime-rate is three to five hundred thousand; the number
> of unemployed is expected to reach four hundred thousand in two
> months; energy restrictions are expected. There seems to be little
> chance that the country can evade a few years when shadows
> grow bigger. This period—primarily depending on how many years

it will last—will be an important socialization period in itself for hundreds of thousands (if not millions) of people. (p. 34)

Indeed, the effect of these conditions is reflected in the following observation of a 15-year-old girl who attended a vocational school:

> I don't know how much we needed this change. The living standard decreased. There is a lot of violence. People still kill each other because they don't have any money. The multiparty system is the spice of it. And all together it's just a big mess.

By the time of the second set of interviews in Pécs in winter 1993–94, it appeared that almost all students were more aware of the changes and had more definite feelings about them. Only ten percent of the students said they "couldn't decide" what the changes meant. Most students' opinions and feelings were positive overall, but included some critical aspects.

> In my opinion, these days it's not bad to be a teenager. We can see the changes with our own eyes. They say that there is no money. But despite it, we see a lot of new buildings. Stores are more beautiful. The shelves are full of products. You can buy everything. Of course prices rose a lot. Fortunately, I have everything I need.
>
> 17-year-old girl, academic school, 1993

As we have noted, this student's focus on her own life was typical. She and the secondary school students in Pécs appeared somewhat more optimistic than adults in national polls. However, adults, too, appeared more optimistic in some polls in 1993–94 than they had in the later polls of 1990. Although the majority of adults still responded that their financial situation had deteriorated, more replied that their living situation was about equal (e.g., Gallup Hungary Ltd. 1994).

In 1993–94, students' relatively good feelings about the changes suggested a possible cohort effect. Once again, it seems that these students, who were younger at the time of the major changes, did not remember better economic times. However, they were aware that the many optimistic predictions some people had made at the beginning of the changes had not been realized. Therefore their responses reflected their own more cautious optimism in their expectations for the future.

In both the 1991 and 1993–94 interviews, the students were generally more positive when discussing how they themselves felt than when they discussed how others felt. In some ways, these results appear counterintuitive because of the concerns students expressed regarding the social situation, e.g., unemployment, poverty, inflation, violence. Perhaps these apparent differences may be explained in the following way. It appears that these adolescents express opinions based on two frames of reference. The first is their own view of themselves and their environment. They feel generally good about their own lives. The second frame of reference includes the views they hear expressed in the media. Thus, their seemingly contrasting opinions may express their own emotional world on the one hand, and the consciousness created by the media on the other.

The students' discussions of their emotional responses to the changes indicated that the emotional saliency of those changes lay in the students' perception of differences in their family's well being. Once again they referred to their family in ways that showed it was their key microsystem, the system that was the touchstone for truly important changes and their reactions to them. Again, school and clubs were rarely mentioned. Once more students' responses reflected a pattern of trust in regard to their family and mistrust regarding the macrosystem, particularly the government. Students emphasized that their parents provided what they needed. At the same time we found that many students talked about how critical their parents were of the economic and political changes, often quoting their parents indirectly or even directly.

My parents talk a lot about the events in the country.

My father usually reads the news to my mother from the newspaper. My father always says, "Did we need that?!" Nothing is working now. Before everybody had a job. Money had value. Not like today.

15-year-old vocational school boy, 1991

※

My mother doesn't care about politics. She quarrels about money. My father decided that the multiparty system is very good, but he says that the old politicians are foolish, they don't know anything. He says they destroyed the economy. They shouldn't have closed the trade market to the U.S.S.R. because we exported 50% of the total of Hungarian products there. In my father's opinion, everything is bad now.

17-year-old academic school boy, 1993

Several national polls of adults have assessed public feelings in terms of "satisfaction" with the political and economic situation. Pataki (1992) discussed findings from a national poll carried out by the Median Market and Opinion Research Institute between May 29 and June 12, 1992 in which a total of 72% expressed dissatisfaction with the political situation and only 21% expressed satisfaction. Respondents indicated even less satisfaction with the economic situation: 87% were dissatisfied, and only 11% were satisfied.

Students' Perceptions of Their Classmates' Feelings about the Changes

I don't know my classmates' opinions. We usually don't talk about these questions.

In 1991, this was the most common answer to the item about how their peers felt about the changes. Most students were able to give their own opinions about the changes and spoke about how their parents felt, but nearly 90% said that they had no idea what opinions their friends had. At the same time, more than 50% said that they thought that their friends had generally negative opinions, e.g., "they consider the changes bad for sure." The response of a 16-year-old boy from a vocational school was typical:

In my group of friends we don't speak as much about the political changes as we do in class. We just care about our own things. We talk about music, sports, and about girls. We talk about our clothes too. If I started to talk about economics or politics they would laugh at me. I'm sure they would say, "Let's go to the Parliament so you could talk there!"

This was the common pattern in 1993–94 as well. Csaba was typical when he said, "I don't know if my friends or other youngsters can perceive anything of it. But I am not interested in this anyway. We don't talk about things like this." Yet by 1993–94, there was an increase in the percentage of students who said that they thought their classmates felt positively about the changes. There was also both more acceptance and interest in talking with peers about the changes in their country:

> The same number of my friends think the changes are good as those that think they are bad. We talk a lot about it. We usually agree that the change itself is not bad, but how it is going [after the change], that is the problem.
>
> 17-year-old academic school boy, 1994

The Relationships between Students' Satisfaction with Their Own Lives, Pécs, Hungary, and Europe

Adel was a 16-year-old student at an academic high school at the time of her interview. Toward the end of the interview, Adel responded to the series of items relating to her level of satisfaction with her life before, at the time of the interview, and her predicted future satisfaction. She was then asked to rate her level of satisfaction with Hungary at those three time periods, her satisfaction with Europe, and with the world. Figure 4.1 shows Adel's responses to these questions.

Adel's answers illustrated that when she compared the present situation in Hungary to that prior to the changes, she was currently more satisfied. They also illustrated that she was optimistic about the improvement of the national situation, when her rating of six at the time of her interview in 1991 increased to nine for her future in the year 2001. Adel's pattern of response represented the most common pattern for the students in Pécs. Adel's responses were also typical in that she was generally optimistic about becoming increasingly satisfied with her own life, the conditions in her city, country, and in Europe.

In addition, Adel's pattern was typical in that she was at least as satisfied with her own life as she was with the present conditions in Pécs or Hungary. Students' ratings of their satisfaction with their own lives in the past, the present, and for the future were consistently, though only slightly, higher than their ratings for their city, Hungary, and, in general, for Europe.

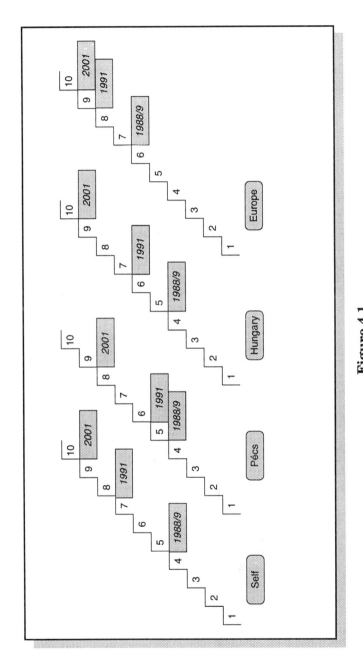

Figure 4.1
Adel's Levels of Satisfaction: Before the Changes, at Present, and in the Future

Between 1991 and 1993–94, students' ratings of their present satisfaction with their own lives and conditions in Pécs and Hungary improved significantly. In 1991, students' estimates of how they would rate their satisfaction with Hungary ten years in the future was relatively high, reflecting their optimism about the outcomes of the changes. For example, in 1991, the mean rating for Hungary was 4.72 for the present, and 7.20 for the future. However, in 1993–94, although ratings for the future remained higher than the present, all predictions of future satisfaction declined. For example, the mean rating for Hungary in 1993–94 increased from 4.72 to 5.08 while the mean rating for Hungary for the year 2004 decreased from 7.20 to 6.55.

Interestingly, the adolescents' mean level of satisfaction for themselves was higher than their ratings for both their city and their country for all three time periods. Thus, while they were fairly optimistic regarding their own future and that of their city, they remained relatively less optimistic regarding Hungary's future.

Commentary

Subtle differences in responses of students interviewed in 1991 and 1993–94 suggest the emergence of a new cohort, even within this brief period. The students interviewed in 1993–94 seemed to remember the time before the changes in a vague way. More time had elapsed since the previous regime than for those interviewed in 1991. But there was also an importance age difference: those interviewed in 1993–94 were younger at the time of the major societal transitions. Their memories of "the time before the changes" are therefore memories of younger children, less extensive and complex. Likewise, the feelings they associate with that time are the feelings of younger children. Perhaps their memories and feelings are also more apt to be influenced by what they currently hear from others, especially their parents, about what things were like at that time. As the omega-alpha generation, these students' adolescent sense of identity had developed during the time of transitions.

Not only did the group interviewed in 1993–94 fail to remember as much about the period prior to the changes, but their responses conveyed a greater sense of normalcy about the current period. By 1993–94 the rapid pace of the transitions had slowed. These young people had a more restricted perspective for understanding "normal" times since most of their adolescent experiences had taken place during rapid transitions. Reflecting this greater sense of normalcy, fewer referred to negative feelings associated with the changes, and fewer talked about the transitions leading to a brighter future.

A far more striking finding relates to consistency across interview year, school type, and gender. When asked to talk about the effects of the major changes, most students talked very briefly about the effects on Hungary and said nothing about the effects on their city, Pécs, or nearby village. Instead, they focused upon their family, talking about themselves in relation to family issues.

It appeared that these youth formed their opinions about the political, economic, and social changes and their effects primarily in the context of their families. As shown in the illustrative examples, most viewed their parents and other family members as uninterested in political issues, just "living their own lives." The students did not perceive their families or friends as valuing activities that relate to the macrosystem level. Students' responses indicated that they had had few opportunities to take part in conversations about these issues.

In Hungary, young persons have generally depended on their family much more, and family control is greater than in western Europe (Komlósi, 1974). This still appears to be the case with respect to the recent transitions. Although strong family control does not foster a strong sense of personal independence and autonomy in adolescents, the family serves as an effective private space where members can find refuge as well as reveal their own selves (Hankiss, Manchin, Füstös & Szakolczai 1982).

These results of the interviews suggest that the families of these students provided an effective private space that functioned like a filter system, protecting the adolescents and guarding against the adolescents' awareness of environmental changes. If this is the case, families help adolescents maintain a greater level of equilibrium with the conditions from a previous era for a longer time and, therefore, adapt at a slower pace to the changing conditions. Perhaps, in Hungary, the family has traditionally functioned in this way as a means of providing security against powerful outside forces that might upset the calmer, harmonious balance of the individual and the family. During this century as well as in past centuries, power and oppression have taken many forms. The greater the pressure from outside, the greater the family loyalty that may develop. This may have been one source of the unexpectedly strong relationship Pataki (1993) reported between adolescents and their parents.

In addition to the microsystem of the family which inhibited students' interest and trust in macrosocial processes, the students' second most important microsystem, their peers, similarly inhibited the growth of positive affect regarding the changing political system. Bronfenbrenner (1993) defines the mesosystem as comprising the linkages between two microsystems. When both microsystems, family and friends, are characterized by features that inhibit development, the effects can be synergistic. This seems the case with these adolescents in Pécs where multiple microsocial processes maximize trust within the circle of family and friends, and minimize trust outside the circle, particularly at the national and international levels.

Understanding Political Concepts: Views from the Sidelines

People say that our life is totally different, but I don't feel this. I cannot decide if it is good or bad for us or what really happened.
16-year-old girl, technical school, 1991

※

Everybody became free. There is democracy. Of course, the economy became bankrupt. We sold half of our goods to the Soviets, and now we're left with those goods. But it is still better than it used to be.
17-year-old boy, academic school, 1991

※

Our situation is better. We are free. We can talk about everything. Until now everything belonged to the State. Now they start selling the land and the companies. Western people buy a lot these days. Lots of people have become wealthy, but lots of people's lives have become harder.
17-year-old boy, vocational school, 1994

Despite the strength of their "family filters" the students in Pécs consistently emphasized democratization, particularly "freedom," and also the move toward a capitalist economy as the most important changes at the national level. This is related to Erikson's construct of psychosocial identity formation which includes the development of abstract conceptualizations about one's society.

In this section we discuss items relating to the topic *Understanding Political Concepts*: the purpose of government, democracy, freedom, free market economy, citizenship, political involvement, patriotism, and nationalism. The adolescents in Pécs were just developing ideas such as democracy, free market economy, and citizenship at the time when, within their macrosystem, the population at large was developing these same concepts. At the same time, new institutions intended to be congruent with the new ideas were being developed. At the time of the first and second set of interviews in Pécs, the adult population had not yet developed a consistent understanding of what these concepts meant. Like the adults around them, these adolescents struggled to articulate the evolving political constructs that had become part of national discourse in the macrosystem.

In addition, students' identity as citizens in a particular democratic country with a free market economy was based on their development of a balance of trust and mistrust in the new government. This also requires the development of national institutions that are consistent with these new ideas and generally deserving of the citizens' trust. In fact, Sigel and Hoskin (1981) make the point that the idea of a relatively high level of citizens' trust is inherent in the concept of a democracy.

Sigel and Hoskin describe the key components of political cognition as factual knowledge, awareness of important current sociopolitical issues, and comprehension of key constructs of the political system. Students' responses to the items related to this theme as well as *Living History* showed that, although their levels of cognition were often low, they were cognizant of the most important issues of the day. Furthermore, as their answers indicate, their level of cognition was consistently higher than their level of trust.

Sigel and Hoskin discuss political behavior in terms of conformity behavior, allegiance behavior, and influence-exerting behavior. Students' responses to these items showed that they saw themselves as law-abiding citizens who carried out their daily tasks at home and at school. However, as Sigel and Hoskin found in their U.S. study, the students in Pécs did not view their participation in their daily school activities as political behaviors. Rather, their examples of individuals' political behaviors related to voting or demonstrating, behaviors more explicitly connected to macrosocial issues.

The students' responses to the items in this section demonstrate that the development of political understandings takes both time and the development of trust. Differences between the 1991 and 1993–94 responses suggest some consistent patterns reflective of different cohorts. In 1991, many found it difficult to distinguish between democracy and free market economy, and many were unfamiliar with the term "nationalism." By 1993–94, students were more familiar with and knowledgeable about those concepts.

Overall, the students in Pécs gave brief responses to the items in this section. Most students appeared to have very concrete understandings of these abstract terms. For the most part, their definitions concerned their perceptions of the current situation in Hungary, rather than more abstract concepts of governmental systems. As many of the quotations illustrate, students' responses provide insight into their personal needs as well as their desires for a better society. Students assimilated these concepts into their own frame of reference as adolescents.

The Purpose of a Government

Almost all students said that the specific purpose of the Hungarian government was to meet the needs of the current domestic situation. The pervasive theme was that the major role of the government was to improve the lives of people. Few students talked about the purpose of governments in a general sense.

> The government wants to bring the economy in balance and it would like us to have a stable economy. They would like the country to improve. They say they would like to cut down unemployment and inflation.
>
> 17-year-old boy, academic school, 1994

More than a third of the students in 1991 declared that they didn't see that government had any purpose since it was not being effective.

> I cannot see that the government is doing anything. They say this and that, but nothing can be seen. Perhaps the opposite of what they are talking about is happening. Prices are rising, more people are unemployed, but they—on the other hand—live well.
>
> 16-year-old boy, vocational school, 1991

In 1993–94 the percentage of students who responded that the government had no role dropped to 10%. Perhaps this reflects students' growing experience with this form of government and their views of the government as active, even if they disagreed with its activity.

In 1991 the second most common answer was, "promote progress of the country." Here, too, students' elaborations often indicated that they were referring to the government's role in improving people's lives economically. More than 25% of the students made a comment related to this role. By 1993–94 fewer than ten percent of the students mentioned this role. This, too, seems to reflect the same growing acceptance, if not agreement, with the new form of government. There was a similar decrease in the number of students who mentioned the role of the government to control the crisis. The following quote is typical of students' realization of public discussions and conflicting opinions regarding the government's attempts to solve Hungary's problems:

> Our economy is in a serious crisis. Crowds of people are fired from their jobs in heavy industries. I do not know if it is right or wrong. The government is always negotiating about managing the crisis. There are a lot of arguments about it on TV as well. The government would like to overcome the crisis and solve the problems.
>
> 17-year-old boy, technical school, 1991

Fostering a better standard of living, and "catching up to the West" were mentioned by a few students in both years.

> There is a wide variety of goods in the shops. We can buy anything. Beautiful shops of Western quality are opened all the time. The government lets everything in from the West so that we can gradually have a life like they have.
>
> 16-year-old girl, technical school, 1994

Democracy

> Thank God there is democracy. Now not only one party can appear on the scene, but many parties can be formed. Luckily, the party that won the election wants something else, wants a free country and free people. The time that one person can do anything and another can do nothing is over. There is equality between people. Laws apply to everybody equally.
>
> 17-year-old girl, academic school, 1991

✖

> The country could elect her leaders freely. Everybody can express their opinions without getting into any trouble. For example, TV and newspapers are full of criticism of the government. They say that the government is doing nothing well. I do not really believe it, but I don't know about it. I enjoy it. Today everything can be written and can be said. Everything gets publicity. We can go to church freely.
>
> 16-year-old girl, technical school, 1994

In his description of a constitutional state, one student juxtaposed the 1956 Revolution and students' rights:

> Finally we live in a constitutional state. A policeman cannot beat a person just because he likes doing it. Today he has to be responsible for everything! People and soldiers who killed others in the 1956 Revolution were taken out and brought to trial. You cannot do everything to students in schools.
>
> 16-year-old boy, vocational school, 1991

"Freedom of speech" was the most common characteristic of students' definitions of democracy in both years: 40% of the students mentioning it in 1991 and 52% in 1993–94. A number of students discussed their own experiences with free speech in the microsystem of school, such as to the right to criticize teachers and others at their schools. For example, one student reported, "My father said that teachers can't stop students from disagreeing with them. Today every student can tell their opinion." Students' comments sometimes showed the difficulties of going from the ideal of free speech to the practice. For example, one student commented in 1991 that, "recently I told my teacher that he was a dirty fellow."

The 1993–94 responses reflected more tempered opinions. A few students, including Mária, discussed the nuances of the rights of free speech. One student explained:

> There is freedom of speech, but you cannot say everything. You can gently talk about anything but you have to find the appropriate way.
>
> 17-year-old boy, academic school, 1994

Students' responses suggested a subtle change of emphasis between 1991 and 1993–94. In 1991 more students talked about the rights of citizens, particularly free speech and, specifically, the right to criticize the government, and also equality among people. By 1993–94 a larger proportion of students talked about a free press, reflecting great public and media attention to the relationships between the media and the government.

In 1991 equality was mentioned by one-third of the students, making it the second most commonly identified feature of a democracy. Some students discussed equality before the law as well as civil rights. The following is a quote from a 16-year-old female technical school student:

> Equality among people is an essential characteristic of democracy. It does not mean that no hierarchy is allowed, but nobody has more rights to do anything. Until now there was no equality. We might have it from now on.

More students discussed economic equality in 1991. Perhaps in the earlier years of the transitions, the students, like many adults, hoped that the relative economic equality among people would remain and that everyone's standard of living would improve. A national survey of adults carried out in 1994 show that, faced with the forced-choice item, "Is individual freedom or equality more important?" 60% responded that equality was more important. However, by 1994, equality was mentioned by fewer than one-tenth of our students. This might be an acknowledgment that economic inequalities were coexisting with free elections, free speech, and, perhaps, equality before the law.

The 1993–94 responses reflected students' experiences with the changing social conditions. By that time they had already witnessed several elections. Almost a fourth mentioned freedom of the press, which was a major current issue in 1993–94, compared to only one-tenth who gave this answer in 1991. In 1993–94 more than a third of the students discussed pluralism or free elections compared to less than 20% in 1991.

> The existence of democracy is shown by freely electing without fear those people whose politics you prefer. People pay more attention to what different parties say. If they did not vote well, they cannot say it wasn't they who decided. Of course, people can be cheated.
>
> 17-year-old boy, academic school, 1994

※

> Today everything can appear in the press. You can criticize even the Minister. Sometimes it seems to me that it is the custom to discredit the government. Of course, there is truth behind the news. Naturally, I cannot decide what is the truth. Sometimes I believe in what I hear on TV, sometimes I don't.
>
> 17-year-old boy, technical school, 1994

Freedom

> Freedom is a good thing. I can do everything. Of course, freedom cannot be at other people's expenses. People can decide freely but they have to take responsibility.
>
> 17-year-old boy, academic school, 1994

One of the most significant differences we found between students interviewed in 1991 and those interviewed in 1993–94 was the latter's more widespread understanding that freedom did not mean unrestricted behavior. In 1993–94 the students consistently added to the definition of freedom that they could not hurt or interfere with the freedom of others. This represents a more complex framework of freedom.

The most salient feature of "freedom" mentioned in both 1991 and 1993–94 was "individual rights." This is consistent with students' understandings of freedom as central to democracy. The most frequent definitions of freedom in 1991 were phrased with reference to the respondent, and sounded quintessentially adolescent: "I can do whatever I want to" or "I can say whatever I want to." Csaba's response included a similar statement, "for me, freedom is that nobody interferes in my business. I do whatever I want." This illustrates adolescents' assimilation of the macrosocial political changes to their own individual psychosocial issues of identity development.

> Everybody does what they want to do. People are not restricted. They can say what they want to say. I am not restricted where I go, what I do, what time I go home.
>
>   17-year-old boy, technical school, 1991

"I can say whatever I want to" was mentioned by one-third of the students in both 1991 and 1993–94. There was a subtle but important shift between 1991 and 1993–94. In 1991, "I can do whatever I want to" was mentioned by about 48% of the students, but only about 13% used this phrase or a similar one in 1993–94. Instead, 28% responded, "I can do whatever I want to—as long as it doesn't hurt others" compared to 2% in 1991.

Other features of freedom that students mentioned in 1991 and 1993–94 were people having rights (16% and 4%) and national independence (15% and 17%). Csaba referred to national independence when he said, "For a country, [freedom] means that it is not dependent upon other countries."

In 1991 another student provided this more reflective response:

> Freedom does not concern me only. The country has become independent as well. Every Russian left the country. This is quite a big thing. Freedom starts somewhere here I think. We are not dependent on other countries. We have to form new relations economically, too. Finally, we can be Hungarians.
>
>   17-year-old boy, academic school, 1991

Free Market Economy

Students' responses concerning the features of a free market economy were similar in 1991 and 1993–94. In both years, the most common answer was "I don't know" (23% of the students in 1991 and 28% in 1993–94 gave this answer). The most common feature mentioned in each year was "free prices," by 22% of the students in 1991 and 20% in 1993–94.

In 1993–94 the typical response to this item was more complex, as can be seen from the following response:

> The free market system is good and bad as well. In the beginning
> it was bad for us, later it became better. Now cheaper goods arrive
> here from every part of the world, and they are sold here, at
> higher prices, of course. The quality is not acceptable in many
> cases. Hungarian goods are driven out of the market [by foreign
> goods]. Home production is not improving, so it cannot be market-
> able for a long time.
>
> academic school, 1993–94

In 1991 and 1993–94 some students discussed increases in
imports and exports (15% in 1991 and 10% in 1993–94). "Free
commercial competition" was named by about 15% in both years.
Being able to start a business was mentioned by students in both
years (12% in 1991; 19% in 1993–94). Overall it appeared that the
students in 1993–94 had a more in-depth understanding of the
political concept of free market economy and could apply the concept to their own lives.

Citizenship, Patriotism, Nationalism, and National Identity

Students' responses to questions about nationalism, patriotism, and citizenship suggested that they had limited understanding of these concepts. Some confused nationalism and patriotism.
However, their responses also showed a consistent absence of jingoistic nationalism. There was no indication that these students
thought that Hungary was a superior nation with special rights.
Most students who defined the term voiced their opinion that jingoistic nationalism was a negative influence on a country.

Students' understandings of the terms citizen, patriot, nationalism, and national identity can only be understood within
the historical context of Hungary and central Europe. As we indicated in the brief introduction to Hungarian history, and according to history books used in Hungarian schools, during the
time of the Austro-Hungarian Monarchy, a patriot was one who
worked for the independence of Hungary. In that context, citizenship carried neither civil rights nor a sense of civic responsibili-

ties. During World War II when Hungary fought on the side of the Axis powers and after the war when Hungary was a member of the Warsaw Pact, the word "patriot" was used by different groups in different ways. Once again, in these highly politicized and divided contexts it might have been dangerous to talk freely about patriotism. Similarly, Hungarians use the term "nationalistic" to convey both the positive and negative dimensions of the dictionary definitions. Some Hungarians currently use the term to mean one who supports independence and is proud of their country. Others use the term to mean one who is jingoistic and has a chauvinistic sense of national superiority. At the time of our study the word patriot was widely understood to mean that one was loyal to the nation and valued preserving it; however, to some Hungarians the term was still associated with the negative meanings of nationalism.

In general, the concept of citizen is also more complicated in central Europe than in western Europe or, especially, the United States. Many Hungarians, like other central Europeans, see a difference between citizens and those who belong to the Hungarian "nation." Csepeli and Örkény (1993) explain that because eastern European nations were previously part of larger empires or were states that lacked stable boundaries, the concept of citizen did not develop as it did in the more stable nations in western Europe. Members of central European nations have had to identify members of their national communities in other ways, e.g., shared language, customs, and values. This has resulted in conflicts between defining who is a citizen in legal terms and who belongs to the nation in psychological and cultural terms. For example, in 1989 Csepeli and Örkény conducted a survey among the intelligencia in Budapest to find out how this group conceptualized a "citizen." They reported that:

> Over 50% rejected citizenship as a primary criterion for membership in the Hungarian community. This confirmed our position that modern citizenship status and citizenship criteria for defining the nation (which are increasingly prevalent in the West) are almost absent from intellectuals' everyday interpretations of national integration in this part of the world. Among this group, there was a clear preference for criteria of culture, language, and consciousness of being Hungarian ... (p. 128)

Csepeli and Örkény (1993) suggest that nationalism in Hungary may take a form that differs from that in other nations. The existence of this alternate form helps explain some of the responses, particularly those of the students who simply said, "national feeling." Csepeli and Örkény explain that Hungarians are conscious of their sense of "otherness," that they are not part of western Europe nor part of eastern Europe; they are not like their Slav nor their Germanic neighbors. "This type of nationalism opposes any broader framework of states or nation having any power over their own nation" (Csepeli and Örkény, 1993, p. 58). In this sense, "nationalism" conveys the meaning of "just having the right to be a nation" rather than the meaning of "one nation desiring power over another."

In 1991 and 1993–94 the most common characteristic of a citizen, as described by our students, was a person who would "obey laws," the response about half the students gave and one that reflected their understanding of what individuals can do in their everyday life. Particularly in 1993–94 this was the most salient response, one that was similar to "do one's daily tasks properly," the response of about half the students.

> A good citizen is one who keeps the law. A good citizen does not disobey the laws and helps the country progress. They love their country. They do the work that they are given.
> 16-year-old boy, vocational school, 1991

In 1993–94 there were increases in the small number of students who included voting and contributing to society, perhaps reflecting an increase in democratic values. Some responses regarding contributing to one's country's progress and loving one's country appeared more abstract, more reflective of an understanding of citizenship as a relationship to one's nation.

> The good citizen does not do anything against the law. They don't take advantage of the weaknesses in the legal system . . . They feel responsible for their country. They don't just look out for their interests. They like working. They take part in public life, in the elections and they are useful to society.
> 17-year-old girl, academic school, 1994

It is unclear from consideration of these responses alone, however, whether they reflect these students' more organized level of understanding based upon explanations available in their social context, or simply that these explanations were being repeated without deeper understanding. Furthermore, the student quoted above was unusual in that few of her peers discussed the ways in which citizenship related to democracy, e.g., though voting, working for candidates, etc.

The focus on obeying the laws is similar to that obtained by Jennings and Niemi (1981) in their studies of U.S. high school students in the classes of 1965 and 1973. In contrast to the open-ended format in our study, they used a questionnaire that asked students to pick the most important of six choices. In both years, two-thirds or more of the students gave the same four choices: obey the laws, proud of their country, vote in elections, and tolerance of other races, nationalities, and religions.

In examining how the adolescents we interviewed compared "citizen" and "patriot" it appeared that many saw these two concepts as synonymous. When they made a distinction, it was that the patriot's service to the nation was a noble one whereas the average citizen carries out ordinary daily tasks. Many elaborated upon the concept of patriotism.

> Patriotism is not only a feeling. It is a unique relationship with the country, where not talking but actions are important. Good patriots are not always known throughout their own neighborhood that they are good patriots, but only by those who know their actions. Later, of course, if people find out, they will respect them. He [the patriot] acts, works, and decides correctly. Temper does not lead him. They always work for something and never against somebody. They know that a more colorful society having more cultures living together in peace is a more valuable society.
> 17-year-old girl, vocational art school, 1991

In 1991, more than half the students responded that they "did not know" or gave no answer to the question about nationalism.

> I do not know what nationalism means. I have never dealt with and never heard about anything like this. These days it's often mentioned on TV, but I still don't know.
> 17-year-old boy, technical school, 1991

There was a significant change in 1993–94 when the majority of students offered a definition. It is important to underscore that

none of the students responded with a definition that clearly
reflected personal chauvinistic beliefs. By 1993–94, far more students said that nationalism had increased. These data are difficult
to interpret because many students referred explicitly to the war in
the nations of the former Yugoslavia. Most students who answered
this question explained that people were nationalistic when they
emphasized national consciousness at the expense of other countries. (See Appendix B, Table 3 for a summary of Pécs' students
understanding of nationalism.)

The following quotes illustrate the range of students' understandings and reactions to nationalism:

> Nationalism is a very bad thing. It incites the nationalities against
> each other. Since they know neither their own culture nor the
> other's, they emphasize one feature of the other's culture that
> proves their own culture to be more valuable and the other's culture
> less valuable. Stupid people can be made to believe in it.
>
> 17-year-old boy, academic school, 1994

> Nationalism is an action against other nations or nationalities by
> over-emphasizing their own national things. Today, the press is
> full of articles about increases in nationalism in Hungary. I have
> not met anything like this yet. It is not a topic for us although I
> have Swabian, Croatian, and Gypsy classmates and schoolmates.
> We are O.K. together. My father said that it was in somebody
> else's interest to discredit us in the eyes of the West. He said, "the
> offended generate nationalism." Soon you won't be able to say
> "Hungarian" because you will be marked as a nationalist.
>
> 17-year-old boy, academic school, 1994

Citizenship Education

In a paper presented at a 1988 conference, prior to the change
in government, Szábo (1991) described the school curriculum at
that time:

> In primary school there is a short . . . subject called "citizenship."
> No such subject exists in high school. Students get a certain pic-
> ture of the present social-political system through social philoso-
> phy and history. Political education in universities and colleges is

provided in the subject "scientific socialism" which handles the political theory of Marxism and which will be changed to political science in the future. (p. 67)

When asked what they were currently learning, almost all the students we interviewed responded that they were not learning anything in this area, a finding with important implications for education.

Some student's responses indicated that while citizenship education was not formally included in their schools' present curriculum, some informal instruction was taking place:

> We studied all of our citizenship education in history lessons in the 8th class of primary school. I cannot really recall what this was about. About the structure of the state, about the ministries, about the role of the Communist Party, but I cannot remember more. I cannot even recall what these were about. Now, during the lessons we talk about politics . . . Of course, not about up-to-date government politics, but about what really happened. These things are not in the subject matter, of course. Something like citizenship education is not in the syllabus today.
>
> 17-year-old boy, academic school, 1991

> I think officially it is not prescribed in the school program. But in our lessons we talk a lot about the present events, about a person's responsibility to the society, [and] to the neighborhood. Other moral values are emphasized in our lives. For us it includes the effectiveness of our studies in order to serve our communities and the country later. The importance of spreading real art comes up in music lessons as well. In this we will have our responsibilities, too.
>
> 17-year-old girl, vocational school, 1994

Finally, a handful of students, like Mária, said that there was "talk about citizenship, the good habits of the citizen." Mária pointed to a problemmatic area when she added, "They [the teachers] never had to think about this, so they are not comfortable with this topic."

The difficulty many students had in defining political concepts, and perhaps their lack of interest in politics, may be related to the lack of civics education in the schools, including teachers' discomfort in discussing these topics. At about the same time that we completed theses interviews, the Hungarian Ministry of Education addressed the lack of citizenship curriculum. It is possible that most Hungarian secondary school students are now receiving more education in this area, and that their understanding of these concepts is becoming more abstract and complex than the adolescents we interviewed.

Political Involvement

Their responses to these questions demonstrated that the students did not view the changes as resulting from the political activity of any people they knew. Overall they showed little interest in politics or political activity. Instead, students perceived their families as uninterested in politics and often perceived their friends as altogether antagonistic toward anything they considered political. One of the few students who had an interest in politics commented on the apathy of his peers:

> I have been working in the students' autonomy [similar to a student government] for two years. We have a good relationship with the FIDESZ Party [Young Democrats]. I like working for my fellow students very much. I argue a lot with my teachers as well, but as I see they are with us. Some people in my school say I am stupid and that it's all meaningless. But I see it is a good thing to represent our interests on a higher level. And it is also effective. I already got money for sporting activities, excursions, literary, and artistic competitions.
>
> 17-year-old boy, academic school, 1994

Researchers have proposed a number of reasons which could work in concert to account for the lack of interest in politics we found among this sample of students in Pécs. First, Gazsó (as cited in Szábo 1991) noted that Hungarian youth view "politics" as the foreign policy issues observed on television. Thus, these events are considered to be far away at the level of the macrosystem and therefore irrelevant to their everyday lives, their important microsystems. Secondly, there is the issue of mistrust in the changing political process. When Bruszt and Simon (1991) surveyed a national sample, they found a group of young people who were not interested in being involved in politics because they felt they would regret it if they became involved. These authors also reported that there was less interest in being involved in politics as one moves from highly urban to rural settings. Pécs is the capital of a province. Perhaps the level of interest in politics of people in Pécs is midway between that of people in Budapest and those in rural areas.

Commentary

Many students evidenced a great deal of apathy toward the government. Their responses to these items also illustrated the influence of people within the students' key microsystems, their family and, secondarily, their friends. Family members and friends also stood on the sidelines of politics. According to these students their family members and friends showed little interest in politics. Few family members or others they knew were involved in "politics" either prior to or during the changes, or at the time of the interview. Students often explained that their friends, in particular, were often anti-political and discouraged conversations about political issues. Consistent with the findings presented in *Living History*, these results also suggest that political information from the media was "filtered" through family discussions that reflected a lack of political trust, or through the more subtle filter of the purposeful absence of discussions. Both "filters" fostered a low degree of political involvement.

Students in both years had a strong sense that a fundamental role of government was to improve the lives of the people. Despite this, few students were either interested in politics themselves or had close contact with anyone who was politically involved. The use of Sigel and Hoskin's (1981) framework of political involvement to examine students' responses to these items helped us understand that their political affect was characterized by a pervasive sense of mistrust as well as a lack of confidence in the ability of the government to fulfill its promises. Students were dissatisfied with the government in general and critical of its specific policies.

In sum, students watched politics from the sidelines along with their families and friends. Most were developing a rudimentary understanding of the concepts but were not engaged. Like the important adults in their lives, most seem to seek protection and security from the changes, rather than become involved in influencing the changes, a course they felt was both more risky and uncertain.

CHAPTER FIVE

The Budapest Study

Portraits of Two Students in Budapest: Márta and Péter

Márta

Márta was seventeen and in her third year of the five year program at the dual language school when she was first interviewed by Van Hoorn in 1991. She was nineteen at the time of her second interview, just a few months from graduation. Márta was twenty-two, and attending both a university and a commercial college program when Tomás interviewed her in 1995. During the four year time span of our research, Márta lived with her family in Budapest. Both Márta's parents were university graduates and both worked as professionals, her mother as a college physical education teacher and her father as an engineer.

Growing Up in Changing Times

In 1991, Márta describes herself as a student who likes to study languages, history, and geography. She expresses a strong interest in travel, and says that she is very involved in sports. The groups that Márta identifies as important reflect her interest in the world as well as her close relationships. In addition to her "school group, family, and sports club," Martha mentions, "friends all over the world."

Toward the beginning of this first interview, Márta spontaneously voices her concerns about the unstable social conditions in her country and her wish for a good career. When asked about her wishes, she reiterates the importance of wise career choice and, when questioned about her greatest fears, she once again expresses fears about an uncertain future, specifically, difficulties in getting a good job. However, when asked to indicate how optimistic or pessimistic she feels, Márta replies "very optimistic" without hesitation. At this interview Márta expresses the belief that if she has a good job, her individual strengths and hard work will protect her from hard times.

During the second interview in 1993, Márta talks spontaneously about changes in the national economic situation and how these changes affect her family life, explaining that her family is cutting back on their expenses. Reviewing the interests she had discussed in 1991, she says that she is less actively involved in sports now, due to an injury, but she expresses more interest in languages and travel. This interview took place a few months prior to graduation, at a time when Márta had to make decisions about university applications. Márta is now much more specific about her career plans. In addition to university, she has decided to attend a commercial college to study the travel business. Márta's comments about her level of optimism/pessimism once again underscore the importance she gives to obtaining a good job:

> I'm still pretty optimistic. It's not worth it to study if I'm not optimistic. I think I can get a good job. I'm not afraid if I get a good job.

Márta's 1993 self-description also reflects a growing confidence in her sociable nature. After reading her 1991 self-description, Márta reflects, "I am [now] more clever and sociable. I like my friends, and I'm cheery." In planning to work in the travel business, Márta has selected a field that capitalizes on these personal traits as well as on her continuing interest in languages and travel.

At the time of her third interview in 1995, Márta again names her main interests as travel, languages, sports, and now adds, "organizing events," an important skill for her future success in the tourist industry. Márta's most important values as well as her interests remain highly consistent across the four years: family life, health, and a good job. At twenty-one, she presents this additional description related to the social nature of her personality, "the respect, sometimes love, of my colleagues and friends."

From the beginning of her first interview Márta showed that she was aware of the social changes in her country and how they affected her present life and future plans. Across all three interviews she was particularly thoughtful when asked to talk about how the changes might affect her overall development.

1991:

It depends on the possibilities to do things, [like the] opportunities to learn. For example, this school is new. This is very important. There are better possibilities to have a job than people had a few years ago.

1993:

I hope that I will think that it is a good period. It's interesting that it was a changing period. Maybe it's good because I know what it was like in the communist regime and what it is now, and I know the difference and how much better it is and appreciate it. And I'm sure there were interesting things in the communist years, too. We had the youth party. We had lots of fun with that. We went to camps and you were singing. It was interesting. [Now] we have scouts. All the grandmothers and grandfathers live their youth again and go with their kids and dress them up.

1995:

[The changes] have made me tougher, given me a better education. They gave me good chances for the future.

When we look at Márta's psychosocial identity development, we find that over the course of the four years, she maintained a good deal of stability in her perception of her personality and had grown into a young adult with clear career and personal goals. Erikson emphasizes the importance of time and place in the development of identity. From her first interview, Márta showed an awareness that instability in the national macrosystem could affect her personal plans for a stable and fulfilling adulthood. She compensated for lack of trust in the macrosystem with trust in her own developing abilities. By 1993 she demonstrated considerable initiative in planning for a career that combined her interests and talents with the newly expanding opportunities to succeed in the emerging market economy. By 1995 she clearly demonstrated substantial industriousness, developing competencies by attending both a business school and a university so that she could be prepared for work both in the tourist industry and a professional job requiring a university degree.

Living History

In 1991 Márta notes that, overall, the political changes are "very good, . . . democracy and the multiparty elections are very good." She explains why they occurred and some of the problems that have resulted:

> [L]ife was harder, people wanted to be themselves.
>
> . . . In other European countries, capitalistic countries, things were very different. We saw that they lived in a better way. We try to copy their political system. People saw the Hungarian system was not good. Everyone was fed up with communism.

Márta thinks that ordinary people influenced the course of the changes because "they were the ones who were not satisfied," and that she herself knows people who influenced the changes, "people, friends . . . (although) part of the country didn't do much directly."

When discussing the changes, Márta's enthusiasm about the political changes is subdued by her view that the economy is "getting worse . . . The living standard is worse for most people" and that people expect too much. She continues:

> The changes were too fast. People couldn't take it. In the 1970s people kind of accepted the system . . . .[because] the standard of living was OK. People didn't look at the obstacles . . . they weren't important. Now . . . people want more and more . . . [but can't get everything at once].

During the interviews Márta responds to the series of items about the effects of both the political and economic changes on her country, city, neighborhood, family, and herself. Her responses show that she knows about several specific sociopolitical and economic changes, particularly those that she perceives as affecting her family and her own life.

1991:

Democracy may help us [Hungarians] do what we want, elect the minister, express ourselves. The economy is worse. Many people live below the living standard. [It's better] only for the rich. Poor people can't buy what they want.

[Budapest] is similar to other cities.

Definitely [it affects my family]. We have to think more about our expenses, like going to a restaurant.

Maybe it's better for me. My future. It's a chance for me, for example, [to get] good jobs.

1993:

It's the same [as my 1991 response]. Inflation is pretty big. We have democracy. This is the first government. I'm sure the political situation could be better. I'm afraid about the economy. The difference between lower and upper layers [of society] increases. People need good jobs to survive.

I don't like the government now, especially the Minister of Foreign Affairs who is the son-in-law of the Prime Minister. I don't like the Minister of Education. He said we [our school] don't need British support. Our school got free books and materials [from the British]. I hope that the other party will be elected in 1994.

We haven't been out [to a restaurant] in years—even once a month. For four people, it's one person's salary. One dish is about 300 forint in a regular restaurant. You have to pay more for rent, electricity, water, food, transportation, everything. Salaries don't increase that much. It's harder to live. My mother has three jobs . . . .She gets paid for two.

. . . You can easily lose your job. Other younger people are coming who have advantages. [They're] the most up-to-date. You still have to study and work [on your skills].

Students are working. Companies give jobs for students—physical work, computers, questionnaires—not regular jobs—newspaper delivery . . . .I've been working for a company that gives jobs to students. It's not a regular job. . . . Students don't get money from their parents [anymore]. One evening out costs about 1000 forint [at the time about nine dollars].

1995:

During her third interview, Márta explains that the changes are going in the same directions as before but that the social problems had become more serious and that "people are not so optimistic." In her discussion, she focuses only on economic changes, although she emphasizes the systemic nature of the changes, "the two, political and economic changes, are strongly related to each other." She thinks that young people favor the economic changes the most and are the most optimistic, while "older people around their 50's" favor these changes the least.

> After the political changes, it [economic changes] got emphasized . . . Before the state gave more money to the social arena, etc. [Now there's] no more money. Everyone tries to solve the situation.
>
> [In Hungary] it should have good effects on a few. People can travel freely. [In Budapest there's] big development, a new bridge, better stores, new construction. [In my area, there are] more new houses, better cars around.
>
> [In my family] . . . the standard of living is lower, but we have a new house, and a new car from abroad.
>
> [For myself,] my high school gave me opportunities—in the English language.

Márta was asked to rate her overall satisfaction with herself, Hungary, and the world at three time periods, prior to the changs, at present, and ten years in the future. Across the interviews, Márta's self-ratings showed great consistency. For example, in 1991, 1993, and 1995, Márta rates her current satisfaction with herself as 7 on a 10 point scale (10 = most positive). In contrast, Márta's ratings of Hungary showed much greater variation, with a consistently positive trend, from 3 "before the changes," to 4 "at present" in 1991, to 5 in 1993 and 6 in 1995. It is noteworthy that, in all cases, Márta's level of satisfaction with herself at present and in the future exceeded the ratings of her satisfaction with Hungary or Europe.

Across the four years of the interviews, Márta evidenced less political involvement in terms of interest and knowledge about the changes. During the first interview she provided more detailed accounts of the major events and important changes than she did in her later interviews. The exceptions were the changes that influenced her own life, particularly her education which she sees as her path to success.

Márta provided conflicting information when it came to the effects of the changes on her family. Particularly in the 1993 interview, she focused on the great financial difficulties they were having, and the personal cost in terms of hard work. She herself was working, an important change in the life of a Hungarian adolescent. In 1995 she still presented her family as experiencing financial hardships, yet almost casually mentioned that her family had a new house and car. This raises questions about whether her family was working harder not simply because of the inflation which Márta discussed, but because they now had the opportunity to acquire more possessions which Márta had described as characteristic of Western countries. Interestingly, her family had cut back on certain aspects of their lifestyle such as going out to dinner, which Màrta used as a measure of a declining quality of family life.

Although she was most concerned about changes that affect her own life, her own microsystems, Márta consistently demonstrated that she had a social consciousness as well. Throughout the interviews, she considered the plight of the many "poor Hungarians" and spoke about the effects of government policies.

Understanding Political Concepts

In 1991, Márta expresses interest in keeping up with the news during the period of rapid changes, the period that she and others thought of as historic. Márta responds that she was "more interested" in politics than before. Indeed, she adds that politics are "important to my future." She listens to the news every night and to a Voice of America program in the morning. However, by 1995, mirroring her decreased interest in following national and international events, she shows less interest in the news, although she says that she still watches the news on TV. Now she reads the newspaper only for the sports news, reads a weekly business paper, and a monthly fashion-lifestyle magazine.

Márta's definitions and discussions of political and economic concepts show subtle changes from 1991 to 1995. During her first interview she talks about the purpose of a government and explains that "The government should direct the country, make decisions, make laws. (You need a) head of the country." Her 1995 responses begin in a similar way, i.e., a government's purpose is to make laws, but she now adds that it should govern the country "as people want." Although still brief, Márta's 1995 explanation suggests that she now takes it for granted that a government should be inherently democratic.

Her concept of democracy appears to change as well. In 1991 she explains that, "democracy means more parties, elections, you make decisions together, it represents the people. You have representatives to make decisions, not only one person." In 1993 she talks about the importance of political parties having experience, e.g., "Now the parties know what to do ... know what a party is for. (Their) work will be more efficient. It's very important." By 1995 she lists the numerous key features of a democracy such as a multiparty system, free elections, an elected parliament, people's rights, e.g., of forming other groups, and a free media.

Márta's definitions of freedom changed from one that was extremely self-referential to one that focuses on the rights of citizens. In 1991 she said, "I can do what I want. I can say what I want. I have rights. I can decide what I want. For example, where to live, the number of children I want." But by 1995 she explains, "... the right to do what you want that is allowed by laws—democratic ones."

Márta's discussions about government and freedom all reflect some engagement on her part. In contrast, Márta's definitions of free market economy seem to show a developing lack of interest. Her initial 1991 definition states her approval:

> Shop owners have a market and the government doesn't say what cost things are. ... [There are] no restrictions. There's competition between them. That's good.

In contrast, by 1995 Márta simply answers, "private property and free trade."

Márta's answers also show that her overall political involvement decreased from the first two interviews when she seemed interested to the third interview when she seemed quite apathetic. In 1991 and 1993 Márta replies that although she and her family had not participated in politics, she is now more interested and plans to vote.

1991:

> I like the Free Democrats and FIDESZ. They're like the [Free Democrats] and do what they say.

1993:

> I'll vote for FIDESZ. They want the same as I do. They're young, educated reformers. For a better country we need clever, intelligent people. [Unlike the present government] they [FIDESZ] don't just talk about money for people who lost property in the 1950s. Everyone already accepted that. They [the current government] live in the past. First they gave out land, then money for people who were prisoners of war—nothing for the future.

In 1995, however, Mártha replies that she is not likely to be involved in politics and, asked whether she had voted, she responds, "No. I didn't have the chance."

Commentary

Márta had developed a fall-back plan to deal with social instability. Her career choice also showed her eagerness to adapt to the new career structure that was emerging in Hungary in which young people in business have greater opportunities for advancement and higher salaries. Through her career choices, Márta also demonstrated the ways in which youth can contribute their vitality to their society. Márta's psychosocial identity development demonstrated her incipient and growing trust in the newly reorganized macrosystem. The career path she selected showed her autonomy and initiative in adapting, based on this level of trust. Finally, her studies were evidence of her industry, her growing development of the competencies she viewed as important in the changing macrosystem. This brief example illustrates the importance of each variable in Bronfenbrenner's process-person-context-time model.

Márta's analyses of the historical events and major changes were often similar to those of social scientists and media analysts, as well as those of her peers. For example, in her response that the changes were too fast for people to accept, that people had accepted the communist system when the living standards were fairly good, and that people now wanted more immediately, Márta analyzed the relationships between Hungarians and their system of government. Indeed, she included three points that were the subjects of academic analysis as well as public discussion. First, she focused on the widespread agreement that people were under stress because of the rapid changes. Secondly, Márta referred to the "implicit" agreement between Hungary's former communist government and the population at large that the government was accepted as long as economic conditions were favorable, a point widely made by journalists, political scientists, and economists. Thirdly, like Márta, many who wrote about this situation were keenly aware that the rise in most Hungarians' expectations was often too great to be easily satisfied (e.g., Bruszt and Simon 1991).

Across the interviews, there were subtle changes in Márta's political involvement. From 1991 to 1995, Márta's explanations of political concepts such as purpose of a government, democracy, and freedom suggest that the changes in the political and economic system that had occurred during the intervening four years, as well as her experiences growing up during this period had resulted in a more complex understanding of these concepts. On the other hand, across the interviews, we also see Márta's decreased excitement and interest in political activity. In 1991 she said that ordinary people, including people she knew, influenced the changes; yet when the items were more focused on political involvement, she said that no one she knew had been involved in politics. Moreover, Márta had not voted in 1995, despite her criticism of the government and her 1991 statement that "democracy may help us to do what we want."

Péter

Péter was 17 years old and in the second year of the English-Hungarian program when he was first interviewed by Van Hoorn, and 19 years old at the time of his second interview. In 1995 he was 22 years old and attending university when he was interviewed by Tamás. Péter lived with his family in Budapest. His parents were university graduates and both worked as engineers.

Growing Up in Changing Times

From age 17 to when he was 22 years old, Péter's interests expanded from art, literature, and his theatre group (1991), to philosophy and Eastern religion (1993), to skiing, working with young people, cultural anthropology, and traveling in 1995. In 1991, Péter says that the important groups in his life are his family and school friends, but in 1995 he adds groups that encompass the exosystem and macrosystem when he mentions Buda (the part of the city in which he lived), Hungary, and his religion. Throughout each interview he speaks of himself as being "fairly optimistic," and his optimism about his own future is reflected in many of his responses. For example, in 1993 he explains that he considers himself both an optimist and a realist:

> I'm realistic. In Hungary things are going in a bad way—but personally I can find my own way and I will. I am strong enough to be independent from the environment. Many people are pessimistic. There are real dangers. But they're not dangers for me. I can work hard. I accept these circumstances. I don't want to change the world. I want to change myself. I'm fairly optimistic about my own future. I see myself changing everyday to be more independent from the environment, to find a meaning in everything, and not to distinguish between good and bad. I am more relaxed than two years ago. Most people at 17 are kind of aggressive and anarchistic. I see myself and now I can accept myself.

During each of the three interviews, when speaking about how living through these times of change might affect his development as a person, Péter focuses on the greater freedom he feels to study what he wishes as well as his feelings of growing personal independence from social conditions. For example, in 1993 he explains:

> It's not something that is exciting. Only the names have changed. People are the same. They make careers. I became more independent from such things. It had more importance in my life than it should have. The political situation is useful. We can learn that we put too much emphasis on change. It's like a swing. It could be better. It's something to learn from.

> The main change for me is that the political changes [led] to spiritual changes. Spiritual [i.e., religious choices] became free. . . . Now there's a mass of excellent books. You are able to study any kind of what used to be secret knowledge. This is the only way that my personality was affected. From one side Hungary is chaos. [From the other] it's a spiritual center. Many people are involved in this kind of searching. Many books are published which were written decades ago. [There is a] rediscovery of Hungarian writers . . .

Although close to his family, Péter, like Márta, is someone who thinks a great deal about his own development as an individual. Péter is content with his own maturational processes. Over the course of the three interviews, he appears pleased that his interests are varied and have continued to expand.

Living History

Across the five years of the interviews, Péter's interest in the news increases. In 1991 and 1993 he indicates that he reads the paper occasionally and sometimes watches or listens to the news. In 1995 he usually listens to the news, but watches TV news and reads the newspapers once or twice a week.

Throughout the interviews, Péter responds to the numerous items about his perceptions of the transitions and their effects with answers that suggest that he has thought a great deal about these issues. When asked to discuss the major changes in his 1991 interview, Péter first identifies "a free passport for me" but then goes on to explain that "the changes were not revolutionary." He thinks that the major changes in Hungary are "the new businesses, the new way of thinking. It's fashionable to start something new, a business. (There are) foreign influences." During this discussion, he also talks about the social problem of inflation and about people facing increased economic hardships. According to Péter, these changes are particularly noticeable in Budapest. However, his family members are more free to do the kind of work they want to do, and that "quite luckily" his family is not having economic difficulty due to inflation.

In 1993, after Péter reviews the responses from his first interview, he discusses the changes that have occurred since then. His growing sense of dissatisfaction, disengagement, and hopelessness is apparent:

> Now there are more differences. . . . The rich who were lucky. . . . Many are very poor. Enough Hungarians are suffering.

> In the political field, many disgusting arguments about ideology. [There's] racism and anti-Semitism . . . many skinheads. [They] made noise so the President couldn't make his speech. The government is friendly with the skinheads. The President is [opposed]. The Minister of the Interior didn't do anything. There are rumors

that the military transported them [to Budapest for the demonstration]—and knew about it. [There's] ... strong propaganda for nationalism, e.g., that there are more Jews in the opposition party. And statements that there should be only ["ethnic"] Hungarian opposition. The government wanted to control the TV and the radio. They started a nasty campaign against the leader of the TV and radio ...

Two years ago I was more optimistic. Now it doesn't fascinate me any more. It isn't as important. There was a time when everyone was very excited. We used to watch Parliament. We used to want to know the up-to-date political situation. It's all over. I'm disappointed. I wanted to see more change. Now the original impulse is over. Now I don't know what to say.

In 1995 Péter identifies economic and political changes as the major changes that have occurred since his 1993 interview. He discusses both the more open economic system and increased unemployment. When discussing the economic changes in detail, he explains that before 1992–93 people had been more equal, that there "hadn't been such an obvious distance between poor and rich.... (Now you) can buy more things than before, (but there are) more starving people." He thinks that this change had happened quite quickly, and that it happened because of the poor conditions in Hungary. In talking about these effects, Péter explains, "It affected everybody's life. It's not a bad thing that people became different in an economic respect. It affected the behavior of Hungarians. Life became more serious than before."

Péter explains that the effects on his country are that Hungary is "trying to become a European country. It has made a big step." Péter also notes major changes in Budapest: "parts of the city became very rich, or very poor ..." His own neighborhood is improving. Péter points to the newly opened shops, but comments that it is "basically the same." And his family? "Not real changes—together as a family."

By 1995 Péter's answers showed that he thinks that he, his family, and most people in Hungary are becoming generally more content with the economic changes. In both 1991 and 1993, Péter rates his feelings about economic changes as 3 on a scale of 1 to 7 (7 = very positive). He thinks that most Hungarians would rate themselves between 3 and 5. In contrast, in both years he thinks that his mother would rate her feelings as 2. Talking about his father, in 1993 Péter explains that "my father became pessimistic." He adds that his father had been the most optimistic at first, but is now the most pessimistic of the family. "He thinks it will get worse, that perhaps there will be a civil war between the East and West." In 1995, however, Péter is feeling more generally satisfied about economic changes, rating his feelings as 5, his mother as 3, and his father as 4. He thinks that most of his friends are even more satisfied, and rates them as 6.

In describing political changes in more depth, Péter points to the more open society, to democracy. Discussing the changes, he refers to the situation in 1989, explaining that the reasons the changes happened was that the Soviet Union collapsed. When asked about the role of "ordinary people" he says that they influenced these changes, because it was "our own choice" and that, although no one he knows personally participated, other young people had.

In discussing the effects of the political changes on Hungary, Péter says that there is "more free press, people know about more things, people are more nervous, more confident about things around them." Describing the effects on Budapest, Péter mentions "lots of political happenings—it's the center of political movements, demonstrations." In contrast, Péter doesn't think that there have been any real changes in the villages. He is aware of new local papers in his neighborhood. But when asked about the effects on his family and himself, Péter responds "no real ones" and "not personally." In 1995 Péter indicates that he and his family, as well as most of his friends and most Hungarians, feel very positively about the specific political changes he described. All Péter's ratings for political changes are between 5 and 7. In contrast to 1993 when he discussed increased political extremism, Péter indicates that he now no longer thinks that there is an increase in militant nationalism.

Understanding Political Concepts

In 1991 Péter likens current political activity in Hungary to a wave. Prior to the changes, neither he nor his family were involved in politics, but they are now more likely to participate. He supports FIDESZ and the Free Democrats, as do his parents. In 1993 he adds that he trusts FIDESZ because they are intelligent and young. "I have a problem with older people. They're more selfish . . . as a group."

By 1995 Péter says that he is no longer interested in becoming politically active, but supports the Free Democrats.

Compared to his explanations of his development as an individual and his description of the sociopolitical transitions and their effects, Péter's definitions of political and economic concepts are brief throughout the interviews. For example, in 1995 Péter defines democracy as "free elections and free press." To have freedom in a country means that a country can "follow its own rules." A free market economy means that "customers can choose from lots of different things—what they can afford." Péter is most expansive when discussing the purpose of a government. For example, in 1995 he replies, "social stability . . . the social basics (such as) redistribute goods (through) taxation . . . and judicial power."

Commentary

Like Márta, Péter works to become independent from the social conditions that might affect his plans for a happy adulthood, which includes having a family as well as living and working in his own house in the suburbs. But unlike Márta who looks outward and is developing career plans based on her assessment of the current possibilities and alternatives in case these conditions change, Péter is looking inward and developing his spiritual side so that he will be content whatever the social situation.

From the first interview, Péter seemed aware of changes in the broader social environment, particularly the national macrosystem. Péter also talked at some length about transitions in Budapest which he considered the hub of the country. Particularly, in 1991 he seemed knowledgeable about many political happenings at both the national and municipal levels. By 1993 the extent of his knowledge but particularly his interest had begun to diminish.

Péter seems particularly attuned to the emotional tone of the macrosystem. Although many psychologists, political scientists, journalists as well as Péter's peers discussed the multiple stresses of the rapid changes, Péter demonstrates considerable insight when he characterizes the change in the affect or tone of Hungarians, from a people who enjoyed life to ones for whom life is more serious. Indeed, if this is accurate, the atmosphere that Péter describes is a quality of national, community, and family feeling that could have substantial effects on young people's development.

The Budapest Study

The adolescents we interviewed in Budapest were living in the capital city, the political, commercial, media, and artistic hub of their country. They all attended a specialized, Hungarian-English academic school with a cosmopolitan, international character. This innovative school was planned in 1985–86 and opened in 1987. It represented a new direction on the part of the Ministry of Education which was moving toward more creative and open programs in secondary education. The establishment of these foreign language schools illustrates that prior to the cataclysmic changes in 1989–90, there were gradual transitions occurring in the macrosystem that affected the young people in our study.

The Hungarian-English language program in this school was a five year, rather than the typical four year, academic secondary school program. The first year was spent on intensive English instruction prior to the subject courses taken in English during the next four years.

Prospective students took a highly competitive entrance exam that differed from most entrance exams. The purpose was to assess students' ways of thinking in addition to their subject-matter knowledge. Several other admission guidelines affected the composition of the student body. At the time of the first interviews in 1991 there was a mandate that a high percentage of students should come from workers' families. About 35% of the students had parents who had not attended college. This was higher than the proportion that was typical of other highly competitive academic high schools. Approximately 25% of the students we interviewed indicated that neither parent had attended college or university.

Because of the rigorous academic program emphasizing English and the opportunity all students had for travel, these students were not representative of those at more typical schools. The students who chose to apply were interested in languages but, even more importantly for this study, they were interested in learning about other cultures and in traveling.

The school provided daily experiences within a microsystem in which students could relate their experiences growing up in Hungary to a broader multinational perspective. The school's informal as well as formal curriculum stressed being open-minded about differences of opinion and tolerant of differences among people. Attendance at the school meant an opportunjty to interact with Hungarian students and faculty with similar interests and attitudes. The majority of the staff were Hungarians fluent in English. Additionally, there were always several staff members from English-speaking countries, English-speaking visitors from abroad, and exchange students from numerous countries. Almost all students had experiences as exchange students, attending schools and living with families in English-speaking countries such as Great Britain or the United States for three or more months.

The Budapest study consists of a total of sixty-seven interviews of a population of thirty students, conducted between 1991 and 1995. Of the 30 students, 13 were interviewed three times, in 1991, 1993, and 1995. Eleven were interviewed twice (six in 1991 and 1995; five in 1991 and 1993). Six were interviewed once in 1991. All interviews were conducted in English.

As previously discussed, the interviews conducted in 1991 were planned initially as part of the procedure to refine the interview protocol. After the first interviews in Pécs had been completed later in spring 1991, we became aware that the Budapest interviews were rich in depth and breadth, and provided a useful complement to the interviews from Pécs. It also turned out that we were able to follow the same group of students in Budapest from 1991 to 1995.

In 1991, the thirty students Van Hoorn interviewed were 16–18 years old. Their average age was 17.3 years. Sixteen were female and fourteen were male. They were completing their third or fourth year in the English-only program, and all were fluent in English. The length of the average interview was one hour—a class period of forty-five minutes with a fifteen minute break between classes. This contrasts with the interviews in Pécs and Gdańsk, which were typically 90–120 minutes long.

In 1993 Van Hoorn conducted 17 follow-up interviews. About half the students, those who had been interviewed during the third year of the five year program, still attended the school. With the continued support from Dr. Anikó Bognár, the program director, Van Hoorn was again able to interview 14 of the students who attended the school. In addition, with the gracious assistance of

Ms. Tünde Tamás, the school librarian who had coordinated the scheduling of the initial interviews, three of the graduated students attending universities were contacted and returned to the school for interviews. The students were 18–20 years old. Their average age was 19.1 years. Ten were female and seven were male.

The second interview protocol differed from the first. Rather than use all the exact same items after two years, the students were first asked to discuss the changes that had occurred in their lives and in Hungary since Van Hoorn had last spoken with them in 1991. Each student was then shown his or her own 1991 protocol and asked to discuss his or her previous responses. Students were asked to comment upon what they viewed as both the continuities and the changes in their responses between 1991 and 1993.

This second interview required a higher level of abstraction since students were asked to reflect upon the relationships between themselves and their society over time. Developmental processes across time are a key aspect of the ecological perspective. The discussions throughout this section on Budapest illustrate how students' responses reflected their development as young adults within Hungary's changing macrosystem.

The third set of interviews was conducted in 1995. Tünde Tamás was able to contact twenty former participants in our study, all of whom agreed to be interviewed. By this time, these former adolescents were now young adults, 21 to 23 years old. Their average age was 21.9 years, and they had graduated from high school two to four years previously. There were eleven females and nine males.

Van Hoorn conducted one interview herself and a second interview jointly with Tamás. Tamás interviewed the remaining 18 young people. Since approximately four years had passed since the initial interviews, we returned to the original interview format and structure. This time there was no time constraint, and most interviews took 90–120 minutes.

Growing Up in Changing Times: Becoming My Own Person

You become more of a person if you go through things that are really hard to deal with. It strengthens your personality. I think many teenagers like me will be leaders. We are [more] optimistic people.

Initial Self-descriptions

Although the students in Budapest mentioned their close relationships with their families, they spoke mostly about their individual interests and their career goals. Many pointed out that they had numerous interests. The most popular were sports, reading and literature, music, and language. Many also indicated a great interest in specific academic subjects, such as languages, literature, music, history, and the sciences, interests connected with the courses available at their school, a key microsystem in their lives. Often they discussed a vocational interest, reflecting orientation toward the future, e.g., "I'm interested in computer science."

In 1993 when the students looked over their previous answers, most responded with nods and statements of agreement. This similarity in their self-descriptions across time seems striking when one considers that, according to Erikson, adolescence is marked by a sense of discontinuity (identity confusion) as well as continuity (identity).

In 1995, these young adults were not shown their previous answers, but were asked to "describe their interests," a more specific question than the first open-ended item about self-description asked in the 1991 interview. Once again, there was a strong pattern of continuity. Like Péter, almost all respondents included two or three interests that they had mentioned four years before in 1991 and often added a few new ones. The most common interests that lasted across time were interests in reading, language, travel and learning about other cultures, theater/acting/dance, history, and sports. Although several mentioned their interest in history as they had in 1991, few of the students mentioned the news. None mentioned politics.

These young adults' interests in travel, language, and other cultures is understandable given that they had chosen to apply to a dual language secondary school. In the Hungarian macrosystems and exosystems, the importance of learning English and other languages of western Europe increased after 1990. For these students, the importance of studying foreign languages and cultures was also important within their microsystems at school, including their peer groups. In addition, their experiences in secondary school had strengthened these interests. All the students had also participated in exchange programs abroad and all spoke English fluently.

In 1995 all the students were strong academic achievers and were attending a college or university (in almost every case, the most prestigious university program in their chosen field). One student had already graduated from college. As one might expect from 21- to 23-year-olds, most also included interests related to their future professional goals, field of study, or current work. In Hungary, as in most of Europe, university programs focus on a specialized course of study rather than liberal arts. For example, the two students who were in medical school both mentioned their interest in medicine, those in computer science mentioned computers, etc.

Thinking about Oneself as Part of a Group

The major theme that emerged across all three interview periods was students' connectedness to their families and friends, particularly school friends. In 1991 and 1993 most students first mentioned family and then friends in their list of important groups. "School" or "my school class" was mentioned almost as frequently as friends, with many students, such as Péter, explaining that most of their good friends were classmates. Both these answers reflect the importance the microsystem of this school had in the lives of these students. Indeed, many students talked about the importance of the people at the dual-language school throughout their three interviews.

For these young people in Budapest, school was a pivotal microsystem in their lives for many reasons. They had had the initiative to apply for admission and the industry to take on the rigors of a program taught in a foreign language. Their choice of school reflected their developing sense of self. This developing psychosocial identity included their interest in other countries and languages, plans for their futures which envisioned opportunities in an international context, and strong academic abilities. They were bright and hard working. They saw that the microsystem of school provided a way to obtain the overall orientation and specific skills they would need to succeed in Hungary's changing macrosystem. When they thought about their future work environment, they knew they would need not only English language skills, but the flexibility to work with different people in different settings.

The dual language school provided a microsystem in which they could further develop these competencies and interests.

Bronfenbrenner (e.g., 1983) discusses the importance of influences in the microsystem that work in concert. These students were not only learning another language, but were interacting with Hungarian peers and teachers with similar interests, getting to know foreign students, teachers, and visitors, and having experiences abroad as international students. Indeed, having international contacts has been found to influence adolescents' views of the world (Farnen, 1993).

Although they were told that they could name as many groups as they wished, relatively few talked about other groups. For example, in 1991 "Hungarian" was spontaneously mentioned by only four students; their religious affiliation by three; "living in Budapest" by one; and "world citizen" by another.

When the 1995 responses are compared with the 1991 responses, the overall stability of the importance of the same basic microsystems is striking: family as the first response and friends as the second. The importance of the students' school or, in 1995, their university or faculty (i.e., department), likewise remained a common response. However, a change can be seen in the increasing inclusion of groups that tied students' identity to the broader community, the world of work, and the nation. In 1995, more students included their national or religious identification, and four of the twenty young adults included their city or community, perhaps an indication that they were beginning to view themselves as adults in a larger world. One respondent who had started his own business included his business colleagues as an important group in his life.

Facing the Future

Within each interview, there was great consistency in each student's responses to the many items that focused on the future. In addition, many common patterns were evidenced across interviews. Throughout the interviews, the students in Budapest demonstrated an individualistic future orientation. This was reflected in their discussion of career plans and in their optimism that they could succeed.

In contrast to their discussions about themselves and their interests, when the students were asked about their wishes, fears, and values, their responses were more global and general, and they seemed less engaged. All the students were questioned about wishes and fears in 1991 but of few in 1995. Questions about values were asked of all students in 1995, but of few in 1991. Since the responses to these items are related and the data for each are incomplete, we discuss them together.

In 1991 students' wishes were fairly evenly divided between those relating to the personal realm, themselves and their microsystems (particularly happiness, happy family, good friends, and good career), and those that related to the social realm, the encompassing macrosystems (particularly peace, a cleaner environment, and an end to hunger and disease). In most cases, the social wishes were also personal wishes, for example, the most common social wishes for peace and for a cleaner environment could be expressions of hopes for a better personal future. The most commonly articulated social fears were, in one student's words, "the same as the wishes": "fear of war, fear of the damage to the environment, and fear of diseases." Personal fears also paralleled personal wishes. Students were most concerned about not realizing their potential in their work or losing someone they loved.

In 1995 all students discussed their values. In most cases, a student's values related to his or her own 1991 wishes and fears. For example, their most commonly mentioned values of harmonious relationships, understanding, good friends, love, a successful job, and peace are parallel to their wishes for a happy family, good friends, a good career, and peace.

Several items questioned students directly about their sense of hope for their future. Students seemed particularly reflective when answering these items and often elaborated on the reasons for their responses. Many students were very introspective and aware of their feelings. In 1991 and 1995, students gave similar responses to an item that used a Likert scale to measure their level of optimism-pessimism (1 = very optimistic; 5 = very pessimistic). In 1991, roughly a fourth of the students described themselves as very optimistic (1), a third as fairly optimistic (2), a third as sometimes pessimistic and sometimes optimistic (3), and the few others as pessimistic or very pessimistic (4 or 5).

In 1993, few students changed their previous ratings. Those that did indicated that they were feeling increasingly pessimistic. These students were often the ones who discussed social problems such as increased right-wing political activity as well as their anxiety about university entrance exams.

In 1995, participants were slightly more optimistic than in 1991 or 1993. None responded that they were fairly or very pessimistic (4 or 5). Their sense of their future might be connected to their success in their university programs and to what they perceived as the somewhat improved social conditions.

In these discussions, particularly in 1991, several students spontaneously added that they tried to "be optimistic." Some explained to the American interviewer that Hungarians often thought of themselves as pessimistic. In general, students had an optimistic outlook that the future would work out well. Moreover, for these students this was not an optimism grounded only in dreams, but in their hard academic work and university programs that they consider instrumental to what they consider a successful adult life, consistent with their values.

Satisfaction with Self and Society

In 1991, students were asked to rate their satisfaction with themselves, Hungary, Europe, and the world for three time periods: before the changes (about 1988), at present (1991), and in the future (2001). The purpose of this item was to compare students' satisfaction with themselves as individuals to their satisfaction with three dimensions of their social ecology and to examine their past and future perspectives. In 1993, twelve students were shown their previous response and asked to rate their current (1993) satisfaction and, if they wished, to change their rating for 2001. In 1995, twenty students were again asked to rate their current levels of satisfaction as well as their future (2005) predictions. In addition, they were asked to recall their previous responses as best they could. (Table 5.1 summarizes the results.)

In response to these items, as elsewhere, these young people were relatively optimistic about their own future. During the first two sets of interviews, the students rated their current feelings of satisfaction in 1991 higher than their memories of how satisfied they felt in 1987–88. This may reflect their growing confidence and satisfaction as older rather than younger adolescents as well as their satisfaction with their special school. Indeed, throughout the interviews most indicated that they felt that they were acquiring the abilities and making future occupational plans that would allow them to succeed despite societal or global conditions. The belief

Table 5.1
Budapest Students' Levels of Satisfaction Related to the Self, Hungary, Europe, and the World

	1987–88	1991	1993	1995	2001	2001*	2005
myself	6.42	7.17	7.31	7.05	8.04	8.50	8.35
Hungary	4.92	6.25	5.65	4.15	8.21	6.05	6.40
Europe	6.50	8.00	6.54	6.00	9.40	8.30	7.05
World	5.80	6.25	3.21	6.15	7.38	5.75	6.11

*1993 interview predictions

that education would allow them to achieve their goals was common. For example, when Márta responded to this item in 1991 she commented on the importance of the dual language school in helping her acquire the abilities to achieve her goals. In 1993, most students were in their last year of secondary school, still relatively carefree and, on average, indicated still higher satisfaction.

By 1993 the students were much less sanguine about the future of Hungary, Europe, and the world. For example, in 1993 and, to a lesser extent in 1995, they had become more dissatisfied with the current conditions in Hungary and Europe compared to 1991. They revised downward their estimations of their future satisfaction with Hungary, Europe, and the world in 2001 and 2005.

A Good Life in Twenty Years

After discussing their values, wishes and fears, and their levels of optimism-pessimism, the students were asked to discuss their dreams for the future by pretending that twenty years had passed and they were telling the interviewer what their life was like. Overall, the descriptions were optimistic and often paralleled their wishes. Although many students had included more detailed plans in responses to other items, this item called forth basic elements: a happy family (usually a spouse, children, often, good relations with parents), a good job, good income, and a nice house.

> Hopefully I'll be a top leader, a manager. I'll own my own company. Hopefully I'll have a happy family. The house [my parents and I have been building] is probably finished.
>
> 18-year-old student, 1991

In 1991, all but two of the thirty students interviewed mentioned a family, and only one expressly stated her plan not to get married. About half the girls wished for three or four children. By 1993, several of these young women, now in their late teens or early twenties, had reevaluated the combination of family and career. One explained that she was no longer as optimistic about combining work and a large family, and that she really wanted to work. Two others said that they would like to stay home with their children. When describing their job aspirations, quite a few, like Márta, mentioned travel as an important aspect of their future professions as biologist, archeologist, or someone working in the music or tourist industries. Some of the vocations they envisioned were "dream jobs" that students understood were rare in Hungary.

In 1995, all participants were attending college or university with the exception of one who had just graduated. Many had part time jobs. Their greater maturity did not appear to change the essential features of their dreams. Fourteen of the twenty interviewed again mentioned three of the common wishes: to be married with children (though more mentioned two children rather than more), to live in a house, and to do work they found interesting. There was still an emphasis on travel but there was also an added emphasis on "a normal life" and four respondents included "good health" among the conditions for a happy life. More students specified a particular career. These choices were also increasingly what older adults would usually term "realistic," yet they still showed the high levels of confidence these young adults express in their abilities and their future. By 1995, being an entrepreneur in Hungary was often perceived as working for a more upscale life and being in the forefront of change. But many of our group still chose professions in social services, environmental work, or academic fields. These choices were also reflective of the values these students described.

Students' Views on How Growing Up during Transitions may Influence Their Individual Development

> People can learn to live on the top of an ice block . . . (Interviewer asked for an explanation) . . . It doesn't matter how hard it gets, you can live. Compared to 1989 we live in an open world. Financially we're more insecure but you can make contact with a lot of people, compared to the old era with financial security but a closed

world. Now we have an open world but less security. I like this
world better.

21-year-old student, 1995

During the first set of interviews, a number of students commented on the question itself, saying that it was interesting and
that they had not previously thought about the issue. Many pon-
dered on the potentially different affects:

It's hard to decide what causes the changes within myself. I'm
more open. My thinking is more open, more . . . realistic. Before I
had more daydreams. I didn't have such optimistic views of the
world. Now I look at things differently.

17-year-old student, 1991

During the 1991 interviews, several said that they were inex-
perienced at coping with the social changes that were occurring in
their lives, but pointed out that their grandparents had had many
such experiences, thus suggesting that some of these young people
looked to their grandparents as role models. One student commented that he saw his grandfather as "more of a person" because
of his difficult life experiences. Coming from a country such as
Hungary that has experienced many changes, and growing up with
grandparents who can recount stories of living through changes,
may influence the way in which these young people faced the
changes that were confronting them.

In 1991 these adolescents generally predicted that political and
economic conditions would improve, and that the effects of the changes
on their lives would be generally positive. The following comments
are representative of the majority of students who thought that the
changes allowed them freedom to develop as they wished: "I'm free
to develop my own opinions." " I feel that I can personally change
something." "Freedom creates a special atmosphere that affects me."

Although most responses were largely positive, a few students
reflected on what they viewed as the negative consequences, for
example, "I'm not so trustful anymore . . . and I don't believe politicians." But students pointed to other factors as well, e.g., the
effects of facing difficult conditions. One observed that, "If you are
brought up in an atmosphere where you can't talk about what you
think, where you are restricted in school . . . later, if there is a
change, you don't believe it will work."

Also, in 1991, one student emphasized that adolescence is usually a period of great change and questioned whether there would be any effects at all from the transitions: "I don't think that the changes influenced my development. This is a period in my life and everyone's life when we change the most."

In 1993, many of the students' responses reflected their increased disillusionment combined with the continued development of abstract thinking:

> You don't meet the political situation on the street. It's indirect. I can look at people [and they are] sad, tired . . . that might be an influence. I stay out of politics . . . .[But it's] interesting to be . . . [on the] outside of the great crowd of people arguing about things . . . [This is] useful [to my development].

Students' 1993 responses also reflected more definite career plans as well as problems in planning for the future. For example, these two students thought it was going to be difficult to establish themselves in their chosen professions, given the lack of stability in Hungary:

> I can't imagine my life and being a doctor here . . . .[I plan on] going to a foreign country and working there . . . I don't know if it's a result of the political situation [i.e., the rise in right wing politics].

※

> Rather negative [effects] . . . At this time when you have to make serious decisions, it's very important to have something that's stable. When you have everything changing all around you, you don't have a [reference] point to be secure. You can't be sure how it will be within months or years. You have to be very decided [i.e., planning for a particular field at the university].

There were still those who remained basically optimistic when thinking about the effects on their lives. For example, one student commented that, "I hope that I will think it is a good period. I know about both systems . . . good things now and then." Another explained, "Maybe I've become more self-confident and feel like I'm someone."

By 1995, participants generally appeared less anxious than they had in 1993, although many still expressed feelings of pessimism and voiced concerns about their being able to plan for their future. The following comments are representative:

> I need security around. Not much security [now] except for family and friends.

※

> [With these financial difficulties] I can't buy books . . . go to the cinema and theater . . . [experiences] that could help [further] my development.

Once again, there was a dominant theme of becoming "tougher" or more "persistent" due to going through a hard time. In 1995, there was also a growing sense that they would "get by" as individuals. One student put it this way:

> I've changed my way of thinking [because of the] economic effects. I'm much more careful. I have become wiser, learned how to deal with people and money. [It made me] work much harder.

Several students related the importance of their good education to their positive outlook. One said, "getting into university affected my whole future. I'm more optimistic." Another commented that it, "made me tougher . . . [Having] a better education . . . [gives me] a good chance for the future."

Commentary

These students in Budapest were well aware of the challenges they faced in creating the futures they desired. They had hoped that the transitions would quickly provide a better economy and an ideal political situation. Instead, many experienced a stressful economic situation within their families as well as disappointments regarding municipal and national politics. By the time of the 1995 interviews, they still had a personal sense of initiative and were more focused on their need to develop into individuals who, they thought, could be flexible and succeed whatever the circumstances. As young adults they were working toward more practical career paths at a time when increased privatization in the macrosystem provided more opportunities for entrepreneurs. Working in business provided opportunities to make more money and be considered part of the new generation.

The students were developing psychosocial identities characterized by individualistic orientations to their future, e.g., "becoming their own persons." Such dispositions are important considerations in discussions of psychosocial identity. They discussed their specific interests, skills, and competencies but they also focused on their dispositions and feelings, being tough, persistent, and hardworking as key to achieving the happy adult lives they envisioned. When talking about the future, most conveyed the belief that, even in rough times, they believed that they would be the exceptions.

Living History:
The Inspiring Historical Moment has Passed

Our students were developing into adults at a time when the history of their country was changing in an often unpredictable manner. In this section we explore students' 1991, 1993, and 1995 responses regarding what they often spoke of as history in the making. In order to understand students' perceptions within a more complete context, we have chosen to present the section on their interest in the news here, rather than in the previous discussion on self-descriptions. We next examine what they considered to be the events of historic importance—the events they chose to include on a historic timeline we asked them to complete, and then turn to their lengthy discussions of the continuities and changes.

Interest in the News

Living in Budapest, and attending a dual-language school, many students saw themselves as living at the center of national life and the transitions. As a group, they were comparatively interested in the news and relatively knowledgeable about the major events that had taken place.

We asked how often our students sought out the news in newspapers, on TV, and on radio. As one would expect, there was a tendency for those who were interested in the news to be more knowledgeable about current events. In addition, the number of times per week that students read the news in a newspaper, heard news on the radio, or watched it on television appeared related not just to their level of interest, but also to news-seeking habits of family members, the family income needed for newspapers or satellite dishes, and the student's course of study. Often students' interests in and opinions about social changes were influenced by the political orientation and level of analysis of particular news sources.

In 1991, the most popular news source was television, followed by newspaper and radio news. About half said that they watched the news or read a newspaper daily. The recent dramatic changes seemed to stimulate the students' interests in following the news. Márta was typical of her peers when she commented, "I'm more interested (in the news). I listen to the news every night. In the morning I listen to Voice of America. It's important to my future." Indeed, she was one of the group of "news-seekers" who obtained news from two or more sources at least four or five times per week. Listening to the Voice of America was among the many Western influences on her development. Most students indicated an interest in politics or current events. Their interest in the news reflected the ways in which they felt a part of history. They were a new generation. Their parents, teachers, and friends at school were also interested. However, there was a small group of students who deliberately avoided the news, emphasizing that they never watched or read news stories.

In 1995, there were several "drop outs" whose news-seeking behavior decreased and who generally declared themselves "fed up with politics." One joked with Van Hoorn that just as a vegetarian doesn't eat meat on principle, so she purposely avoided all contact with the news—she didn't watch, listen, or read about the news "on principle!"

About a third of those interviewed in 1995 said that they rarely or never watched, listened to, or read the news. The overall proportion of news-seekers decreased from that in 1991. Yet more than half still said that they obtained the news from one or more sources at least four times per week. Therefore, although they may have perceived their level of their knowledge and interest as decreasing, it was probably high relative to their peers in the population at large. There were still a few high level news-seekers who expressed a keen interest in keeping up with the news. As one would expect, these news-seeking students were also more interested in politics.

These findings are consistent with those from previous items. Even though our students grew older, had more experience with the changing social system, and were increasingly more capable of abstract thinking in their field of study, their interest in the news and their interest in politics decreased over the time of our study.

Making History: Students Construct a Timeline

In order to discover what these adolescents and, later, young adults viewed as "key events," they were asked to draw a timeline during each interview. They were given a blank piece of paper with a vertical line and asked to place important events on this timeline. These timelines inform us as to how they construct their ideas of history.

In addition to discrete events, some students also included more gradual changes in their timelines. The distinction between gradual changes and events is sometimes quite blurred however. For example, "Hungary declared a republic," "people can participate in politics," and "more liberal laws" were all included in timelines. The first one, "Hungary declared a republic" is associated with a date but it is more difficult to determine whether the other two items are events or gradual changes.

In 1991, students were told to begin the timeline with the year they considered the beginning of the major changes in Hungary. Most students began the timeline in 1988 or 1989 and included five to seven events. It was clear that most recognized that the political changes had, in fact, started earlier in the 1980s. For example, Márta said, "the changes began before 1989, but after (1990) the political changes got emphasized." The most common events the students included were: being able to travel outside of Hungary; the death of Kádár who had been General Secretary for thirty years under the previous regime; the declaration of Hungary as a republic; the establishment of the multiparty system; the first national and local elections; the opening of borders with Austria (which permitted East Germans to go to West Germany); the rehabilitation of the leaders of the 1956 Revolution; and the taxi drivers' strike that protested a rise in gas prices.

In 1993, when students were asked to include events that had occurred since their last interview in 1991, they included fewer events. In addition to the shorter time span, this may reflect their decreased interest in news. Students focused on the new government and also mentioned new laws such as those instituting re-privatization of land and religious education.

In 1995, they were again asked to list the important events since the 1991 interview. Most students began the timeline with the first elections which were held in 1990, prior to the first interview. Every participant included the 1994 elections. Eight students recalled the death of President József Antall in 1993. Three students mentioned the taxi drivers' strike. Seven specifically included the economic plan developed by Economic Minister Bokros. And seven included the establishment of university tuition fees. Other events mentioned were privatization, the beginning of the war in the former Yugoslavia, the rise of radical right wing parties, the devaluation of the forint, the closing of hospitals, the resignation of two ministers in 1995, the privatization of electricity and water. Compared to previous years, more students mentioned international events such as the Middle East peace plan and the peace agreements in Bosnia.

When we compared the 1991, 1993, and 1995 timelines, we found that students listed the greatest number of events on their 1991 timelines and more frequently discussed the events as historic. This was also the time when the students reported the highest level of interest in politics and the highest level of interest in keeping up with the news. It was also the time when all were students at the dual-language school.

Discussing the Major Changes

Although the rapid pace of change slowed between the 1991 and 1995 interviews, conditions in Hungary continued to change over the years of our study. In 1991 the new political economic and social system was becoming institutionalized. Discussions in the Parliament were televised and important new laws affecting fundamental changes in the macrosystem were passed. The unstable economic conditions were marked by increased inflation (30%) and growing unemployment. Our 1993 interviews occurred during a period of continued consolidation of the new system, but also a time during which the economy was still in disarray. The national deficit remained among the highest in Europe, inflation was at 20%, and Hungarian currency was again devalued. The challenge of militant nationalistic forces that had become evident in 1992 continued. By 1995, this challenge was reduced. Legislation affecting national and municipal polices had become more consistent. The 1994 elections had resulted in a coalition of the Socialist Party and the Alliance of Free Democrats. Contrary to voters' expectations, the new government carried out an economic austerity program, including the imposition of university tuition fees. At the time of the 1995 interviews inflation was still high (25%) and the currency had been devalued once again.

The illustrations below show how two typical students, Ildikó and Jeno, talked about the major changes during their interviews. Ildikó's 1991 response shows her to be cautiously optimistic, with a sense of how the changes are affecting her life as well as her country's. By 1993 she is disappointed and disengaged. In her last interview, she shows increasing concern about social issues, particularly the growing gulf between her own social status and that of many others. At the same time, however, she presents the positive features of a democracy—an open society—with more complexity than in her previous interviews:

1991:

The major changes are a free passport for me. The changes aren't revolutionary. We face inflation. My family is quite lucky . . . In Hungary there are new businesses, a new way of thinking. It's fashionable to start something new—a business. There's more foreign influence. (Note: Hungarians could get a passport for international travel easily after 1987.)

1993:

Two years ago I was more optimistic. Now it doesn't fascinate me any more. It isn't as important . . . There was a time when everyone was very excited. We used to watch Parliament. We wanted to know the up-to-date political situation. It's all over. I'm disappointed. I wanted to see more change. Now the original impulse is over.

1995:

Lots of changes . . . a break [between rich and poor] within the Hungarian society. . . . [The most important changes are] the economic changes—unemployment, an open economic system, and the political changes. Before people were more equal—there wasn't such an obvious distance between poor and rich. Now you can buy more things than before, but there are more starving people . . . [Economic changes] affected everybody's life. It's not a bad thing that people became more different in an economic respect. It affected the behavior of Hungarians. Life became more serious than before . . . [Important political changes] are the open society, the democracy. Now you can have any opinion. You can choose your favorite party. It's the democratic system. [The effects on Hungary include] more free press. People know about more things . . . Budapest has lots of political happening . . . It's the center of political movements and demonstrations.

Jeno's responses were less optimistic than Ildikó's throughout the time span of the interviews, but reveal some of the same patterns. He is less certain about the future of democracy in 1993 but, even though he says he is less informed about politics in 1995, he seems more confident about democracy being institutionalized. In 1993, Jeno discusses the increased number of poor people and ties people's growing dissatisfaction to growing nationalism. Similarly, in 1995, he discusses further polarization among people and their increasing pessimism.

1991:

People are losing control over their greed. The new government doesn't work. The new leaders aren't ready to lead the country . . . . I feel more uncertain, unsafe. At the same time, it's challenging. I hope the country will develop.

1993:

The leading parties are trying to maintain power, not democracy . . . I think that people mix a definition of democracy with a definition of 'I can do whatever I want to.' It's a way of not strengthening the law, but the weakening the law. People are getting angry. . .

Nationalism became worse. There are more poor people. I see the tendency that when people aren't satisfied they need people to blame. Some politicians use this to worsen this national crisis.

1995:

There's further polarization, less optimism, [people are] shifting attention either towards the materialistic world—of money or the transcendental-metaphysical sects like New Age, Body Control, Dianetics . . . [The most important changes] were the elections. The popularity of MSP [the Hungarian Socialist Party] and, afterwards, the loss of popularity again, partly the result of radical monetary cuts—by Bokros [the Minister of Finance] . . . But I'm not well informed about this and don't ever argue about it with anyone, as I have no time at the moment to delve into the subject. And without the deeper understanding of these things, I could only repeat some rumors in which I don't believe.

The analysis of students' responses across time reveals a shift in their affect. At the time of the 1991 interviews, most students felt that the height of the transitions passed and, to the disappointment of some, the directions of the changes had veered from what they had hoped. Despite this, students' responses still reflected a sense of optimism and an idealism about the possibility for a better society. Their idealistic hopes can be considered typical expressions of adolescents, but also, and importantly, they were the hopes of many adults at that time.

The 1993 responses reflected the low point in students' satisfaction with the political situation. Although the Budapest group was still critical of the political situation in 1995, their responses conveyed the sense that they considered the new democratic form of government to be normalized and stable. Overall, students' own perceptions of their levels of optimism also decreased between 1991 and 1995.

In the following discussion, organized by year, we focus in more detail on specific aspects of the major changes the students discussed: systemic changes, political changes, and economic changes. In examining the type of changes that they listed as important, we found that the students demonstrated fairly high levels of political cognition in terms of their knowledge of the important national sociopolitical events of the time.

In 1991 the changes students discussed mirrored the public discussions of the time. The two types of changes most frequently identified related to politics and economics at the national level. In all, students named twenty-nine changes relating to the political realm, most of which related to civil rights. The change mentioned most frequently was that people could think or speak freely, mentioned by eleven students, and, secondly, the right to travel. The most frequently pointed out change in the political system was the advent of free elections. Students discussed thirty changes related to the economy. Most expressed optimism as they talked about "more job possibilities," "privatization of factories," and "more goods in the shops." However, eleven of the thirty responses related to a worsening economy, e.g., inflation and increased unemployment. Although approximately a third of the students identified a systemic change that influenced many areas of life, none went on to discuss the truly systemic nature of the change in a complex fashion. Instead, the changes were named like items on a list, e.g., "freedom of the whole system," "open to the West." Appendix C, Table 1 lists all the changes the students discussed in 1991 and presents several themes we used when organizing them.

Many students appeared disappointed that the transitions did not match their own ideals of "transitions to . . . ." Nine of the thirty pointed out that the various changes they discussed were not that significant. As students emphasized to the American interviewer, "you foreigners are always talking about changes much more than we do." Another student reflected that "the height of the changes is decreasing." In 1991, many of these students went on to explain that their lives as well as the lives of family members and friends remained relatively untouched by changes that others considered major. Therefore, although they could and did discuss changes, they were aware of the abstract, faraway dimension to their discussions. They were referring to the qualitative differences they felt between changes in the macrosystem that were not perceptibly related to those in their microsystems. For them, these changes in the macrosystem had not yet "hit home" in 1991.

By 1993, this had changed. Students' responses evidenced not only greater detail, but a move toward a more systemic analysis of the changes. Importantly, many students spoke spontaneously, in greater detail or for the first time, about how the effects of changes that had occurred at the national level were affecting their city, neighborhood, families, and themselves. Changes in the macrosystems became more salient when they affected the students' microsystems directly.

Although their enthusiasm regarding the political changes had diminished by 1993, all but one student still mentioned at least one positive political change. Most of their discussions, however, were pessimistic in tone and tended to focus on blocks to democracy such as corruption, the difficulty in learning the truth from the media, and challenges to freedom of the press. Several emphasized their own dissatisfaction, like Péter who said, "Two years ago I was more optimistic. Now it doesn't fascinate me anymore. It isn't as important." These students pointed out that most Hungarians were dissatisfied with politics, e.g. "people are more dissatisfied . . . impatient" or "people feel betrayed by politicians." Another commented on public apathy, "people are becoming really fed up. They don't care about what's happening."

Like Jeno, half those interviewed spontaneously called the interviewer's attention to increased nationalism, anti-Semitism, and right wing activity among such important politicians as István Csurka. They also pointed to the spectre of rising neo-fascism and the visibility of the skinheads, particularly an incident in which the skinheads had stopped the Hungarian President from speaking, the same incident that Péter had recalled. Two other students explained:

> Partly Hungary wants to open to the West; partly [Hungary is becoming] more national socialist.

> ※

> These changes frighten me to some extent. The right wing is getting stronger. It can lead to violence. People aren't understanding each other.

Between 1991 and 1993 there were great differences in emphasis when students discussed changes related to the economy. In 1991 they tended to emphasize the positive and talked about the increased job possibilities, new businesses, and people's ability to make their own decisions about their work. These students saw increased possibilities for their own futures resulting from these economic changes in the macrosystem. Many related their own experiences at home or on the city streets to the national situation. Economic changes were also widely discussed in 1993, by twelve of seventeen students. But as with discussions of political changes, the tenor of these discussions was different. With few exceptions, students' remarks were exclusively pessimistic. Seven students focused on rising unemployment; five on continued inflation. One student summed up the situation by pointing out that money had now become the key force in most areas of life. Another commented that, "privatization is selling out the country." Throughout their interviews, five students repeatedly emphasized that many people were becoming poor. Several related personal anecdotes about "the really poor" who sold their few possessions in the streets or begged for money in the Metro. Many students discussed their own family's situation. A few, including Márta, had taken jobs to help out their families.

By 1993 many more students mentioned systemic changes, and began to analyze these changes rather than merely listing them. Fifteen of the seventeen respondents talked about the "new government" or the "political changes" and then related this political change to economic and social changes such as the new governmental economic plan. Many discussed systemic changes in terms of the worsening, chaotic social situation and its psychological consequences. Another systemic change emphasized and analyzed by more students in 1993 was Westernization. For example, one made the point that, "Western influences . . . were good and bad . . . a balance: new shops, supermarkets, etc. (but) chaos at the individual level." Some students pointed out that they saw many more Western goods in the stores, but that the goods cost too much. They were also unhappy that they saw fewer Hungarian goods in the stores and explained that they missed Hungarian products.

In keeping with their perceptions of more negative changes, many students also emphasized that the mood of the average Hungarian was getting darker. They pointed out that there were actually fewer major changes taking place, but that the changes which had taken place now "affect everyone."

The personal changes the students experienced in their own lives, such as a change in their family's finances, may have contributed to their more detailed discussions in 1993, an illustration of the link between macrosocial and microsocial processes. This stands in sharp contrast to the 1991 responses when these same students told the same interviewer that most people's lives were not noticeably affected. For example, in 1993 Márta described how her family was affected by the change in their family finances, focusing on how expensive it had become for the family to go to a restaurant.

In 1995 the students tended to give still more detailed responses than they had in their 1993 interviews. Their concern about the economy and their dissatisfaction with the political changes continued to be prominent features. By 1995 most of the twenty young people did not appear to be any more hopeful regarding the economic situation, but most had become more satisfied with the fundamental nature of the political system although they were still critical of particular politicians and politics.

In 1995, many of the students spoke about their widespread dissatisfaction with the government that had been elected in the spring of 1990, prior to their first interviews. They also talked disparagingly about the new socialist government that had come to power in the 1994 elections. Seven talked about the program carried out by the Minister of Finance which had decreased funding for social programs, including government support for the education of university students such as themselves. For these students who could remember a time when university education was free for those who qualified, the introduction of tuition was a hard reality of the changed political system, one that related most directly to their own microsystems.

> Before this September we didn't have to pay, only for books. There were no extra fees. Now the basic fee is 2,000 forint and the university can decide about extra fees.
>
> 21-year-old student, 1995

This student went on to explain that the government did not have enough money, but that the students—including herself—went on strike to prevent the imposition of fees. Despite harsh criticism of the government and its economic policies, there was a decreased emphasis on "blocks to democracy" compared to 1993 when many students had expressed discouragement about what they considered the shaky state of democracy in their country. During those 1993 interviews students had pointed to the arguments occurring in Parliament, to the government's use of power to influence the media, and to the rise of the "radical right wing" nationalistic and anti-minority politicians and groups. In 1995, only one student spontaneously mentioned increased nationalism as a continuing problem. Although students voiced many criticisms of the current government, they did not talk about the unstable nature of the new form of government. This suggests that by 1995 these students thought that democracy had become "normalized."

Almost all students continued to voice concern about the growing gap between rich and poor, and the difficulties of the middle class. Nine of the twenty students emphasized the increasing social differences, five talking about the relationship between unemployment and inflation, and four mentioning a worsening social life. Once again in response to this series of items, university tuition surfaced as an issue that students clearly saw as both economic and political, and one that strongly affected them personally. A few students did present more positive views of the changing economic system. Two talked about the continued increase of free enterprise; another about increased technology; another pointed to increases in new construction.

Overall, the pattern of response that was most notable in 1995 was the more systemic perspective that these young people had developed. The students emphasized the relationship between political and economic changes. The development of a more complex, systemic understanding is consistent with the students' development of more abstract thinking, particularly in those areas of greater interest and experience. In this case, however, evidence of increased ability paralleled decreased interest.

Their lowered level of interest may relate to their age as well as to their change of school. At university, few were enrolled in courses in which current macrosocial changes and related issues were discussed. They were being challenged to apply their developing capacities for abstract thought in areas focused on their discipline and not on analyses of their changing society.

Explaining Why the Changes Occurred

How these adolescents and then young adults explained why particular changes came about provides insight into both the political changes going on around them and their own psychosocial development. Across the three interviews these students' explanations for the changes evolved along with the types of changes they mentioned.

In 1991, students talked about the major changes to democracy and capitalism, emphasizing that "it just had to happen," that the changes happened because "forty years was enough of a one-party system," " people couldn't go back," and that "we couldn't go on like that." Other students commented that, "the Communist Party weakened" or that the changes were "connected with changes in the Soviet Union." One summed it this way, "The whole world is changing." Although students named a large number of changes in 1991, they mentioned far fewer reasons and described the reasons they did mention in a more cursory manner. (The complete list of explanations the students discussed is presented in Appendix C, Table 2.)

In 1993, students looked over their previous responses and discussed subsequent changes. While in 1991 they clearly considered the changes historic, by 1993 few discussed the more recent changes with much interest or in any depth. They focused on the negative when explaining why the recent changes occurred, pointing to the "bad economy," to the fact that "it is easy to sway people to the (extreme political) right," and to the "lack of political leadership." When talking about the arguments in Parliament or the difficulties within government, several students explained that the politicians had no previous experience with democracy. Many students explained that the growing economic and social inequalities contributed to other kinds of changes. Several pointed out that many leaders of companies during the old regime were still the leaders in this new regime. Some students were cynical but others explained that it was reasonable that people with experience and expertise would stay in leadership positions.

In 1995, students were again asked to identify and discuss the major changes and give their opinions about why the changes had occurred. Most students focused on the reasons for the change in government. They explained that people had grown dissatisfied with the previous government and had voted them out of office. As a group, these students focused on the imposition of tuition, a change that directly affected their own lives and one that students talked about a great deal.

Effects on Hungary, Their City, Their Families, and Themselves

During the interviews students discussions of the effects of the changes were strikingly consistent with their discussions of what the important events were, their explanations of why they occurred, and their reflections on how they and others felt about the changes.

In 1991, when considering the effects the changes were having on Hungary as a whole, almost all participants discussed some aspect of the political changes from a positive perspective. The theme of freedom was a common one although it bothered them that politicians were always arguing:

> People feel they can speak more freely.... Hungary is more open to Europe.... Maybe something has started which can make things better.... People are getting more open. [They're] just starting to realize that they can say anything they want and no one will say anything.

Students generally emphasized the negative outcomes that the economic changes were having on Hungary. Many emphasized that Hungary was being sold out or taken advantage of by foreign business, saying, for example, "[they're] selling Hungary to the West ... hotels, (etc.) ... most profit goes to the West." When discussing the negative economic changes, most comments concerned the continued deteriorating conditions for average people, e.g., "bad effects ... no jobs. People are pessimistic." The following comment was also typical: "People had money before the changes ... (now) many people feel pessimistic, tired. I see the problems in their faces."

Nevertheless, a few students expressed a sense of hopefulness about the future. As one student said: "We can make more business in the West. The West is interested in Hungary."

In 1993, the students described fewer changes and fewer effects on their environment. Several commented that the number of changes, or the rate of changes, had slowed down so that there were fewer effects to describe. There were no longer any hopeful comments about the effects of democratization. Only two students described any definitely positive effects reminiscent of the comments in 1991, e.g., one said, "more freedom ... more books, knowledge...." Instead, students' descriptions of the effects of the changes on Hungary tended to focus on the negative economic and political effects and their psychological consequences. Students also mentioned the economic difficulties, often emphasizing the differences between the rich and the poor: "It's going in the direction of South American countries. Ten percent rich and ninety percent poor." They pointed to unfulfilled expectations: "People are less and less optimistic. They thought that everything would be different in a few weeks." And expressed increased cynicism: "Money rules in a lot of fields."

A few commented that the situation seemed less stable or that government didn't seem able to cope with unemployment or inflation. These comments were prescient of the outcomes of the 1994 elections, which resulted in a change of government. In 1995, participants again emphasized economic changes. The changes and the effects were usually the same, e.g., increased differences between rich and poor, unemployment, and, once again, the imposition of college tuition fees. When discussing the effects of changes on Hungary, observations included: "Hungary becomes more European and (Hungary is being) assimilated into the West." A few students focused on the negative psychological consequences of the changes: "I see more and more shallow people who are behaving unnaturally, on one hand, and lots of sad, painful faces (on the other hand)."

As in other analyses, many students presented more complex pictures, including both positive and negative dimensions. For example:

> More homeless people, worse wages, higher prices, generally bad social life . . . but no socialism, better communication with the other countries, higher technology. [Hungary is] beginning to be like the West.

Students' descriptions of the effects of the changes on Budapest were relatively simple compared to the richness and complexity of their discussions of the changes in the national macrosystem. At the same time, students echoed the same themes they had discussed in relation to changes in Hungary. Most responses focused on highly visible changes relating to the economy.

In 1991, students emphasized the observable consequences of lowered economic standards for many people. On the streets of Budapest they saw more homeless people and more people begging or selling their personal things on the streets:

> [There are] old women who cannot pay their expenses.

> The mayor tries to keep things in order . . . but life is worsening.

Only about half included one or more effects they viewed as positive, such new buildings, new gas stations, more tourists, and more modern new hotels.

In 1993, when asked to look over their 1991 responses, quite a few students said that things were about the same in Budapest and that they did not want to make changes in their responses. If they elaborated on any changes at all, they focused on the "economy getting harder," "people becoming more pessimistic," and the increased observable differences between the rich and the poor.

The emphasis on their frequent personal observations of differences between rich and poor mirrored in city life was even more evident in the 1995 responses. Only a few students pointed to positive changes such as "new homes and better cars," and "new shops and businesses" or to "new buildings and a bridge." But more focused on the contrasts between the haves and have nots. Some of the same students who had described the poor or sad people they were seeing in 1991 or 1993 did so again in 1995. One student explained that "parts of the city are becoming very poor or rich." Another talked about her neighborhood changing from a "workers' neighborhood to a rich neighborhood."

The students were asked how the changes had affected their family and themselves. Because the answers to the two questions about family and self were so similar we discuss these results together. For example, few talked about their plans for the future without including their family. Even in 1995, as these young adults were preparing to join the workforce, the strong ties between family and self was evident.

In both the 1993 and 1995 interviews, students were much more animated when talking about themselves and their families than when discussing the effects of the changes on Budapest. Their responses illustrate once again that the saliency of particular macrosocial changes increases as processes of change move from the level of the macrosystem to the level of the microsystem. They related the changes of the macrosystem to experiences in their families, their primary microsystem. The redundancy in these responses provides additional evidence for the trustworthiness of these responses.

Some examples related to economic transitions. In 1993 one student gave the example of her sister's friend whose parents were out of work. For the first time the family had so little money that it was difficult for them to buy enough food. The student reported that her sister's friend consistently showed up at their house just before dinner time. The student's family was confronted with a dilemma. They felt compassion for the girl's family, who had to send their daughter to eat with another family. Yet they, too, were short of money and found it difficult to feed the girl.

There were other examples that related to the tumultuous political situation. In 1993 one student spoke about her disappointment and disillusion with her father's political views. She and her father were walking down the street when she noticed a graffiti of a Nazi Cross on a building. When she pointed it out to her father and told him that it was "fascist" and "disgusting," he replied that it was nothing for her to worry about, that it was "just a cross."

Their responses also suggest changes in the role of adolescents within Hungarian society. In the 1991 interviews, some of the students told the American interviewer that when they were exchange students in the U.S. they were surprised to find that so many American teenagers worked. As we have noted, between 1991 and 1995 more of our students took jobs to earn the pocket money their families were no longer able to give them. In 1993 one student told the interviewer that she needed to work now to help support her mother and herself. She observed that some of the other students felt sorry for her, but that she was happy to work several part-time jobs so that her mother would be less troubled.

During the 1991 interviews, approximately two-thirds of the students said that their lives and their families were basically unaffected by the changes. About one-third discussed increased economic concerns within their family:

> We have to think more about our expenses.
>
> ※
>
> [My] father has to work much harder.
>
> ※
>
> Three years ago my parents could save. Now their salary is hardly enough.

Some of these students described a decrease in the quality of relationships, particularly the sense of harmony within their family life. Tensions at home had increased with the financial insecurities. For example, one student confided, "my father is nervous because of decisions to make." Some explained that they had less time to spend together as a family since their parents were working longer hours. In some families, less money for nonessentials also meant less time for family vacations which these students who loved to travel missed greatly.

The two-thirds of the students who reported that their personal lives were relatively unchanged also said their family situation was unchanged. In most cases they explained that their family was fortunate because they were doing well, and that the positive personal relationships within the family remained stable. These students tended to see positive effects of changes on their lives. They traveled more and could buy goods of higher quality.

During the second interviews in 1993, the great majority of students who described all or mostly negative effects on their families in 1991 continued to do so, focusing on their parents' nervousness, job insecurity, and increasing prices. Many more of the students appeared very aware of their parents' financial situation. Changes in parental employment accounted for the most dramatic changes that students described. The issue of parental employment was also key in the more common instances in which students talked about parents who had lost jobs, or had to work much harder. Compared to many of her peers in 1993, Márta went into more detail about family expenses. Márta's understanding of her family's finances and her comments about how easy it was to lose a job also went beyond the comments of many students, showing the perspective of an adult worker.

Only a few pointed to any other positive outcomes for themselves or their families. One said that her generation was going to have a "different way of thinking." Not surprisingly, the students who mentioned the positive effects of the changes tended to be better off financially than those who had seen their family's financial situation deteriorate. One student who, in 1991, talked about how hard it was for his parents to make a living, had become more optimistic about his family's condition in 1993 because his father was able to buy a small business. But they also acknowledged the tradeoffs, e.g., "I'm lucky because my parents' salary is quite high, but my parents have to work harder." Those few students who reported positive personal and family effects in 1991 still tended to report generally positive effects in 1993. For example, the student who had talked about "increased opportunities" in 1991, spoke of being able to go abroad without a visa during the 1993 interview.

By 1995 almost three-fourths of the students spoke about the financial difficulties that their families were experiencing and, again, some spoke about the related change of mood in their homes. Many of these discussions arose in relationship to their descriptions of more general changes, such as the change in government or harder economic times, and more specific changes such as increased unemployment rates:

We have to work harder to maintain ourselves.

... worsened situation for my larger [extended] family.

Our income is getting lower.

The economic problems were often discussed in relationship to their psychological consequences. The students clearly saw the connection between their family's economic situation and the psychological state of their parents:

> My father is unemployed. It's hurt him a lot. . . . Now he has a job below his qualifications.

> [My family] feels kind of morose.

In 1995 the key change in responses was that the great majority of students now put more emphasis on personal rather than family difficulties, particularly those concerning the new university fees:

> I have to work more . . . and look to my parents for more support.

> I work to help my parents [pay for my education].

> From last September we have to pay for university. Before we had no fees at all. In my own life, the price of gas, electricity, rent goes up. It's easier for people who live with their parents. If we will have to pay we will think more about skipping classes and what we expect from teachers.

A minority, about one-fourth of the students, said that their family situation had not changed or had improved compared to the three-fourths who felt that it had deteriorated. One commented that her family was "lucky." The few students who said that there were no effects on their family also said that there were no changes in their own lives.

There were inconsistencies regarding some students' perceptions of their families' financial situation and their descriptions about family life. For example, Márta spoke of the financial difficulties her parents were having, but also mentioned that they had recently bought a new house and a new car. Perhaps they, like others, now viewed their financial situation in terms relative to the changing economy with its greatly expanded opportunities for consumer goods.

Feelings about the Changes

As another measure of how students felt about the changes Hungary had undergone, they were asked to rate how they, their peers, their family members, and "most Hungarians" felt. The following patterns of results were found across time for 1991, 1993, and 1995. As expected, students' ratings regarding levels of satisfaction were positive when they spoke about changes such as freedom of speech, freedom of the press, and freedom to travel. Their ratings regarding levels of satisfaction about changes such as increased unemployment and inflation were negative. In 1991 there was an overall higher level of hopefulness. Students spoke about changes such as democratization and the change to a market economy that they said had not yet personally affected them but that they hoped would positively influence their lives. In 1995 students spoke with more feeling about the changes which they said had already influenced their lives.

Across items, when asked to estimate how their mothers and fathers would rate their degree of satisfaction with changes, most students indicated that both parents felt more negatively about the changes than they did. This finding was true of both positive and negative changes. This further underscores the students' opinions that older people felt more negatively about the changes than did younger people. When asked to predict their mothers' and fathers' ratings separately, most students estimated that their fathers' ratings would be lower than that of their mothers for most changes discussed. If the students' estimations are accurate, this may be partly explained by the students' future orientation and relative optimism about the future based upon their development of useful competencies, such as speaking English. The relative optimism of these adolescents was also an expression of what Erikson viewed as youth's contributions of vitality to society's renewal. A heightened level of optimism may be particularly needed if the "omega-alpha" generation is to contribute to its rapidly changing society.

Students' estimates of their parents' feelings may also reflect their understanding of their parents' responsibilities and their parents' consequent orientation to the present rather than the future. Many students further reported that their parents had taken on the financial responsibilities for grandparents who had inadequate pensions.

Most students thought that their friends had somewhat more positive feelings about the changes than they. This is a curious finding. If this is indeed so, it may relate to adolescents' focus on their own problems and their common perception that others are having an easier time. It could also be explained by the lack of discussion among peers on these topics.

Students were also asked to identify the groups whom they believed favored the changes the most as well as the groups who favored the changes the least. There was widespread agreement. The students believed that young people, new business people, and the new people in power were the most enthusiastic about the changes. They believed that poor people, factory workers, retired people, and the people who were previously in power favored the changes the least. Interestingly, they usually failed to make the explicit connection that they would be the young people about whom they spoke. Many are both young and preparing to be the "new business people" as well as leaders in their fields, i.e., "people with power."

Feelings about the Situation in Hungary

In 1991, students were asked to rate their satisfaction with themselves, Hungary, Europe, and the world for three time periods: "before the changes," "at present" (1991), and in the future (2001). A 10-point rating scale was used, with very dissatisfied equaling one and very satisfied equaling ten. In 1993, twelve of the same students were shown their previous responses and asked to rate their current (1993) satisfaction and, if they wished, to change their rating for 2001.

Table 5.2 summarizes these results relating to their satisfaction with the situation in Hungary.

In 1995, students were asked to estimate their rating for satisfaction with Hungary at the time of their last interview. Most had been interviewed in 1993, but there were a few whose last interview was in 1991. The general pattern that emerged was that students tended to underestimate their previous level of satisfaction, i.e., they recalled that they were more dissatisfied than they had indicated at the time of the last interview.

Commentary

In their 1991 interviews, students reflected that the upbeat, historical moment had passed quickly. Most of these adolescents, like many adults around them, complained that they were confused by the pace of the changes and disappointed by some of the outcomes, yet at the same time that they pointed to the new "openness" and new possibilities for careers. By 1993 a growing proportion were concerned about the challenges to the new democracy from anti-democratic forces. Like Csepeli (1993), they wondered about the course of a democracy with few democrats. There was an increased sense that the changes were not only to be seen out in the streets, but in their homes as well.

By 1995 these young adults were less concerned about the future of democracy but more aware of how economic changes affected all levels of their social ecology. Although they pointed to the positive outcomes, they were not only aware of differences in

Table 5.2
Budapest Students' Levels of Satisfaction
Related to Hungary

Budapest students	1987–88	1991	1993	1995	2001	2005
1991 (n = 23)	4.92	6.25			8.21	
1993 (n = 12)			5.65		6.05	
1995 (n = 20)		——6.0——*		4.15		6.40

their own lives but also remained concerned about the lives of the many people who were becoming poorer. These students were individualistically-oriented with respect to preparing themselves to succeed whatever the future might bring, and optimistic that they could do well. Yet, at the same time that they were focused on their individual success, they evidenced a collectivist sensibility in their concern that the changes should not harm the less fortunate.

Understanding Political Concepts:
Growing Apathy at the Vortex

Even in 1991, all of the students in Budapest were able to provide some explanation for all the political and economic concepts they were asked to discuss. In order for us to obtain additional information about their political involvement, we asked the students to discuss their past and present interest in politics, and the political involvement of others they knew. In 1993, the students were shown their 1991 responses and asked whether they had anything to add or change. Very few students did so. Therefore, in 1995 we did not show the students their previous responses, but asked them to explain and then discuss the same concepts once more.

The Purpose of a Government

> A government is like a pyramid: people, then the representative, then parliament, then the government, then the prime minister. Each level should adjust decisions to what's under them.

When we examined the patterns of responses from 1991 to 1995, it appeared that the students' concepts of the purpose of government had developed from more concrete and simplistic views to more complex and integrated views. Their responses related to three governmental purposes: (1) organizational, (2) problem intervention, and (3) support and care for citizens.

In 1991 most students discussed one or two purposes. The most common theme related to the organization of the government. Of the fifteen or so specific purposes described, the most common was to "organize the country." Four students emphasized that the government should "organize foreign affairs" and three students mentioned the related purpose, "make laws."

At one level, these organizational descriptions appear to be simplistic, concrete responses. At another level, the students were accurately describing the first order of business of the new government which came into power in 1990. Indeed this government's first goal was to get organized and construct a vastly changed political and economic landscape.

The theme that a government should care for and support people was also common. Typical supporting, caring descriptions were that a government should help the society improve and "make good decisions for people." This theme is illustrated rather eloquently by the following response:

> The purpose of a government is to give aims and hope to people . . . to cooperate with parties who are in government . . . to get the best ideas and try to make them real.

As expressed by the students, both themes present the government as the active agent and the people as passive agents: governmental purposes do not appear to reflect citizen responsibilities. Our students consistently emphasized their endorsement of a truly new democratic order, but expressed democratic processes in a top-down (government to citizens) rather than a bottom-up (citizens to government) manner.

In 1995, the themes of organization, and support and care were still important, but a third theme emerged, problem intervention. After five years and two national elections, the students' responses were also more complex and complete. The 1995 responses also reflected a small shift toward viewing citizens as active agents. Two other findings lend support for the notion that democratization was becoming normalized in 1995. First, there was a change in the way that students talked about the organizational role of government. Secondly, much of what the students said about the role of government was in response to a general question about government, rather than to the specific question about democracy.

Although "organizing the country" was still mentioned by three students, most tended to focus on the more specific aspects of organizing the country, including both internal and foreign affairs.

For example, "establish good relations with other countries," "communicate with other nations," and "keep the peace" were mentioned. Once again, the second theme of support and caring was emphasized. Students' comments reflecting this included, "develop the country to a higher standard of living," promote social stability, ensure social basics, provide for education, and maintain a balance through "taxation and the redistribution of wealth."

A major shift in 1995 was the importance of a third theme of problem intervention. Students described government functions such as, "prevent injustice" and "protect minorities." The other important role that was mentioned was maintaining democracy. Several students mentioned ensuring democracy or ensuring that "citizens had rights." This theme may reflect students' sense of the continued institutionalization of democracy.

Democracy

> People who have different thoughts can vote for different parties. . . . People don't feel the difference of opinion in everyday life. . . . All parts [of society] should be represented.

Throughout the interviews, these students discussed their support for democratic concepts and governments. Lázsló and Farkas (1997) found that, between 1990 and 1995, Hungarian university students' concepts of democracy became less idealistic and influenced more by an awareness of the complexities of their nation's situation. This was true for the students in Budapest as well.

In 1991 students were very interested in talking about their ideals and ideas of democracy. They named most frequently a representative government with a multiparty system that allowed differences of opinion to be expressed in Parliament. Equality and civil rights for citizens, such as the right to voice any opinion and the ability to influence political leaders, were also mentioned.

In 1995, students' definitions included more details than their 1991 responses. Their discussions related to their experiences with the new democracy as well as their ideals about democracy. Ten students mentioned free elections; nine students said free media/press; nine said free speech; and four mentioned a representative government or parliament.

In 1995 participants also began to include and discuss their ideals for democracy. This included the theme of an informed and active citizenry:

People willing to participate in elections.

※

People should feel happy about their rights and exercise them.

※

Decisions can be made together [with the people].

※

Somewhat intelligent and independent middle class.

※

Ordinary people can take part in politics.

Another theme that emerged more strongly in 1995 was that government should serve the interests of the people:

A law system that assures freedom and equality.

※

Trustworthy politicians.

※

The government should serve the people's interests.

※

People have the feeling that powerful people don't control everything.

The third theme that emerged was that it was important that people have a good standard of living in order to ensure that they could continue to be active and informed citizens in a democracy:

A [good] standard of living.

※

Economic well being.

※

Equal chance regarding [getting an] education.

As with their description of government, when the students talked about democracy in 1995, their responses were generally more complex and related specifically to the role of government. In 1991 most did not link the concept of democracy with the purpose of a government. By 1995 many students made this connection:

> Peaceful coexistence of different views about the world [some may even be anti-democratic], opportunity of the population to elect its leaders, law system that assures freedom and equality.

Freedom

There were also differences between 1991 and 1995 in students' discussions of the concept of freedom. In 1991 most students emphasized civil rights. The most common definitions of freedom focused on the individual citizen's civil rights, e.g., "free press," "human rights," "people can do what they want," "free speech," "freedom to travel." Márta's response that, "I can do what I want. I can say what I want. I have rights. I can decide what I want," was typical of many her peers, and reflected their adolescent thinking.

A few students talked about freedom from an international perspective: "not to be controlled by other countries." This is not surprising given Hungarian history, but students were in fact referring to relations between Hungary and the Soviet Union, rather than the broader historical context, e.g., Hungary's relationships with Germany during World War II or Austria prior to World War I.

In 1995 there was still an emphasis on civil rights, but students expressed their own rights in a different, more adult way, stressing obeying the laws and not hurting others. These definitions were often phrased in a more complex and linguistically sophisticated manner:

> I think it's basically the feeling of [assuming] that no injustice can happen to them as long as this injustice can be prevented by the political system's structures.

While some still said that one could do what one wanted, in 1995 they added "as long as it didn't hurt others." Several students, including Márta, also discussed freedom in terms of legal restraints. Similarly one of her classmates said that Hungarians now had, "freedom to act within legal boundaries." As in 1991, several students pointed out the association between freedom and the quality of life, e.g., "a good standard of living" and "free medicine."

Free Market Economy

Students' discussions about the free market economy were more limited than those about democracy and freedom. In 1991 most definitions were quite brief. Students emphasized that the market was not controlled by the government, that everything could be private, that people were free to start businesses or patent inventions, that prices were "free," determined by supply and demand, and that people were free to bring foreign capital into Hungary.

Their 1995 discussions reflected a growing sense of pessimism about the economic system. The definitions themselves were similar to those in 1991, e.g., "no controls on production or sales," "free trade," and "supply controlled by demand." Péter, for example, said that, "customers can choose from lots of different things—what they can afford." None of the students spoke of the quality of goods increasing at the same time that the prices decreased, as some had in 1991. Instead, the problems caused by totally unregulated prices emerged in several responses. One student said that, "customers have choices depending on what they can afford." Another suggested that the government should set some limits, that "competition should be influenced by the political and economic system."

Involvement in Politics

Students were asked a series of questions about their political involvement, covering such topics as what the students thought about political changes, their support for a particular party, and whether they intended to vote or had voted. With few exceptions, they spoke about issues at the national and international levels. This is consistent with other findings. Szabó (1991) cites Gazso (1987) who found that, prior to the change of regime, young people thought of politics as "faraway," as exemplified by foreign policy issues rather than as something closer and more personal.

It appeared that interest in politics had actually peaked prior to the 1991 Budapest interviews. Once again, in response to these items, in 1991 approximately one-fourth of the thirty students responded that they were interested in politics. These students also indicated that they followed the news closely. Two students, however, pointed out that relatively few people, and few students, were interested in politics. When these two students were asked to estimate the percent of students at the school who were interested, they both guessed about 15–20%. They were probably quite accurate, 20–25% of the students interviewed indicated interest. Similarly, few students reported that they had parents or friends who were interested or involved, either prior to the changes or at present. When asked how they would vote if they could, the most popular party was FIDESZ which students liked because the party had young, educated candidates who emphasized that they spoke for youth.

By 1993, most of the students who had previously indicated their interest were no longer interested. Some had become quite discouraged. Others seemed matter of fact about their loss of interest. A few pointed out that they were busy preparing for university exams and had less time. Between 1991 and 1993 no student developed a new interest in politics.

In 1995, only three of the twenty participants expressed interest in national politics but a few expressed some interest in local or university activities. Only two said that they supported a particular political party, while seventeen said that there was no party or program they supported. Almost all, however, said that they had voted, most for the Free Democrats or FIDESZ.

Most students had had the expectation that they would find a party that represented all their opinions and commonly expressed their disappointment that no such party existed. Another factor in their lack of involvement could be related to the meaning of "party member," which, for some, may have carried a negative connotation from the previous regime. This finding provides further insight into respondents' adaptations to the changing macrosystem (e.g., the process of democratization). If this response is common among young people, it also suggests additional reasons for decreased interest and low voter turnout at the national level.

Patriotism and Nationalism

As we have discussed, in the late 1980s and the early 1990s, there was concern both within Hungary and elsewhere that Hungarians would become nationalistic, in the sense of being jingoistic. At several points in the interview, we asked questions related to the students' views and feelings about their nationality. Several items related to patriotism and nationalism. Some students in Budapest spoke about "being Hungarian" in response to the item on the important groups in their lives. Later in the interview these students were asked to discuss what made them proud and what made them not so proud to be Hungarians.

The responses were strikingly similar in 1991 and 1995. The majority mentioned being proud of at least two of the following: Hungary's history; intelligent, clever people or famous people— particularly scientists; the Hungarian language; the Hungarian countryside; and Hungarian cooking. The students' responses often reflected interests they had spoken of in their self description such as history and science. This illustrates once again the interrelationship of the responses to many items. For example, Márta reflected her interest in a career in the tourist business, and, indeed, spoke like a travel agent when she said that she was proud of "the friendly people, beautiful country, nice history, traditions and customs, and the peaceful changes." Three other students talked about the changes toward peace; one noted that the image of Hungary had changed and that now "others think better of us."

When asked a related question about what made them "not so proud to be Hungarian," the students were most critical of people's "way of thinking" and that "socialism could last for 40 years." One student, who had decried increased Westernization in her responses to other items, responded to this item in 1991 by saying that "we tend to learn things by imitation" and in 1995, "(we're) buying everything that's Western." Another suggested that the conditions in Hungary were not always supportive of success, commenting with a smile that, "(famous Hungarians) have become successful and famous outside Hungary."

Despite the fact that in 1995 more students said they were "Hungarian" when discussing their group identities, these young people reflected a sense of satisfaction with Hungary without a sense of superiority or exclusivity. None gave any response that could appear to be chauvinistic or jingoistic.

Commentary

These young people's understanding of political concepts reflected experiences such as attendance in a school with an international influence, travels as exchange students, ongoing experiences with social, political, and economic changes, as well as their development from middle adolescence to early adulthood. In 1991, in school and at home, they talked about more interest in discussing these concepts. In 1995, they attended different faculties at universities where political and economic issues were rarely discussed outside those particular fields of study. Consequently, at the same time that the students were becoming more competent in their fields of study, most were becoming less interested in political, social, and economic issues.

They were frustrated that the government had not turned on democracy as if it were a a lightbulb. Almost all underscored the importance of voting and identified their own party preference during the 1991 interview but, as young adults in 1995, some had not voted in the most recent election or had let their parents decide how they should vote. Despite their experiences as exchange students, they also focused on the national situation as the only source of economic problems. Few connected the economic problems they discussed with international forces, e.g., only one student mentioned the role of the World Bank in Hungarian economic policy. Thus, despite their increasing sophistication in other areas, these young adults in Budapest viewed the new government as completely responsible for the political, economic, and social policies that affected many aspects of their lives. And while they expressed the importance of the role of active citizens, in responses to numerous items, most students portrayed the government as the active agent and the citizenry as passive.

Our findings bear some striking similarities to those from the Hungarian national survey of adolescents carried out in 1995, the year of our last interviews in Budapest, as part of a multinational European study, Youth and History (Kéri & Békés 1997). Students viewed themselves as unlikely to do any political work (2.48 on a scale of 1–5). At the same time, when asked about their own future, they were more sure that Hungary would remain democratic (3.24 on a scale of 1–5). Kéri and Békés point out that this survey was conducted in the spring of 1995, right after the imposition of harsh economic austerity measures. In this national survey, as in our interviews in Budapest, there was widespread agreement with the position that democracy involves social welfare. Here, again, we see that although the students in Budapest were an elite academic group, their views often paralleled those of their peers across the country.

PART THREE

Poland

CHAPTER SIX

An Introduction to Poland
and its History

The Republic of Poland is a country of 120,728 square miles with a 1996 population of approximately thirty-nine million people. Poland is situated in central Europe and shares borders with Germany, the Czech Republic, Slovakia, Ukraine, Belarus, Lithuania, and Russia. Poland's capital, Warsaw, is also its largest city with a population of 1,640,700. Poland has a labor force of approximately seventeen million adults. The largest number of people are employed in the category of agriculture, with manufacturing jobs a close second (Europa World Year Book 1996).

Poland's borders have shifted frequently and Poles have both been ruled by and have ruled other peoples throughout their history (Stefanowicz 1996). The following brief history of Poland and the recent transitions is intended to give the reader a context in which to better understand the development of the adolescents interviewed in Gdańsk. In order to familiarize readers with historical materials that these secondary students would have encountered, this overview emphasizes major historical changes.

The Distant Past

In their history classes, these students in Gdańsk learn that Poland has ancient roots and was part of the Piast Dynasty, founded circa 850. The country became Christian in 966 when its ruler, Duke Mieszko, was baptized (Halecki 1957). Since then the Catholic Church has played an important role in Polish history. Poland

199

was ruled by a series of princes of the Piast Dynasty and the country was repeatedly divided up among different rulers until 1338 when Poland was reunited under Casimir III, the only king whom the Poles refer to as "the great." His death ended the dynasty in 1370.

During this time, the influence of the order of Teutonic Knights grew in the area near Gdańsk. Malbork, their stronghold, was situated near the Baltic sea close to the present day city. Most secondary students in this region, and probably all who were interviewed, have visited Malbork and learned the history of these powerful knights and of their defeat by the Polish Jagiellonion Dynasty.

From 1386 to 1572 Poland was ruled by the Jagiellonian Dynasty. Starting with the marriage of Jadwiga of Poland and Grand Duke Władyslaw Jagiełło of Lithuania, this period also represented a union between Poland and Lithuania (Gieysztor, Kieniewicz, Rostworowski, Tazbir & Wereszykhi, 1979).

Toward the end of the Polish Renaissance, the first elected king of Poland, Henry of Valois, was installed in 1573 through a process in which nobles of all ranks voted. During this period of elected kings, the king had more obligations to the country. The Polish people had more rights, including more religious freedom, than did their ancestors. This was also a time when modern cities with a growing middle class and humanistic traditions began to emerge (Gieysztor et al. 1979).

During this period, several foreign kings were elected. The nobles believed that they would be able to exercise more power without a strong dynasty (Curtis 1994). For example, in 1587 Sigismund III of Sweden was elected because the nobles thought that a union with Sweden was attractive because it would result in joint control of the Baltic and provide united opposition to Russia (Halecki 1957). In fact, the ensuing twenty years were ones of turmoil for Poles, marked by internal struggles and external invasions, including battles with the Ottoman Turks. By 1688 much of the territory was no longer Poland and, as a result, Poland's population was halved. Students and historians know of this time as "the deluge" or years of crisis (Gieysztor et al. 1979).

Russia's Catherine II intervened in 1764 and brought about the election of Stanisław Poniatowski as king. She assumed that he would be a loyal ally but, surprisingly, he challenged Russian intervention, facilitated modernization, and enacted more democratic and humanistic policies.

Polish secondary school students learn about the numerous territorial gains and, more frequently, losses that occurred throughout the eighteenth century. Austria, Prussia, and Russia began the partition and annexation of Poland into smaller regions and incorporated vast regions into their own countries. The Poles revolted, led by Tadeusz Kosciuszko, the Polish revolutionary who is also honored by Americans for his participation in the American Revolutionary War. The Polish revolution was quelled and Russia, Prussia, and Austria subsequently divided the spoils, "erasing the commonwealth . . . from the map and pledging never to let it return" (Curtis 1994, p. 22).

In 1795 the last partition of Poland ended its existence as a sovereign state. Thus, the eighteenth century was a particularly traumatic time, a period Dziewanowski (1977) describes as "the search of lost independence," a tide of longing for an independent Poland that grew from early support among the wealthy and educated to widespread support that included the peasants as well. Polish nationalism took many forms, from the wish for a recognized homeland to disdain for other ethnic groups.

Poland was not reborn as a state until after World War I. Living in the territory of Russia, Germany, and Austria-Hungary, Poles fought on both sides of the war for different reasons, and both sides courted their support. The end of the war was marked by complex intrigues, uprisings as well as negotiations, as the newly recreated state sought to secure boundaries that would include historically Polish lands. New borders were determined in 1921. In mid-1921 a democratic, parliamentary constitution was enacted that guaranteed civil rights, including freedom of education, association, and many private property rights (Gieysztor et al. 1979).

Recent History

This is the past remembered by the grandparents and great grandparents of these students in Gdańsk. Poland was the largest of the new states formed after World War I. In 1918, Józef Pilsudski was named the provisional president. His government faced many challenges, including the lack of defined national boundaries, and the absence of a legal or judiciary system. None of the many political parties had a majority, resulting in a series of coalition governments. There was little separation between church and state, and the Catholic Church enjoyed privileged status. During this time Poland was still largely agricultural with two-thirds of its population depending on farming as their source of income. Poverty was widespread. Only the areas previously held under German rule had developed a sizable industry. In addition, the newly reconstructed Poland included large numbers of ethnic Ukrainians, Lithuanians, Jews, and Germans, many of whom opposed Polish rule.

By the eve of World War II in 1939, Poland had become more stable after a difficult struggle to develop into an independent nation. By then illiteracy had decreased greatly, higher education rose, and the arts flourished (Dziewanowski 1977). Poland's great potential to become an industrialized nation ended with the opening of World War II.

In September 1939 Germany invaded Poland, including Gdańsk, home of the students in this study. During the war the Germans used the Gdańsk shipyards (the shipyards the students know well) to build ships for the German Navy. Sixteen days after the German attack on Gdańsk, with Poland in turmoil and unaided by Britain or France, the Soviet Union occupied the eastern portion of Poland. An exiled Polish government was established in Paris, then moved to London after the fall of France. Almost immediately after the Nazi and Soviet invasions, two major underground resistance groups were organized inside Poland (Derleth 1997). Indeed, by the end of the war, Poles made up the fourth largest contingent of Allied forces (Nelson 1983).

The Nazis declared most of Poland a German colony, a *General-gouvernement,* viewing it as a resource to be exploited. They closed all Polish public schools, artistic and cultural activities were severely circumscribed, and a ban on political activity imposed (Korboński 1992). Roughly four and a half million Poles died in the concentration camps during the war, including three million of Poland's 3.3 million Jews. After the war, only about one percent of the prewar Jewish population remained.

At the end of the war the Germans fought to keep control of Warsaw. In 1944, as the Soviet Army approached the capital, Polish partisan forces and the civilian population rose up to liberate the city. The Soviet Army did not intervene and the Poles withstood devastating loses. The city was almost totally destroyed and one-fourth of its population killed. By the war's end, Poland was in ruins. Its population had decreased by over six million (Curtis 1994).

At the Yalta Conference in February 1945, Roosevelt, Churchill, and Stalin agreed to leave Poland under Soviet control. Its boundaries were shifted so that part of eastern Poland was annexed to Russia, and part of Germany. The city of Gdańsk became part of Poland. Germans, Ukrainians, and Belorussians were resettled outside Poland and ten million Poles were resettled within the new borders of Poland (Halecki 1957). Families of some of the students in the study were undoubtedly some of those relocated after the war.

The Polish Committee of National Liberation was formed by Communist factions. By January 1945, it became a provisional government and was recognized by the Soviet Union (Curtis 1994). In 1948 the Polish United Workers Party (PZPR) and the Polish Socialist Party were formed and in 1952 a Soviet-style constitution was adopted (Derleth 1997). Poland joined the Warsaw Pact in 1955 (Nelson 1983).

During this post-war period, industry and agriculture were collectivized, and many civil and religious organizations were restricted (Nelson 1983). In 1956, following a major general strike, Władayslaw Gomułka, who was considered to be a "moderate" Communist (Curtis 1994), was named the First Secretary of the PZPR replacing the more hard-line leadership of the previous First Secretary (Nelson 1983). Gomułka promised to develop a more "Polish" form of communism for Poland. He ended agricultural collectivization, defied some of Stalin's policies, and gave the Catholic church more power. Many considered him both a "patriot and a staunch anti-Stalinist" (Taras 1996, p. 49). However, Gomułka was not able to enact the economic reforms necessary to halt the continued economic decline of Poland. In an attempt to improve the economic situation of the country, he increased the heavily subsidized retail prices (Derleth 1997).

By the spring of 1968, many Poles, like others in central and eastern Europe, were hopeful that Poland, too, would experience "socialism with a human face." As elsewhere, however, demonstrations were dispersed and leaders arrested. Dissent grew, centered on food shortages and high prices. Workers in cities such as Gdańsk protested price increases. Edward Gierek, replacing Gomułka as First Secretary in 1970, rescinded the price increases, but while there was a short-term positive effect on Poland's economy, Gierek was forced to raise prices again in 1976. The now routine pattern of strikes and demonstrations followed this latest price increase

(Derleth 1997). In 1976, the Committee for the Defense of the Workers (KOR) was formed to represent workers. Open confrontation also centered on civil rights. Discontent over prices continued, and in July and August of 1980 there were widespread protests over high meat prices (Korboński 1992). In 1978, an illegal union called the Committee of Free Trade Unions was founded. One of its founding members was Lech Wałęsa.

Major food shortages continued and again workers at the Gdańsk shipyards were the first to protest (Nelson, 1983). Widespread strikes occurred in 1980 after the government made another attempt to increase food prices. Striking shipyard workers demanded the legalization of their union. The result was the legalization of the National Committee of Solidarnosc (Solidarity). This union operated alongside the government until it was outlawed in December 1981 (Korboński 1992). At its peak in 1981, Solidarity and its rural union affiliates had more than twelve million members.

Once again, the strikes led to a change of government with Stanisław Kania replacing Gierek in 1980. In September 1980, General Wojciech Jaruzelski was named prime minister. When *Solidarity* announced that it would organize a national vote of confidence in his government, he appeared on television early one morning and declared a "State of War." Solidarity was outlawed but survived and grew underground. Even though Jaruzelski lifted martial law in 1983, he neither gained the support of the Polish populace nor restored economic stability in Poland.

The economic situation in Poland continued to deteriorate, and in 1988 there were two separate waves of strikes that threatened the stability of Poland. Solidarity was revived by the government and asked to intervene with the striking workers (Korboński 1992). Two important factors in the change that was to come were Soviet President Gorbachev's urging that Jaruzelski consider serious political reforms and Wałęsa's willingness to compromise with Jaruzelski (Rothschild 1993).

The Transitions Gain Momentum

In 1989, the Round Table talks that some students mention in their interviews were held between Solidarity, the government, and the Catholic Church. This led to a new electoral law to govern parliamentary elections in June 1989. Three other important declarations came out of the Round Table talks. These were the legalization of Solidarity, the right of free speech and association, and the establishment of judicial independence (Korboński 1992).

The first free elections in Poland since 1947 resulted in a major victory for Solidarity. Tadeusz Mazowiecki, an intellectual-journalist, became President of Poland. Leszek Balcerowicz was named Minister of Finance. The Balcerowicz Plan, as the new Minister's economic plan was called, attempted to implement a free market economy.

From the beginning there were conflicts between Wałęsa and Mazowiecki. Wałęsa thought that the Mazowiecki was not being aggressive enough in dismissing ex-communist party members from their political and economic positions. In 1990 the economic situation declined sharply. Prices rose by 250 percent and incomes dropped. The conflict soon turned into a split within Solidarity, with intellectuals such as Mazowiecki on one side, and workers and Wałęsa on the other. Both factions formed political parties. The Centre Alliance supported Wałęsa and the Movement for Democratic Action supported Mazowiecki. A bitter rivalry between the two factions dominated the pre-election environment.

In December of 1990, Wałęsa became the first popularly elected Polish president. The election was not a smooth one. Wałęsa, who had declined to be a candidate in the parliamentary elections in 1989 or to become a member of the Mazowiecki cabinet, was forced into a runoff election when he received only 40 percent of the vote (Rothschild 1993). In the first election, voter turnout had been low and to complicate matters, 37 parties ran candidates. In the runoff election, Wałęsa received approximately 74% of the vote (Rothschild 1993).

Wałęsa named economist and private businessman Jan Krzysztof Bielecki to the position of Prime Minister. Bielecki and his cabinet attempted to continue the austere economic policies of the Mazowiecki government but were unable to retain parliamentary support. In November 1991, one year before Suchar interviewed the first students in Gdańsk, polls indicated that 60 percent of the public believed that the economy was worse than the previous year (Dydynski 1993). Bielecki resigned after only one year in office. Wałęsa then appointed Jan Olszewski as Prime Minister but relations between Wałęsa and the new Prime Minister soon worsened as Wałęsa pushed for an amendment to the Constitution to give the office of Presidency more power. Olszewski held the office for only five months before leaving without being able to form a workable government (Derleth 1997).

The Gdańsk Study Begins (1992–1994)

The interviews in Gdańsk took place during the ensuing two years of conflict and change. In June 1992, following a controversy over attempts to expose alleged communist conspirators in the government, Hanna Suchocka, a university professor, was installed as Prime Minister. She formed a seven-party coalition dominated by the Freedom Union (UD), a party with Solidarity roots and ties to Mazowiecki, and the Christian National Union (ZCHN). Suchocka's government became the first to command a parliamentary majority in post-communist Poland. Despite her success in forming a coalition, the new government was immediately challenged by a month-long copper plant strike that was supported by transportation and power worker unions. At the end of 1992, a miner's union went on strike in protest over government plans to restructure the coal industry. Teachers and health-care workers were also on strike. In May 1993, the Sejm (the lower house of parliament) presented a motion of "no confidence" to the Suchocka administration. Wałęsa refused to accept Suchocka's resignation and dissolved the Sejm. New elections were scheduled for September.

Meanwhile, by 1993 many Poles were depressed about the economy. The September elections brought overwhelming support for parties that represented the political left, with the Democratic Left Alliance and the Polish Peasant Party winning the majority of the seats in the Sejm and the Senate. Wałęsa's newly formed Non-Party Bloc for Reform party won only 16 seats in the Sejm and two in the Senate. The new Prime Minister, Waldemar Pawlak, formed a coalition government with the Democratic Left Alliance and the Polish Peasant Party (The Europa World Year Book 1996).

In 1994, 20,000 people took part in a demonstration in Warsaw demanding that the government increase investment in the public sector and combat unemployment. Numerous work stoppages occurred during the early part of 1994 but plans for a general strike were canceled when coal-miners returned to work after the government promised pay increases. The conflict between the legislature and Wałęsa continued. It was during this period that the last of the interviews in Gdańsk occurred, and some of the students interviewed during this year referred to these conflicts.

CHAPTER SEVEN

The Gdańsk Study

Portraits of Two Students in Gdańsk:
Adam and Joanna

Adam (interviewed by Suchar in 1993)

Adam is 18-years-old and in his third year of the academic secondary school. He lives with his family which is considered middle class. Both his parents graduated from a technical college and both work outside of the home.

Growing Up in Changing Times

Adam describes himself as interested in "music, girls, money, and sports." Adam first says that he is "persistant" but adds that he is "impulsive and lazy." He talks about his childhood as having been "normal," saying that "nothing very special" has ever happened to him.

He points to family and friends as important groups and does not mention any formal organizations, religion, or being Polish. The values Adam names are "friendship, honor, dignity, and faithfulness." He indicates that his values are congruent with those of his parents but not necessarily in line with his friends.

When asked about his wishes Adam says:

I would like to be young and healthy forever. I would like to meet a wonderful woman but this may be impossible. I would like to be happy.

Discussing his fears, Adam indicates that he is afraid of getting "old or ill" and is afraid of an "uncertain future." He explains that his fear of an uncertain future is related to his concern that the new government will not keep Poland on the right track. This concern is also reflected in his comments about how his life compares to his parents'. Despite saying he feels his life is better than his parents' lives were at his age, he says that he is worried that environmental pollution will have a negative impact on his children's quality of life. Though Adam thinks that his children will have a better life in "a materialistic way," he fears that their overall quality of life may be lower since increased pollution may mean that his children "will not be able to have a close relationship with nature."

Adam says he is optimistic about his own future. He plans to continue his studies and wants to travel outside Poland. Adam says that he does not often look very far into the future except for his concern about the environment.

When asked to estimate his satisfaction with his life before the changes, at present, and his estimate of his satisfaction with his life ten years in the future, Adam marks six on a ten-point scale for the past and present, but marks nine for the future. Describing a good life twenty years in the future, Adam hopes to be a healthy 38-year-old man with a "fantastic woman," children, and money.

Adam was asked about how living during this time of change might affect his development as a person:

> This present situation is very important—the changes are very important. We have better international contact and better positions. I think that these changes will positively influence my future situation.

Living History

Though Adam talks about several changes in Poland and emphasizes the problem of pollution, surprisingly, he evidences no interest in the news. He says he doesn't read the newspaper and rarely watches television. He listens to the radio, but only to music stations.

When asked about what has remained unchanged in Poland, Adam first talks about what has remained unchanged for him personally, saying, "my very positive attitude towards girls. I'm still very interested in girls." When he turns his attention to what is unchanged in Poland, Adam expresses a rather pessimistic evaluation of Poles, "in society people are very individualistic, they are rather stupid like they always have been. The Polish people are not responsible for what they are doing."

Adam thinks that the changes in the economic system and changes to democracy are the two major types of changes. He cites examples when he discusses these changes, answering questions about why they occurred, how things were before the changes, what the effects of the changes are, and how he and others feel about them:

> The change of the economic system started in 1990. Before there were very few things in the shops, and now we have lots of goods but prices are extremely high. The changes went rather quickly. The reason for these changes was that there was poverty. We didn't have bananas. We didn't have contact with foreign countries.... Ordinary people did not influence the changes.

> In our surroundings [neighborhood] the changes are not so great ... [For my family] the changes are great. We can see them. At home we eat better products and also I can buy more things like cassettes, tapes, and better food to eat.... But of course, the rich people benefit most and the poor people least.

(When asked to mark his feelings about the changes, he indicates 4–5 on a scale from 1–7 (7 = most positive).

> I am happy because of the changes [in the economy], and so are my mother, father, and people my age. But the Polish people feel very differently.

> The second change ... this is the democratic system and the new president. Before we had less political freedom but now we have a great mess in politics so the change is going very slowly.

> [The reason this change happened] is that the people didn't accept the previous system ... [but] many people have different opinions.... People influenced [this] change because they had a chance to vote so it's better now and we can see the changes.

My emotional attitude to this change is 5. I can name the emotions. My father—sometimes he is laughing, sometimes he is angry, sometimes happy. As for my mother and people my age, I don't know. The Polish [people] have different opinions about the [political] change.

[The effects of the changes are] that we have freedom of speech, of the press. So people also influence this change and things are much better. We can see the changes. We have free newspapers, more different and better films. Everyone who gets information benefits from this change, and also the politicians. [He explains that he is happy about his change and so is his father.]

Understanding Political Concepts

Adam says that the purpose of government is to improve the country, particularly living standards:

The government should make the situation in the country better. It should help citizens live better, and develop industry, and care for the ecology. If possible, the government should also take care of people's health.

Adam defines democracy in the following way:

There is freedom of speech, of the press, freedom to express one's opinion. Democracy [also] means good neighborhoods and [a good] country. Also, citizens have their representation in the government and the church does not have great influence in social life.

For Adam, freedom entails the right to "express my ideas and opinions. I have my own rights. All citizens are equal before the law no matter how rich they are." Adam thinks that the changes to a democratic system of government and increased freedom in Poland have not impacted his life at school. "At school we have no freedom. At school we have a great mess!"

Adam defines the concept of a free market economy without hesitation, explaining that in a free market economy citizens have the right to "exchange goods, make mutual agreements, and have the right of free trade."

Adam indicates that he has had little education about citizenship in his school. He appears upset that he and the other students were not given information to help them function under the new system:

> We should know how the government is constituted, about courts, about citizens' rights, and about the constitution. Also the schools should give us some ideas about how to manage life because sometimes they just give us stupid useless information.

Adam defines a patriot as someone who is proud of his nationality and fights for his country. He expresses some conflict in his personal feelings about Poland. First he declares that he is "ashamed of being Polish." Then he takes a more moderate view saying, "I think that we are neither better or worse than any other nation." He lists Poland, along with Sweden, Germany, France, and Austria, as one of the good countries to live in. His personal choice would be to live in Sweden or Austria. He is negative about nationalism saying that the skinheads, whom he criticizes, are nationalists. It may be, therefore, that Adam feels that being proud to be Polish is akin to being nationalistic.

Adam says his family is more interested in politics than he is and that he is not at all active. Adam is one of the few students who mentions a parent who has been politically active. His father was an activist in Solidarity. But Adam insists that he is "not interested." He is not sure if he will vote in the next election and cannot identify any political party he would support. Although Adam says that if he decides to vote he will try to learn about the candidates before the election, he sounds rather apathetic.

Commentary

Adam's values and identification were family-based. He was basically optimistic about his own personal future, but did not discuss any specific vocational plans.

During several points in the interview, Adam expressed concern about the environment. This concern, however, had not translated into action of any kind nor interest in politics. He was not sure he would vote in the next election. He did not seem aware or perhaps was just not interested in the parties such as the Green Party that shared his interest in the environment. He looked to the government to solve the problems, including the environmental problems.

Joanna (interviewed by Suchar in 1994)

Joanna is 17-years-old and in her second year of the academic secondary school. She is from a typical Polish city area of large concrete apartment houses with very small flats. She lives in a two-room flat, sharing her bedroom with her younger sister. Her mother takes care of the family. Although her mother, who is an accountant, works for the state, she is relatively well paid. Joanna's contact with her father is limited.

Growing Up in Changing Times

Joanna describes herself as being interested in sports, culture, and foreign languages. When asked to talk about her personal strengths and weaknesses, Joanna says that she perceives herself as a "stubborn egotistic person," but, on the other hand, she acknowledges that she is "calm and tolerant."

The positive characteristics Joanna names refer to her positive relations with people. The negative characteristics she mentions may refer to her need for continued independence. She considers individual autonomy as the basis of her values. Although she is focused on autonomy in her relationships with people, she incorporates rules from her religion into her concept of an individualist. She points to Christian values in a broad sense as the basis for her own system of values. Among them, she says, love and honesty are the most important:

> I am an individualist following more or less the rules of the Catholic religion. Neither my family nor school influences my way of thinking.

She declares that her future and success depend on her own effort and work. When Joanna is asked to indicate how satisfied she is with her life at present, she rates herself as six on the ten-point scale and also indicates that she thinks that she will be more satisfied with herself in ten years. Joanna's optimism and her plans for her personal future are intertwined with her beliefs about the positive political changes in Poland:

> The changes in Poland are very important for my generation. Although the political and economic situation is presently compli-

cated, I believe it will improve. Maybe we will see improvements in five years.

Living History

Joanna spontaneously declares her interest in politics. When asked to name the three most important changes, Joanna names changes and events that are all political: the breakdown of the socialistic system; the first democratic election to the Parliament; and the election of Lech Wałęsa for president. In reference to the election of the Parliament, Joanna adds, "we needed the election so much, but then when it occurred, the wrong people were elected."

In discussing the reasons for the changes, Joanna describes her perceptions of the negative qualities of the old system:

> The politicians were dogmatic. The policy of the government led to making the economic and social situation worse. The changes had to come. There was no alternative for them.

> We have democracy now . . . freedom of choice . . . of speech. The politicians are quarreling but, probably, this is the way of doing politics in a democratic country.

Joanna's timeline of the transitions starts with the 1989 Round Table talks. She points to the election of the Parliament as the most important event in 1990. For 1991, Joanna includes Lech Wałęsa's election. For 1992, she includes the new government and Hanna Suchocka becoming Prime Minister.

Joanna's discussion of important changes indicates that her points of reference go beyond Poland. She talks about the situation in Europe and the rest of the world. Her analyses of the relations between Poland, Russia, the other former socialist countries, and the U.S. illustrate her comparatively complex understanding:

> Poland-U.S. relations are rather formal now and narrowed to diplomatic visits of both sides. The presidents—Wałęsa and Clinton—are officially declaring common approval and support for each other. But no economic effects on the Polish side are visible. Maybe our direct cooperation is not so close. Besides, the U.S. confronts many internal conflicts and problems that preoccupy Clinton at the moment.

Joanna's analysis of the war in the countries of the former Yugoslavia is also fairly sophisticated. "The international reaction to the conflict came too late. It should have been stopped, controlled just at the beginning." Joanna adds, however, that she understands it is hard for external forces to "engage in internal national conflicts."

Joanna points to the U.S. and Germany as the best countries to live in because of their freedom and wealth. At the same time, she emphatically declares "Poland must stay Poland." She names only positive features of the Polish nation. Joanna once again identifies Lech Wałęsa as someone whom she admires greatly.

Joanna goes on to say that it is the people who are active in private enterprises who benefit from the changes the most. She identifies farmers as the social group who probably benefit the least.

Understanding Political Concepts

In describing the features of democracy Joanna stresses political freedom and pluralism as well as the free expression of one's opinion. She says that the duties of a government include protecting the citizens, and having a social policy that promotes good conditions for society.

When asked whether she supports any particular party, Joanna points to the liberal parties as her political favorites. Joanna knows the names of the parties which are influential in Gdańsk and names a specific party affiliation.

Joanna's identity as a citizen of Poland includes a sense of industry in that she sees herself as a participant in the changes in her country. She says that she, personally, as well as her family and the rest of Polish society participated actively in the changes—either by their participation in the underground opposition or just by denying official propaganda. While she believes that most people think of the changes as positive, she recognizes that not everyone shares in this optimistic view, commenting that:

> My mother is slightly critical of the financial policy of the government. In some cases people may be disappointed, but generally I think they are satisfied.

Commentary

Joanna showed a relatively high interest in and knowledge of politics, and her analyses of current and historical events were relatively complex. Her timeline included many events and she was able to describe the relationships between Poland and other countries. Joanna also knew the names and some information about the positions of the many political parties in Poland. She was frustrated, however, that the "right" people did not always get elected. In defining political terms such as democracy her responses showed a basic level of understanding. Her overall judgment of the new government was somewhat positive. Although she was, in fact, very positive about Poland as a place to live, she indicated that she was aware that many people were disappointed in the changes.

The Gdańsk Study

Gdańsk has a population of approximately 465,000 making it the largest city in northern Poland. Almost 800,000 people live in the Gdańsk greater metropolitan area. These students as well as tourists can view the massive shipyards, play on the sandy beaches of the Baltic sea, promenade beside the rebuilt stately mansions that line the Royal Way where kings entered the city, and examine jewelry with the famous local amber that was carried along ancient trade routes.

For more than a thousand years, Gdańsk's location on a calm gulf in the Baltic has made it an important trading port. During medieval times it was a center of commerce for the Teutonic Knights. During the Middle Ages and into the Renaissance, scientists and artists from many European countries flocked to this wealthy international commercial city which controlled the majority of Poland's trade by the mid-sixteenth century.

From the mid-seventeenth century to the mid-twentieth century, Gdańsk was controlled at times by Poland and at times by Prussia. After World War I, Gdańsk was declared *Wolne Miasto Gdańsk*, the Free City of Gdańsk, and was largely self-governing. It was in Gdańsk that World War II began. By the time the war had ended, most of the city, including the shipyards, was rubble.

Since World War II, the parents and grandparents of the adolescents interviewed for this study participated in the triumphs and vicissitudes of this historic city. After the war, ordinary people helped artisans rebuild the city brick by brick. The magnificent buildings of the reconstructed Main Town, the heart of the ancient city, reflects their dedication and craft. After the war, much of the city's population, and probably many of the students' grandparents, were relocated here from an area in eastern Poland, resettling the destroyed city, and working in the newly reopened shipyards.

As discussed in the brief introduction to Polish history, Gdańsk's shipyards, central to the city's long history, were also central to the story of Polish political upheaval and transformation. The 1970 massive strike there was a major challenge to the regime. In 1980, the Solidarity movement, *Solidarność*, began at the shipyards. By the time of the first interviews in 1992, the students had watched on TV as its leader, Lech Wałęsa, became the first elected President of Poland.

Gdańsk Sample Demographics

When Suchar started the interviews more than three years had passed since July 4th, 1989, the day the first post-communist Parliament was elected. In terms of historical processes a period of three or four years means very little, but it means a great deal in an individual's development, especially in the transition from childhood to adolescence. Most of the students had been thirteen or fourteen, just beginning to develop their identity as Polish citizens, when the rapid systemic changes in Poland began in 1989.

The study in Gdańsk began in 1992. Suchar interviewed a total of fifty-nine students over a twenty-five-month period, with more students interviewed in the first twelve months than during the second thirteen months. We have chosen to treat the youth we interviewed in Poland as one group rather than divide the participants by year for the following reasons. First, the interviews were carried out at fairly regular intervals across the twenty-five months. Secondly, because a smaller number of students were interviewed in the second twelve months, dividing the interviews into two groups would have resulted in a large difference in the size of the groups. While an argument can be made that the data would be best treated as two groups so that comparisons could be made, we think this is the most conservative way to treat these data.

All the students attended the same secondary school and were sixteen to nineteen years of age at the time they were interviewed. Sixty-five percent of the students were female. This was consistent with many academic high schools which at the time of our study had a majority of girls. Most students reported that their parents were "blue collar" workers. Typically both parents worked, which was the common situation in Poland.

The secondary school the students attended was a four-year "general secondary school," in Poland called *Liceum Ogólnoksztatcące*. This particular school was typical of the academic schools in Gdańsk at the time of our study, but atypical of the average secondary school in Gdańsk which placed a greater emphasis on vocational training. *Liceum Ogolnoksztalcace* provide students with preparation for university studies. These students received instruction in humanities, Polish language, history, foreign language, math, physics, chemistry, biology, and geography. Classes in music and drawing were also available. Within the school there were several different programs of specialization such as languages, humanities, science, and computer technology, consistent with the tendency for Polish students to choose a specialty or profession during their secondary school years. This trend toward early career choice and therefore earlier vocational identity development was reflected in the fact that 90% of the students interviewed declared their intention to go on to university studies. This compares with the results from a national survey of secondary students from all types of schools in which 45% of those surveyed viewed university education as an important condition for obtaining a good job.

Students in Poland must take and pass exams to qualify for university study. These exams represent the formal acknowledgment of academic competence for Polish youth. However, data regarding the percentage of students from this *Liceum Ogólnoksztatcące.* who passed the university exam successfully were unavailable. (This information was apparently not compiled by the school's administration.)

In the following discussion of the interviews, we refer to results from the state Public Opinion Research Center (CBOS) surveys from 1992, 1994, and 1996. Of all the survey centers, the CBOS has the longest tradition of studying social awareness of different aspects of everyday life in Poland. Many of the topics in our interviews were also the focus of the CBOS surveys. Each of the CBOS surveys cited used a large, national sample of about 1,200 students ages seventeen though nineteen years old.

Growing Up in Changing Times:
Surrounded by Family and Friends

> I live in a big concrete block [apartment house]. We have three rooms, but I have my own room even though I am living with my mother, my father, my brother, and his wife. We have a good understanding between us and have a lot of fun together.... I have lots of friends. We go to the discos. I also have a boyfriend.

The students viewed their family and friends as their most central and important microsystems. Few of their friends, however, came from their classroom peers, and school did not appear to be an important microsystem to many of these students. During the course of the interviews, few students described relationships between the microsystem of their family and other microsystems such as clubs, friends' families, or church groups.

Self-descriptions

I am the elder sister in our family. I cannot stand my sister but I love her. I have a pet—it's a dog.

❋

I'm Polish, an ex-scout, a member of an ecological organization.

❋

I have red hair, freckles, but I do not resemble Ann of Green Gables.

Most students gave self-descriptions that focused on the here and now, and few spontaneously mentioned plans for the future. The prevailing themes that were mentioned spontaneously in these descriptions were their family, living conditions, and personal interests.

Almost all students referred to their family, either parents or siblings, when describing themselves. Interestingly, when talking about their families and their home situation, more than a third of the students, mostly girls, spontaneously made some reference to the number of rooms in their home or whether they had their own room:

I have two sisters and one younger brother. . . . We have two rooms for all of us.

17-year-old girl

❋

I have an older sister. I live in a big concrete [apartment] house. . . . I have a room of my own.

17-year-old girl

❋

I live in a big apartment complex where there are 200 apartments. We have two bedrooms for me, my younger brother, my

> younger sister, my mother, and my father. There is very little
> space in the apartment but we are happy to be together.
>
> 18-year-old girl

In general, the students lived in small apartments in the large concrete buildings that were built during the Communist regime. The majority of students who had a sibling shared a bedroom. The problem of the lack of "private space" was a common complaint.

Sixty-two percent of adolescents surveyed by CBOS in 1994 described their home atmosphere as "nice, friendly, and warm," whereas 6% of the adolescents surveyed mentioned conflict in the family and 2% mentioned alcoholism as a family problem (CBOS 1994d). Our results were consistent with these findings in that most of the adolescents interviewed indicated that they felt good about their home atmosphere: "I adore and respect my parents. My life conditions are very good. I do not complain, although it would be wonderful to have more pocket money."

During the interviews a few students discussed problems within their family, including conflicts with parents, and feelings of rejection, but none mentioned alcoholism as a family problem. One student discussed conflicts in her family in this way:

> There are four people in my family. I have a younger sister. We
> live in a three room apartment so I don't have a place for myself.
> I am not the favorite child, so very often there are conflicts be-
> tween me and my parents.

There was no pervasive, underlying sense of adolescent rebellion or alliance with peer groups in opposition to parents. In general, students were developing their sense of self and autonomy within the context of their immediate family. There was a strong sense of trust in the family, particularly in parents, and a sense of being a part of a collective family unit. This contrasts with adolescents in societies like the U.S. where identity development is marked by earlier development of autonomy from parents and other immediate family members, and increased identification with peer groups.

About one-third of the students spontaneously mentioned personal interests such as hobbies or pets in their self-descriptions, e.g., "I am interested in photography. I like to travel, and visit new places." When asked about their interests, the two most common themes were parties, going to discos or pubs, mentioned by almost half the students, and sports, mentioned by more than a third. The inclusion of sports is of note given that few students said they belonged to a sports organization or team. Adam was typical in that his interest in sports was limited to watching his favorite team or playing informal games with friends rather than member- ship in a formal sports team. Specific hobbies such as going to the cinema, interest in computers, and photography were mentioned by a few students but were not prevailing themes:

> I love to dance. I go to the discos often. I like swimming, riding horses, I read books, and I'm interested in medicine.
> 16-year-old girl

> I am interested in sports. I also like to read books.
> 18-year-old boy

Although most of the students we interviewed focused on fam- ily, living conditions, or interests when describing themselves, a few spontaneously described their personality characteristics. For example, one boy said, "I am an easy going person." Similarly, one girl described herself as "devoted, sacrificing, (and) someone who easily forgets offenses." When asked specifically abut their person- ality characteristics, the most common negative descriptors given were, "impulsive," "nervous," "envious," or "stubborn." The positive descriptors that were most often given were "helpful," "good- hearted," and "tolerant."

Group Membership

Except for families and friends, few students spontaneously mentioned any group membership when describing themselves. When asked to discuss the groups that were important to them, family and friends returned as the important themes, both men- tioned by approximately 40% of the students. There was substan- tial overlap between the students who mentioned family and those who mentioned friends. For example, one particularly articulate 17-year-old-girl stated, "the most important groups for me are my family and friends. I think that it is thanks to them I can develop my personality." When students talked about friends, they often added comments like, "they accept me as a person" or "We spend leisure time together. We listen to the same music."

In answer to the question about group identity, about one-tenth of the students said that they felt a part of Gdańsk or Poland, and about one-tenth said the "whole world." Those who said the "whole world" made comments like, "in each place I can feel O.K." or "I am a world citizen," indicating that they viewed the larger macrosystem as personally important in their lives. Joanna was one of the students who saw herself as part of the larger world community. Her discussion of the relationship between counties and her concern about the war in the countries of the former Yugoslavia were illustrative of her larger world view.

Though most students presented self-identities that connected them to more widely socially accepted groups such as their family and friends, a few described their identification with fringe groups of young people. One student stated, "I am close to the vanguard— hippies, punks, heavy metal—all those subcultures; I even like skinheads, if they are real."

Ten of the fifty-nine students we interviewed answered "nobody" or "there is no group." The students who said this tended to think of themselves as "self-governing" or extremely "individualist." This group of adolescents described their autonomy in a way that was more similar to the descriptions one finds in societies that place great value on the independence of the individual. It is notable that this was the single group of students who also tended to report conflicts with parents.

Microsystems that are formal organizations such as church and sports teams were only mentioned by a few students. Joanna was one of the few students who spontaneously talked about her religious orientation. This lack of explicit identification with the Catholic Church was a somewhat surprising finding given the prominent place the church has played in the history of *Solidarity* in Gdańsk and in Polish history. We did not ask if the students attended church. It is possible that more students attended church with their family than mentioned any religious identification when talking about themselves. What was apparent was that for the majority of our students church membership was not a highly salient part of their identities. It is also interesting that given the prior history of the Young Pioneers organization and the relative absence of other youth groups under the communist regime, formal organizations were not popular with the Polish adolescents. In the 1994 CBOS survey about 80% reported they did not belong to any formal organization (CBOS 1994b; CBOS 1994d). Our results are congruent with these survey results.

Another group identification not often mentioned by the students was school, including school clubs and school friends. The 1994 CBOS survey data indicate that most adolescents reported that their friends were not from their school (CBOS 1994d). Perhaps the microsystems of the Gdańsk students' school and their good friends showed little overlap because, for most, their school was some distance from their apartments. In addition, most students lived in apartments located in housing blocks with hundreds of other students. Most had probably attended elementary schools near their apartment where their classmates came from the same neighborhood. Perhaps these students' closest friends remained those from their own neighborhoods.

Being Polish

We found no strong trends in the students' feelings about being Polish. The positive association with being Polish included respecting the traditions or history of Poland or how Poland was respected by other nations in eastern Europe. Negative comments included an opposite view of how other nations viewed Poland, for example, one student said, "we don't have a good reputation among other nations." Overall the students in Gdańsk gave short answers when asked about their sense of pride in their country:

> I can be proud of the history of Poland. The Polish people have fought so many times for freedom.
>
> 18-year-old girl

> What makes me proud of being Polish is our rich historical tradition and what I am not proud of is the behavior of Polish people in Western countries.
>
> 18-year-old boy

Facing the Future

Students' responses reflected their family focus as they considered their future as well as their present lives. Their responses to the numerous items about future orientation suggested that they did not have a strong individualistic orientation toward building their future through personal effort and activities such as education and work. Although they were aware of the difficulties of everyday local life as well as national problems connected with the transitional changes, these young people did not perceive themselves as the potential creators of the future of their community or country. Perhaps this perception of their powerlessness to facilitate changes beyond their family kept students from making linkages between their personal lives and the wider social world of their community, city, and nation. The few students who, like Joanna, saw their future as dependent on their own efforts, tended to believe that the changes in Poland would make it possible for them to succeed if they worked hard.

The relatively small group of students who saw connections between what happened in their own microsystems and changes in the larger macrosystems were divided between those who saw their future as bright and those who were pessimistic. Not surprisingly, the students who were most optimistic were those who believed that the political changes in Poland were good for the country. These students saw themselves as having the power to take advantage of the changes that were happening at the level of the macrosystem.

In contrast, students who were pessimistic thought that they were powerless to take advantage of the changes or that the changes were not good for the majority of Poles. Fratczak-Rudnicka (1997) reviewed the results from national polls from 1992–94 and reported the level of pessimism was particularly high in 1992, when a large proportion of students were quite pessimistic. She reported that by 1994 students showed a small decrease in their level of pessimism regarding the future, shown by such measures as interest in entering universities.

Wishes, Fears, and Values.

My wishes are that I would like to have my own horse and lots of animals around me. Then I would like everyone to be happy, in particular that all the people with whom I am close to would be happy. And I wish that I had a fantastic boyfriend. And my fears. I am afraid of losing my parents or my friends. . . . I'm also afraid of pollution in the air and that animals will not survive because of pollution.

17-year-old girl

The most common theme for wishes was "good health" for themselves or for their family. Love was another common theme. Finding a loving partner and having a loving family were also common answers. The third common theme was financial welfare. For example, many students mentioned a better economic situation for the country or family or having a good job. One group of students, like the girl quoted above, was concerned about the environment and this was reflected in their wishes or fears and other responses as well. More personal wishes included success in exams, traveling around the world, having a horse, and becoming a model. Adam's wishes were fairly typical in that he focused on health and happiness.

The most common fears that students mentioned had to do with illness, their own death, or the death of a family member. The second most common answer was war or natural disaster. As we have noted, Adam related his personal fears to his fears for the environment. Being a victim of a crime or a swindle was also a common answer. Failing school exams was mentioned by only a few students. This was somewhat surprising given the importance of the end of year exams to the students' academic careers.

Several female students named personal wishes or fears that indicated a focus on the importance of physical appearance such as "I am afraid to gain weight." Several others wished to be a model or to look like the women in the fashion magazines. In fact, more than a third of the girls indicated that they regularly read fashion, teenage girls', or women's magazines.

The students' wishes and fears focused on the students themselves or on their family. However, the wishes for "peace," or "world peace," or a "clean environment" indicated that some of the adolescents, including Adam, saw the connection between peace in the larger macrosystem and their microsystems.

When asked about their values, the most common response was honesty or being a moral person. Being a loving, faithful friend was also mentioned by most of the students. Wealth was mentioned by only a few students. Patriotism was rarely named.

Measures of optimism and pessimism.   Overall, about one-third of the students interviewed were solidly optimistic about their futures. These students thought that by being personally industrious they could overcome the problems they saw in Poland and secure their personal success. For example, one girl was confident and optimistic about her future, no matter what might happen in Poland because "my fate is in my hands." This student also felt that she could succeed by being on guard: "people can cheat you if you're an honest sucker."

Other students saw their personal futures in an optimistic light but more related to the national macrosystem:

> I am very optimistic about my future. I want to become a lawyer [and] have a good job, happy family, big house, and good car. The only problem might be if I have to pay for my studies—now an education is free in Poland.
>
> 17-year-old girl

A good life in twenty years.   A happy family and money were the overwhelming popular descriptions of a good life. It is interesting that more specific descriptions of the future, such as the type of job they thought they would hold, were rarely mentioned. Joanna's expressed desire to study economics was an exception to this. It is possible that twenty years into the future was such an abstract idea during this period of rapid changes that it was hard for the students to place themselves in this perspective.

> The present situation promises that in five years everybody can live a relatively good life. I have no idea what I will do personally but definitely—in twenty years I will be a rich man, having several big houses all over the world. I can travel without limits. I will earn lots of money!
>
> 18-year-old boy

> [In twenty years] I will be happy. I will have a fantastic loving husband and two children, a boy and a girl. We will be living in a really nice house. It will be a big apartment in a very nice district. My parents will also be able to buy a new flat for themselves and live close to us. . . . We will also have a beautiful car and big dog.
>
> 18-year-old girl

When asked to describe their future in twenty years, the most common theme was having a happy family, mentioned by more than 60% of the students. Most of the students saw children in their future. Being wealthy or having no material needs was the second most common theme. As Adam expressed it:

[In twenty years] I will be thirty-eight years old. I will be healthy, with a fantastic woman. We will have children and we will have money.

Students' Views on How Growing Up during Transitions may Influence Their Individual Development

In response to this item, like the previous ones, the students who felt their future was independent of the larger macrosystem appeared to feel that by being personally industrious they could overcome the problems they saw in Poland and guarantee their success. Other students also saw their personal futures in an optimistic light but related to conditions in the macrosystem:

The situation is bad—nobody except the politicians is satisfied with the changes. When I think about future [in five years]—I will be twenty-three. Maybe I will be a student. Maybe I will work, if there isn't such great unemployment in the country. Maybe I will get married and leave Poland because there are no chances for a good job here. Even if people work their salaries are low—too low for normal life.... I hope that in five years the situation changes.

17-year-old girl, 1992

There were great differences in students' responses to this item. For example, one boy saw a bright future for himself but, unlike the girl quoted above, appeared to avoid thinking about the social situation: "wealth, health, a nice family, and lack of government." He went on to explain, "in five years I will be well educated, bold, and at last there will be no political mess—no government at all."

One 19-year-old boy we interviewed in 1993 linked his optimism to the new democratic system: "I am very optimistic about the future because the democratic system is established and it will be continued." Similarly, one girl interviewed in 1994 said, "the present situation will result in a future where everybody will live relatively well in terms of their financial position."

Not all the students who saw their future as connected to the macrosystem saw their futures in a positive light. For example, in 1992 one girl said:

> The future seems to me fairly pessimistic. Why? From the present perspective I do not see any future for me in Poland. . . . I would like to study but, on the other hand, there are no jobs for well educated people. Quarrels in Parliament, constant changes of governments—nobody cares about young people's future and perspectives.

Commentary

Overall, the students we interviewed did not make connections between the microsystems of their family and friends and the larger macrosystems, such as Poland and, in particular, Europe. The personal identities these students were developing were tied closely to their family and related distantly to the greater political changes around them. These young people have a sense of security that their families have maintained financial stability throughout the changes in the political system. In fact only three students reported that a parent lost a job because of the changes to a free market economy. The great majority of students appeared to be protected from the negative effects of the changes by their families. Almost all the students said they had the material items they needed and wanted. While some students did complain about not having a room of their own or about living in an apartment that was too small, for the most part, the majority saw their economic situation as at least average.

The majority of students in Gdańsk appeared to view themselves and their families as being independent from the changing macrosystem. These students tended to focus on their important microsystems, family and friends, and felt that their future was unrelated to more distant changes.

Living History:
No One Controls the Situation

[The politicians are] gangs of liars and cheaters. Since 1989 we have had only permanent changes of governments, corruption,

and Mafia. My parents and I, all the Polish people are furious
about everything, about politics and politicians. . . . Poland is a
good country, but we must stop treating ourselves as the center
of the world.

17-year-old boy, 1993

✳

There are great chances for Poland. The question is whether Poland
will take advantage of it. . . . Now there are greater possibilities
for young people. We have a chance for a good education and job.

19-year-old boy, 1994

Most students viewed the general directions of the changes
positively, such as the changed form of government. They emphasized that ordinary people had played a role in creating the transitions, albeit in a general way: "the people wanted the changes."
Many, however, made negative comments about politicians and
emphasized that these adults in power didn't care about the average person or about youth. When asked to talk about the major
changes, they focused on the collapse of the old regime. Students
interviewed in 1992 were generally more specific than those interviewed in 1994 about details of the course of the transitions.

Interest in the News

Students' perceptions of the changes and their effects related
to the source of their information. Most learned little about national events through the media. The majority of our students said
they read the newspaper. However, most of the students who read
a newspaper indicated that they read one of the local Gdańsk papers
that were oriented toward local affairs. Few students said they
read papers such as the *Gazeta Wyborcza* that included more national and international news.

About half the students indicated they watched the nightly
TV news regularly. During the two-year-period of our study, three
nationwide news programs that covered social, economic, or political issues were popular in Poland. Only a few students reported
watching one of these popular news programs on a regular basis.
Instead it is probable that the TV news was on in the apartment
and, because apartments were small, these students passively
viewed some of the news. Similarly, few students reported listening

to the news on the radio. Students like Adam who said they listened to the radio tended to listen to music, not news.

Most of the girls reported reading at least one magazine, usually a teenage girls' or women's magazines or magazines about international pop and rock music. The boys often reported that they would rather watch TV than read a magazine.

In sum, these students appeared to obtain little information from the media about social changes in Poland, their history, and effects. When talking about their sense of other people's opinions, it was usually their parents' opinions that they quoted.

Reflecting upon Continuities and Changes

The major, consistent theme that emerged from students' answers was that they knew that changes in the national political and economic structures had occurred but felt that their personal life remained basically the same:

> [My] surrounding are the same. I mean the buildings look the same. Our school looks the same. Also the social conditions and the poverty in the society are the same.... Money is still at the top and there are lots of poor people.

> We have had a change in the political system. Citizens' position in the country changed and we've had a presidential election. I don't remember when it started but before we had a communistic system and it was completely undemocratic.

> Ordinary people had some influence on the changes. The effects of the changes are that there has been some political change. The feelings of the citizens of this country are a little bit better, but the paradox is that the ex-communists also benefited from this change. They still have the money and some power.

> Poor people were not affected by the changes in a positive way.... Me and my parents are angry because the ex-communists were not completely dismissed from positions of power.
>
> 18-year-old boy

Continuities

Students were first asked to discuss what was unchanged. Most students emphasized that their family life had not changed.

For example, one 19-year-old girl said, "we are still a loving family (and) I still have the same friends." This was the most common answer. Even students like Adam who indicated that they had more money or access to more material goods said their home life was not greatly different after 1990.

In fact, the third most popular answer to what had remained the same in students' own lives related to their standard of living. For example, one 17-year-old girl said, "my place of living and my family's life style is the same." A few students also indicated that their attitudes, opinions, faith, or values were what had remained unchanged. (See Appendix D, Table 1 for a summary of the students' responses related to continuities.)

Despite being asked specifically what had remained unchanged, almost half the students answered this question with statements about the worsening economy in Poland. For example, one student commented, "the rich are O.K. but the majority of the society is getting poorer." Another student said, "prices have been increasing but salaries are going down."

About a third of our students said that "nothing had changed." This can be compared to the finding of the national 1992 CBOS survey which reported that 42% of the adolescents they interviewed said nothing had changed (CBOS 1992b). Our results and the CBOS survey findings are interesting given that the peak of political changes occurred prior to 1992. These findings may speak to the relatively young ages of these adolescents when the changes started. Some of these youth didn't clearly remember the situation in Poland before 1989. Therefore, they may have viewed the country as maintaining a state of status quo. It may also be that some of the students saw the changes in the political system as changes in name only and therefore did not consider them real changes. For example, several students underscored the similarities between the old and new governments. One 17-year-old boy put it this way, "the same thieves like the previous ones, the government consists of liars and cheaters . . ."

Most Important Changes

When Suchar asked the students to name the two or three most important changes, most students concentrated on political changes, and secondly, on social changes. The most commonly named themes or events were the end of communism or the change in the political system; changes in the economic system; and Wałęsa becoming president. Each was named by almost half the students. In addition, about a third of the students referred to the public arguments within government. Many students named two or three of these most frequently cited changes:

> The most important changes are that we have many good shops but we have less and less money and there is unemployment in the country. . . . The ordinary people had no influence on the changes, but as a result society is becoming poorer and poorer.
>
> 18-year-old boy

> The most important changes are that we have a a new Parliament, also a Senate, and a new President . . . . Now we have many more goods in the shops but we have little money and there's lots of unemployment so I am not getting my pocket money. I am angry about the changes and my parents [are too]. The young people are rather indifferent but the rest of the Polish people are also angry about the changes.
>
> 17-year-old boy

> The ecological movement is active and visible. . . . Of course it affects older people but younger people are most aware of the positive results of this ecological movement. So we feel the need for further action. My parents accept this idea. They think I am right.
>
> 17-year-old girl

Several students commented on the role of the Catholic Church. Joanna was one of the few students who talked about the church in a positive light. Others, like Adam, emphasized that the church should stay out of peoples' lives.

Other students focused on changes linked to their own personal experience. For example, the son of a *Solidarity* member mentioned the shipyard workers' strike against the communist government but he was the only student to do so. (See Appendix D, Table 2 for a summary of the "most important changes" students named.)

*Students' Perceptions of the Effects of the Changes on Poland,
Gdańsk, Their Families, and Themselves*

Students provided seemingly contradictory responses. They
viewed their lives as relatively unchanged, but many saw the effects on their family as more negative. When they talked about the
effects on themselves, more students felt that the changes had no
effect on them personally rather than a positive or negative effect.
Many declared that they didn't feel the changes had any effect
worth mentioning. In fact, these responses were quite similar to
their reflections on what had remained unchanged:

> I'm still the same person. I have the same dreams, the same
> religion.
>
> ※
>
> Everything is the same—our home, our parents, father's job, my
> friends.
>
> ※
>
> Again, I'm still not the favorite daughter of my parents.
>
> ※
>
> My parents are not in a good mood—this is normal.

When assessing the overall effect on their lives, almost 30% felt
that the changes had had a positive effect, while only a few reported that their lives were worse off than before the changes.

In strong contrast, many students talked about the effects on
their families. More than twice as many students thought the
changes had a negative rather than positive impact on their family's
economic well-being. Similarly, the CBOS national surveys of adolescents found high levels of concern. The 1992 CBOS survey reported that 50% of the students said their family's financial situation
was worse than in 1991. Only 30% of the adolescents participating
in the 1992 CBOS survey said that their family's situation had
remained the same (Fatyga, Fluderska & Wertenstein-Zulawski
1993). Likewise, in 1994, 27% of adolescents participating in the
CBOS survey responded that their family's financial situation was
"bad" (CBOS 1994c).

In talking about the effect of the changes at the national level, students discussed both negative and positive aspects of the changes, with almost half saying that Poland was better off overall:

> The international position of Poland [has been] raised up.... Everyone in this country has better perspectives.... We are a democratic country.
>
> 19-year-old boy, 1994

Examples of students' negative responses include, "it was better before, although there was not much of a variety of goods in the shops," and "(the) economic changes are OK, but the political changes ... I do not care about these changes. The people have a lot against politicians." (See Appendix D, Table 3 for a summary of students' responses to the item about what had changed in their own lives and their families' lives.)

Explaining Why the Changes Occurred

> The change of the economic system started in 1990. Before there were very few things in the shops, and now we have lots of goods but prices are extremely high. The changes went rather quickly. The reason for these changes was that there was poverty. We didn't have bananas. We didn't have contact with foreign countries.... Ordinary people did not influence the changes.
>
> Adam

When Suchar asked the students in Gdańsk why they thought the changes had occurred, "the will of the Polish people, " and "people did not want communism any longer" were the most common themes. Many students started out their comment by saying "the people wanted...." Typical of these responses were: "people wanted to make everything better in Poland" and "people wanted more freedom and better living conditions." One student explained that the changes were caused by people's reactions to "empty shelves in shops, the economy in ruin, and the political bankruptcy of socialism." A few students named more specific events, for example, "there were strikes and protests against the old system." In general, students failed to draw relationships between the transitions and numerous events in the decade prior to 1989.

Students' Perceptions of Effects of the Changes on Their Development

Most students responded that the changes would have no effects on their development or that they simply didn't know. Those students who discussed effects were generally pessimistic and disillusioned. For example, at first this student expressed the idea that the changes would have no effect, but then continued:

> The things that happen now will not influence me very strongly because I will be involved in my own affairs, maybe a family, maybe still a student ... or I will work ... but still I will think about how to survive. But this thought, this idea, the situation in which I am growing up—like unemployment, the fight for surviving on one's salary ... I'm afraid that ... in the future I have to live the same way.
>
> 18-year-old boy

From the beginning, others were more pessimistic, some sounding quite alienated:

> From today's perspective I don't see any future for me in Poland. I think for educated people there are no chances for getting a good job. [In the] near future I don't think that change will be better. Considering the permanent changes of government and conflicts in Parliament, the problem of young people's future will never be solved according to our hopes and expectations.
>
> I think I will still be nervous about the situation because it looks like there will not be a much better future. I don't agree with such politics. Poland is a good country to live in. The problem at the moment is the people who have power ... only care about their own benefit.
>
> 18-year-old girl

❋

> In five years I will be a 23-year-old woman. If I will be lucky enough I will be a student at the university. But if we have to pay for our studies I don't know if I can afford it. So it is possible that I will not be able to continue my education here. I don't see my future in Poland because of the high unemployment. Educated people like teachers and doctors ... earn very little money.
>
> 18-year-old girl

A sizable proportion of these students predicted that their futures would not be as bright as they had hoped. These data suggest that this might be particularly true of students whose parents had not attended university but who, themselves, hoped to attend university and have professional careers. Some students now thought that they would not be able to attend university if tuition fees were imposed. At the same time, these responses also suggest that these students did not have the cultural resources, such as information from parents and teachers, that would help them plan a transition to careers with more opportunities. Some students believed that they would be on dead-end paths in a society with few new roads to success.

Commentary

When the adolescents in Gdańsk talked about the effects of the changes and their feelings about the changes, they were very family-focused. Few discussed the effects of the changes on Poland in any detail. None analyzed the effects of the changes on their city. There was little discussion of any effects of the changes on microsystems such as their school, clubs, or groups of friends. Instead, they talked mostly about what their parents thought about the changes and sometimes gave examples of the effects of the changes on their families.

Most students thought that ordinary people like themselves and their parents did not participate in the changes actively, instead they went though the transformations passively. However, the students attributed many of the changes to what the "people wanted."

Writing prior to the change of regime, Fratczak-Rudnicka (1988) noted that the decisive factor in understanding the political consciousness of the youth in Poland was the economic situation. Czapinski (1994) observed that, since the change of regime, psychological well being is increasingly linked to social indicators, particularly income, which did not vary so greatly under the former regime. The results of these interviews in Gdańsk are interesting in that most students viewed their family both as working class and as working families, yet rarely reported concern about personal finances directly. It may be that the anger and criticism they often leveled at the government is an indirect reflection of lowered life satisfaction and psychological well being within their families.

Yet students generally mentioned their concerns regarding their family's financial situation in an indirect way. For example, one student said that his father didn't work and another mentioned his lack of spending money but neither directly mention a significant effect on their family's financial situation. Instead, students tended to keep their discussions focused on how other people were affected—poor people—rather than on their own family's situation.

How can this be explained? The CBOS survey found that families with adolescents in the home owned twice the number of computers and three times the number of televisions (CBOS 1996c). It would appear that Polish parents were making a sacrifice to see that their children received the material items they wanted from their parents despite financial difficulties within the home.

This may have been even more true of the students in the Gdańsk study and their families. They were attending an academic secondary school and hoped to enter university. Their vocational aspirations differed from their parents' jobs as working class people. They might have been receiving above average support from their families in attaining these academic goals, including encouragement to spend their time studying rather than working, as well as computers, books, and money for transportation to their school.

Understanding Political Concepts: Struggling to Find New Meanings

We have freedom of speech, of publishing, we have citizens' rights, and [these rights] are respected in the country. Everybody is equal under the law and the authorities are telling the truth about society.

18-year-old boy

※

Freedom means that you may walk the streets peacefully, that you may learn and study.

17-year-old girl

※

[A] good citizen is like a politician. [He] knows how to make profit from his position and power.

17-year-old boy

As the students in Gdańsk discussed their understandings of political concepts, many had difficulty defining or discussing concepts such as democracy and free market economy, and the responses they gave were often vague. They gave far more complete answers to questions concerning their microsystems of family or peer groups than they did when asked about political concepts or changes that they viewed as relating to the national macrosystem.

The Purpose of a Government

Almost half the students had difficulty answering this item. For those who answered, a common theme was that the purpose of the government was to care for the Polish people, for example, "take care of ordinary citizens." Students discussed the Polish people's role as passive. Rather than emphasize that the government should create opportunities for people to succeed, the students thought that their government should provide for the people:

> To benefit the country, care about the poor and those who cannot work, and make the situation in Poland better.
>
> 16-year-old girl

※

> To stop the crisis in the country, protect jobs for everyone, provide social and health care, support the education system, and make sure that there is good payment for jobs.
>
> 19-year-old boy

These students' emphasis on the caring role of government is consistent with CBOS survey results. In the 1992 CBOS survey, 87% of the adolescents surveyed agreed with the statement that, "the state should offer work to everyone" (Cichowicz 1993). These survey data from adolescents is also congruent with data for Polish adults. In 1990 and 1991, when forced to choose between the concepts that jobs should be sought by workers or the state should be responsible for full employment, more than half the adults asked chose the latter (Boski 1993).

In 1992 approximately a third of the adolescents we interviewed said that the government should give people hopes and goals, or make those hopes come true. Perhaps the students we interviewed in 1992 still had higher expectations about the changes. By 1993–94, only two students of the twenty-seven interviewed gave that answer. In addition to the themes of caring for the people of Poland, giving people hope, and making laws, organizing Poland was mentioned by many students in 1992 but only a few in 1994. In 1992 there was still much to be done to institutionalize democracy and a free market system. For example, one student said the government needs to "develop a free market economy, free trade and production, (and) regulation of the bank system." (See Appendix D, Table 4 for a summary of the different roles for government the students mentioned.)

Democracy

> Freedom of speech, democratic elections, chances for economic development of the country.
>
> 17-year-old girl

※

> That I can express my opinions openly.
>
> 17-year-old girl

※

> Democracy? Enough food, absolute freedom, justice, and the communists are eliminated.
>
> 18-year-old boy

More than half the students found it difficult to define democracy and identify the key features of a democracy. The most common themes in the students' definitions of democracy were the right to hold elections and freedom, each mentioned by almost half the students. Civil rights was also a common theme. For example, one student said, "personal freedom, freedom of choice, (and) freedom of religion." Another commented that "in our country it is (the) apparent feeling of freedom." Some students, however, voiced frustration with the ambiguous situation. They wanted a democracy instituted quickly, so that "everything should go according to clear rules."

Our results regarding the students' emphasis on freedom are again consistent with the findings of the CBOS survey data from 1992 (Cichowicz 1993; CBOS 1996a) which indicate that "freedom" was the most frequent word Polish adolescents chose to describe a democracy. Adults in Poland appeared to take a similar view of democracy. A 1996 study of adult factory workers, bank employees, teachers, and city aldermen found that, except for teachers, most individuals conceptualized democracy as consisting of institutional structures that protected the freedom of citizens and provided opportunities for personal achievement (Reykowski 1996). It is interesting that, as we noted in the previous section, these students did not focus on providing citizens with the opportunity for personal achievement as a governmental role.

About 20% of our students mentioned a multiparty system as a key feature of democracy. A higher percent of students interviewed in 1992 mentioned this feature than students interviewed in 1994. During this time the political situation in Poland had changed dramatically. Beginning in 1992 and 1993, a large number of new political parties were created. In addition, some of the parties that had been founded in 1989 and 1990 were split into different factions. As a result, by 1993 there was a grand total of 120 political parties in Poland. Thus, by 1994 the change to a multiparty system had resulted in a wide and often confusing choice for voters.

The items asking students to define and identify the features of a democracy prompted some students to make strongly negative comments about the political system in Poland. At the time of our interviews, teenage popular culture presented this view and many songs performed by Polish rock groups voiced harsh criticism. In fact, Polish rock music was known throughout Europe for its stridency.

Like the songs they listened to, the students' criticism reflected a growing disappointment in the emerging democratic form of government. In 1992, 60% of the adolescents in the national CBOS survey responded that democracy was the best political system (Cichowicz 1993) but by 1994 only 24% said that democracy was the best (CBOS 1994a). Similarly, we also noted that students interviewed at the beginning of the study tended to be somewhat more positive about democracy than the students interviewed toward the end. It is possible that for many Polish youth the initial excitement of democracy was associated with high expectations. Experience with the new political system may have lead to disappointment at the slow rate of change and the problems with the system as well as the widely discussed economic problems. For example, a student who was interviewed in 1994 declared emphatically, "it (democracy) is not as good as it should be. . . . There are people who have billions and then some who do not have enough to buy bread."

Freedom

> Citizens' freedom is described or stated in the constitution.....
> Freedom at school? I think that people have the same rights at
> school as in the rest of life.
>
> 18-year-old boy

※

> The meaning of freedom is that you can say what you think, that
> you can do what you want, and you feel secure and safe in your
> country.... In school of course we have the right to express our
> opinion but the consequences may be terrible.
>
> 16-year-old girl

※

> We have freedom of speech, of publishing. We have the rights of
> citizens respected in this country. Everybody is equal under the
> law and the authorities are telling the truth to the people.
>
> 18-year-old boy

When asked to define freedom, more than half the students
mentioned freedom of speech: "Freedom means you can say whatever you want." Adam, for instance, thought that this gave Poles
the information they need to make choices about the future of
Poland. The second most frequent answer was having freedom from
restrictions, being able to do what one pleases. Only four students
mentioned equality for all Poles.

Free Market Economy

> Free market economy means that we can sell everything wher-
> ever we want. You can sell any goods and everybody can start his
> own business.
>
> 16-year-old girl

※

> The newest and, I think, the most effective form of trading that
> has to be developed in the future.
>
> 18-year-old boy

※

> "What is this?"
>
> 17-year-old boy

Most students had great difficulty answering this question. Of those who did, free competition, lack of regulation of prices, and being able to start a business were the most common themes, each mentioned by at least one-fourth of the students. One student put it this way, "we can sell everything wherever we want and everybody can start their own business." Another commented pessimistically, using a Darwinian metaphor, "jungle law, no regulations for trading." Indeed, initially the market was largely unregulated. Like political policies, economic policies were being developed and instituted month by month.

Students who were able to give more complete answers to this question tended to be those who were interviewed in 1994, possibly reflecting changes in the school's curriculum and teachers' knowledge as well as more definitive economic policies. Changes in the educational curriculum lagged behind various social transformations. As with political change, in the early years of Poland's transition to a free market economy, teachers were not prepared to teach students about the changing economic system.

Citizenship Education, Citizenship, and Patriotism

A good citizen [is a] *Solidarity* member.

17-year-old girl

※

A good citizen [is] sociable, practical, open-minded.

17-year-old girl

※

A good citizen obeys the constitution and laws, [an] ordinary person.

19-year-old boy

※

[A good citizen] trusts one's own country and acts for the country's benefit.

18-year-old girl

The students were asked about the role of school in influencing their ideas and feelings about citizenship. When asked to comment on citizenship education before the changes, the most common answers were that they learned about the structure of the Communist Party or the socialist system. However, an overwhelming majority (about 85%) indicated that they had not received any education on citizenship since the transition to democracy. Citizenship education was simply not part of the curriculum in their school. This may be explained by the fact that new curricula had not been developed and the old curriculum was no longer being used. A few students did say they had been taught about citizenship education. For example, one student said, "education now (is) about politics, basic terms connected with political and economic systems." Another student said that the "changes in the country" were the focus of citizenship education in his class. One student who apparently had received a more comprehensive education than most said, "generally we studied (the) constitution and before the presidential election we talked about the candidates."

By 1994, a few more students were able discuss citizenship education. Most of these mentioned political changes as part of the education. But there still appeared to be a lack of comprehensive planned instruction. One student put it this way, "we learn only about pure facts and definitions—government, party, election,—not what it means." Another student made it clear that she thought that the wrong content was being taught, saying, "they stress current political events in the country and the world—it should be more about things like sex, (or) drugs." In 1996 the CBOS survey indicated that only 50% of the students said they received citizenship education at school (CBOS 1996a).

When interpreting the data from the questions about the school's role in teaching citizenship, information about the emotional state of many teachers in Poland in 1992 and 1993 provides an important context. The general condition of the educational system in Poland had worsened. During this time many teachers were experiencing a great deal of stress in their private as well as their professional lives. In 1992 and 1993 teachers' salaries were only about 50% of the average salary of a government worker. In the spring of 1993, a national teachers' strike took place but the strike did not result in any improvement in salary. Teachers' stress undoubtedly affected their interpretation of the systemic changes that were occurring at the time.

We asked the students to explain their perceptions of the characteristics of a good citizen both before and after the changes. About a third said that under the communist regime a good citizen was one who did not interfere in politics. The second most common description was that a good citizen was someone who followed the regime's point of view. About a third said that they had no idea.

When asked to think about current meanings of being a good citizen, the most common response was "contributing to Poland's progress," which was mentioned by more than a third of our students. Being a patriot was also a common answer, as was paying taxes and working hard. Several students said that a good citizen was one who obeyed the laws. Responses to these two items suggest that most students felt that a good citizen involved a more active role after the change of regime.

Several students gave sarcastic responses. One student said, "the more you cheat on taxes, credits, etc.—the more freedom and lack of punishment you may expect." A few students felt that citizenship was not a necessary component of life or else were negative about citizenship. One girl asked, "a good citizen? In what sense? Something like a patriot—but is it really necessary?"

When asked what it meant to be a patriot the most common response was "somebody who loves his country" and "is ready to sacrifice for the nation." A few students said the only patriots left were people in their grandparents' generation.

Political Involvement

> I'm not much interested in politics. My parents and friends are also not interested. I would not get involved with politics at any level. I don't talk to my friends about politics. I don't know much about it.
>
> 16-year-old girl

With the exception of a few students like Joanna, the students we interviewed indicated little interest in politics. A typical answer across all three years was, "I do not care about politics." Although the students were often critical about politicians, they were apathetic about their own interest in what decisions were being made by lawmakers. Most perceived no connection between what was happening in their government and in their own personal lives.

Many of the students' comments reflected a lack of trust in the national government, the macrosystem. In particular, this lack of trust was directed at the adults in power whom students saw as making decisions based on self-interest. One girl's negative comments about the adults who were running her country was typical of those students who held this view:

> In Poland no one treats such institutions like the government, Parliament, church, etc., seriously. What's ridiculous is that the politicians don't even treat themselves seriously, they perform like in a cabaret. . . . People are bored or angry with all the quarrels in politics. No party is attractive to me.

Other comments students made that reflected this pessimistic point of view included: "(the politicians) take care of themselves and forget about the people;" "Only politicians are favored by the changes;" and "The government policy gives us no chance to overcome the crisis."

Our findings are again consistent with those from the 1992 CBOS survey (CBOS 1992b) which found that about 60% of the adolescents surveyed agreed with the statement that, "no one controls the situation in the country" while only 4% agreed with the statement that "Poland is in good hands." It appeared that the young people of Poland did not trust either the old or new systems, and felt they had little control over the political situation. Apparently, many adults as well felt they had little control over the political situation. A survey of adults in 1990 and 1991 found that more than 50% of adults replied that they had no influence on the course of political events in their country. These adults who were alienated showed substantially less inclination to vote. In addition a large majority (86%) felt that it was not possible to know if the decisions made by politicians were good for the country or not (Korzeniowski 1993).

Despite the expressions of criticism toward the present government, some students, nevertheless, indicated potential political interest related to their basically optimistic outlook about Poland's political future. Adam's view was typical of these. He was optimistic that the political future would be brighter, despite his disapproval of the adults in charge as well as his relative lack of current interest in politics.

In addition to asking about students' general interests in politics, we asked questions about students' intent to engage in any political activity, including voting.

> I am not involved with politics and my family is not [involved].
> But I will vote if I am allowed. But I don't know what party I will
> vote for.
>
>   18-year-old boy

※

> I am interested in politics and so is my family. I know that many
> of the parties have problems. I do not support any of them but I
> support the people who fight for the elimination of the abortion
> law. I am against the [Catholic] Church becoming more influential
> in political and social life. I will vote but I don't know whom to
> vote for.
>
>   18-year-old boy

Most of the students showed little political involvement. The typical answer was, "I don't care about politics." The student above who mentioned his position against the abortion law was in a minority of less than ten students who specifically named political issues they felt strongly about. The most commonly named issue was the environment. Joanna was again an exception in the depth of her knowledge about national politics. Even students whose families had been involved in Solidarity didn't appear to be very involved in the current political situation:

> In the 80s my father was one of the strike organizers at his work.
> My grandmother printed illegal flyers at work. We demonstrated
> our solidarity by lighting the candles in the windows of our home.
> This was to demonstrate against the martial law. . . . My interest
> in politics [now]? I see problems in many of the parties. I might
> vote if I find the right candidate. But I am very skeptical.
>
>   18-year-old girl

This girl's skepticism and her related disappointment in political parties was typical. Despite the large number of political parties to choose from, most students indicated that they had no party affiliation. Most were either unsure if they would vote or said they were not planning to vote.

Commentary

To a great extent, the students we interviewed in Gdańsk had only vague understandings of the changing political system in their country. Most were not receiving any explicit instruction on these topics in school. The lack of school instruction on politics and citizenship certainly contributed to some students' lack of rudimentary understanding, but it is also important that the methods of citizenship education need to be consistent with the curriculum. Students pointed to the lack of democratic pedagogy in style as well as factual content. Lack of explicit instruction, combined with the fact that the important adults in these students' lives, such as their parents often had only rudimentary understanding of emerging concepts such as democracy, made it difficult for these students to comprehend the abstract concepts involved in the new political system in Poland.

In sum, these adolescents were not interested in politics. Fratczak-Rudnicka (1997) reporting on the results of yearly national polls, wrote that, "as far as politics is concerned, young people are even more uninterested than they were a few years ago. They are also not very well informed politically" (p. 335).

PART FOUR

Conclusion

CHAPTER EIGHT

Growing Up in Changing Times

> True identity... depends on the support which the young individual receives from the collective sense of identity characterizing the social groups significant to him: his class, his nation, his culture.
>
> Erikson 1964, p. 93

Overview

A premise of our research is that historical transitions influence adolescents' psychosocial development, that there are clear links between lives and times. Rapid social changes would therefore result in reweaving the fabric of identity of family, class, nation, and culture. Yet there are few previous studies that have examined how the political perspectives of young people are influenced by their social contexts. This study of Hungarian and Polish adolescents' sociopolitical identity development during a time of political and economic transitions explored their views of their changing society and the effects of the changes on themselves, their families, their cities, and their nation.

As we began this research in 1990, we raised several questions. First, how would these adolescents view their own identity development? This question was developed into the topic, *Growing Up in Changing Times*. Second, how would they understand what was happening in their society, and, in particular, the relationships between societal changes and their own lives? This question was developed into the topic, *Living History*. Third, how would they understand and respond to the sociopolitical concepts related to the transitions? This question was developed into the topic, *Understanding Political Concepts*. These topics focused on students' political involvement, broadly defined as students' political interest, cognition, affect, and behavior in the context of their everyday lives.

All three topics consider both social and historical dimensions of psychosocial identity. The social context of development is conceptualized as a continuum from self to important microsystems such as family and friends, to the community, the nation, and the global context. The historical context of development is conceptualized as leading from the present moment forward in time to near future and toward the distant future, as well as moving from the present moment back in time to the near past and toward the distant past.

Did these adolescents make explicit connections between their lives and times? Did they think that growing up in changing times affected their development as a person? When we concluded the interviews, we were surprised how consistently the students responded that their lives were relatively unchanged. We were also struck by the similarities in the answers of students who lived far apart and who were interviewed in different years. Although aspects of political and economic changes were similar in both countries and all three cities, we had thought that major differences in historical background and precipitating events, as well as in timing and outcomes, would result in greater differences in students' views.

We found, to the contrary, that the great majority of students believed that the transitions had no significant impact on their development. Few students had strong opinions or talked about major life changes. Even most of those who said that their development might have been influenced by the transitions discussed relatively minor changes. Some talked about the new possibilities for a "new way of thinking" or opportunities for travel and careers. A few discussed how living through hard times would help them become tough and persistent. Most students viewed the social continuum as divided between the far and the near, the public and the private. Their psychosocial identity was grounded in the private and rarely extended to the public. Similarly, their historical perspective was centered on the present. They did not view themselves as a part of a system changing over time. Students' nearsighted vision along both the dimensions of space and time meant not only that they would be less likely to perceive the impacts of the changes but also that they would view perceived changes as less relevant to their daily lives.

Even though at first these findings appear counter to our premise, they are, indeed, consistent. While we found that their lives were, indeed, changed, our research explores young people's understandings of their own lives. As we discuss in greater detail in this chapter, as adult researchers we can understand students' perceptions that their lives were basically unchanged. However, when we consider their sociopolitical identity in relation to the social and historical continua, it appears to us that the changes have, indeed, affected their lives.

Through listening to the voices of these young people, we hoped to better understand their development as the last generation of the old political and economic system and the first generation of the new—the omega-alpha generation. In this chapter we first discuss the major findings from our studies, relating them once again to those aspects of Erikson's and Bronfenbrenner's theoretical work that guided our research. We then consider how our results helped us understand general aspects of adolescent development in rapidly changing societies. We end by addressing a question we raised at the beginning of this book: What implications does the political involvement or lack thereof of this generation of young people have for the vitality of democracy in their countries?

Designing Emergent Research

When we first designed this exploratory research, we planned one set of interviews of students in different countries, at the three types of secondary schools common in eastern Europe, both boys and girls. As we have described, the design changed in response to the continuing nature of the transitions, the opportunities for further studies, and changes in the lives of the researchers. We have referred to this process as emergent research. Other researchers who study the psychology of transitions may find the idea of emergent research useful because it conceptualizes the research design as a continuing process. Furthermore, from this perspective, exploratory research and hypothesis-testing research are viewed as designs along a continuum, rather than contrasting schemes.

During our research, interviews of different populations of students, in different cities and countries, carried out by researchers from different countries, helped us understand development in different contexts. The broad framework of the protocol which permitted flexibility provided the means to examine students' views of the changes that were important to them. The numerous items relating to each topic, including the complementary use of open-ended questions and forced-choice questions, increased the trustworthiness of the results. This was particularly important in those cases in which the finding was that students were ambivalent and confused. The longitudinal study in Budapest allowed us to examine the same students' responses over time. The follow-up study in Pécs allowed us to explore the implications of a student's age at the time of the major changes. The data we collected on the general aspects of these adolescents' psychosocial identity were critical in providing the needed background for a richer understanding of their sociopolitical identity formation.

Perspectives on Growing Up in Changing Times

When we wish to establish a person's identity, we ask what his name is and what station he occupies in his community. Personal identity means more; it includes a subjective sense of continuous existence and a coherent memory. Psychosocial identity has even more elusive characteristics, at once subjective and objective, individual and social.

Erikson 1987, p. 675

The interview protocol reflected our view of adolescent psychosocial development as a holistic process that includes individual and social dimensions. To answer our questions about the relationships between broader aspects of psychosocial identity development and the more specific aspects of sociopolitical identity development, we needed to learn about these "elusive characteristics." How did the students perceived the social and historical context of their development? We understood more clearly why students perceived and responded to the changes as they did after we had heard them talk about their sense of their own identity, the important groups in their lives, their sense of the future, and how they viewed growing up in changing times.

Patterns of Identity

In the preceding chapters on Pécs, Budapest, and Gdańsk, we purposely refrained from drawing comparisons among students from the three cities. The samples of students were not intended to be representative of Hungary and Poland nor of these cities. However, the portraits we provide of specific students attending particular schools and living in three specific cities contain data that can help us understand the dynamics of sociopolitical identity development of adolescents growing up in rapidly changing societies.

Three patterns emerged when we examined students' sense of self in the context of space and time, the social and historical context. There were two contrasting patterns in students' orientation to the social context, along the continuum from the individual self to the global. The adolescents in Pécs and Gdańsk were oriented to their family and friends. In addition to family and friends, the students in Budapest were also oriented toward their individual development and toward their community, nation, and the world.

In Pécs and Gdańsk few students spontaneously emphasized relationships other than family and friends throughout the interview. Not surprisingly, these students' hopes and fears were family-centered as were their visions of a good life in twenty years: "a happy family;" " three children;" "enough money for us to travel;" "a big house with a garden." They mentioned few local groups such as sports teams that would connect them to the broader community, or church membership that would connect them to a national or international community. The relationships among family and friends were their key mesosystems. Based on this finding, it is reasonable to suppose that the lack of other microsystems in addition to family and friends would serve to heighten the synergistic effects of these two primary microsystems (Bronfenbrenner 1993).

In contrast, although the students in Budapest focused on the importance of their families, they also focused on personal dimensions of development such as their interests, experiences, and career plans. They spoke about learning languages and traveling abroad as well as their interest in specific academic subjects often connected with career plans. Almost all these students talked about their close ties with their dual language school and of their close friends from school. Many emphasized their membership in community groups. All had been exchange students abroad, and some discussed their host families or international friends. Their orientation toward development as individuals and their identity as students in an international school, as members of community groups, and as international students shed light on the influence of their mesosystems on their perspectives of living history. What emerged were patterns of mesosystems characterized by a greater number of microsystems, e.g., family, friends, teachers, sports teams, host families, with a greater number of relationships among them.

These two contrasting patterns of adolescents' orientation to the social continuum leads us to expect contrasting patterns of political involvement. In the first case of most adolescents in Pécs and Gdańsk the heightened synergistic effects of their two primary microsystems made it easier to predict their low level political interest, knowledge, affect, and behavior. In the second case, we would expect that the adolescents in Budapest would be more aware of social changes that affected people in their communities and nation, as well as changes that affected the possibilities for their own futures. However, precisely because of these diverse influences, we would also expect that it would be more difficult to predict specific aspects of their future political involvement.

The third pattern that emerged was the way that adolescents, in all three cities, situated themselves in time, the historical context. Their responses about the present time were much more detailed than those about the distant past or far future. We expected to find that adolescents centered on the present moment. However, we also found that this view led students to discuss the transitions within an extremely limited historical framework, giving limited consideration to a greatly truncated near past or near future, e.g., their parents' lives or their own futures. Their inability to situate the history of the transitions within a broader time frame greatly limited the scope of their sociohistorical analyses of the transitions.

The Role of Family

> In some young people, in some classes, at some periods in history, the identity crisis will be noiseless; in other people, classes and periods, the crisis will be clearly marked off as a critical period, a kind of "second birth," either deliberately intensified by collective ritual and indoctrination or spontaneously aggravated by individual conflict.
>
> Erikson, 1987, p. 679

These Hungarian and Polish adolescents' sense of self was deeply rooted in their positive feelings about their family identity. They explicitly discussed the significance of their family when describing their own sense of self. Their family focus was strong and demonstrated consistently in their responses throughout the interviews. Students also talked about their families and friends when asked to describe themselves or talk about the important groups in their lives. For example, in Pécs, 84% of the students interviewed in 1991 and 88% of those interviewed in 1993–94 spontaneously identified their family as one of their "most important groups."

The great majority of these Hungarian and Polish adolescents viewed themselves as members of a close and well-functioning family. In contrast to adolescents in some countries, they did not view this stage in their lives as a time of presumed intergenerational conflict. This was true even among those who talked about some disagreements and arguments with their parents.

For most of these adolescents, development of psychosocial identity appeared a quiet process, unmarked by family and friends as "critical." To the contrary, adolescents generally perceived their families as highly supportive and talked about their parents making financial sacrifices for their happiness, thereby protecting them from the negative effects of the changes. This finding regarding the central and positive nature of family relationships in virtually all the adolescents' descriptions of themselves helps explain why their families were so influential in how these adolescents perceived and responded to the societal changes. This finding points to the importance of studying how cultural differences in family relationships can influence children's perceptions of their changing world.

The Role of the Wider World

Adolescents' sociopolitical identity development includes their participation in national as well as local groups. Some group identifications, such as religious denominations, national clubs, or political parties or orientation, connect adolescents to the broader society, the nation, or the world. These dimensions of psychosocial identity are more directly related to the macrosystem. When developing the protocol, we wondered whether students considered such groups important in their lives and what influences they would have. As we have discussed, none of these students spontaneously mentioned affiliation with a political party. We found that a small minority of students in all three cities mentioned the importance of their religious affiliation or national identity. Only a handful of students talked about any connection between this dimension of their identity and the way that they viewed their changing society. Adolescents spent a great deal of time talking about themselves. Few of the students we interviewed considered the social transitions to be important in their everyday lives.

In 1991 we had included several items on nationalism in the protocol. As adult researchers we thought that this was an important issue to investigate at a time when relations between ethnic groups were changing and state borders were shifting. We found it surprising that many students had difficulty discussing this term. Only a few students in each of the cities and in each of the sets of interviews spontaneously identified themselves by their nationality. However, Pécs, Budapest, and Gdańsk, adolescents' sense of national identity showed that nationality was something that they assumed as a matter of course, rather than a facet of identity that had to be defended or demonstrated actively. There was no indication among the students we interviewed that they were nationalistic in a jingoistic sense.

This is an important finding considering the growth of jingoistic, nationalist groups in neighboring countries as well as the groups that existed in both Hungary and Poland at that time. The apparent lack of jingoistic nationalism suggests that this orientation was not supported in their important microsystems such as their families or peer groups. It also suggests that these students would not interpret social changes or define political concepts from a jingoistic perspective. Indeed, in 1993 some students in Pécs and Budapest were worried about militant nationalism in their areas. The students in Pécs talked about the fighting in nearby Croatia fueled by ethnic hatred, and the students in Budapest discussed the activities of militantly nationalistic, anti-Semitic groups in their city.

It is important to note here that this information was uncovered only through casting a wide research net. It also demonstrates the importance of carrying out longitudinal or follow-up studies when studying the nature of transitions. If we had only conducted the initial set of 1991 interviews, we would have concluded that students were not knowledgeable or interested, and would not have witnessed the changes in their knowledge and interest.

The large majority of students in all cities painted their own future as bright, generally brighter than that of their country. This rosy outlook was especially strong among two groups of students: one group focused on family strength, the second focused on individual strength. Here we find the same pattern but two different explanations. The first group was made up of students who had a strong inward focus on their family and a weak outward focus on political, economic, and social changes. This included many students in Pécs and Gdańsk. Their more collective sense of identity involved their membership in a strong family where family members took care of one another. Although many of these students referred to wanting a good job, few talked about individual initiatives such as particular training or the outlook for a particular field of work.

The second group of highly optimistic students was made up of individually-oriented students working toward individual competencies. This group included many students in Budapest. They conveyed a strong sense of feeling that they would be successful in realizing their goals through their own hard work and personal achievement, even if the future national situation would not be bright. For example, as the students in Budapest grew into young adults, they talked more about career plans that were often flexible and based upon the realities of employment opportunities.

The relatively small proportions of students who were quite pessimistic about their futures viewed their prospects as highly dependent on that of their country, Hungary or Poland. They were pessimistic about the national outlook and pointed to economic or political problems that they thought would not be solved. Several declared that they could not "imagine" themselves having a good future unless they moved abroad. A recurring theme among these students was that they could succeed if only they lived in a solid and stable economic climate.

Once again, these contrasting orientations toward the future would affect how these groups of adolescents would perceive future changes and their effects. Based on these findings, we would expect that the adolescents whose optimism was based on their sense of strong family support would be sensitive to future changes that affected their family, but that this sensitivity would be relatively weaker because they would expect protection from their families, even in future times of hardship. Such students would be less likely to venture out to create new possibilities for themselves. In the future, as a group, they would have more limited possibilities, but might be able to withstand greater social changes, except for those that threatened the family.

In contrast, those adolescents who are more individually oriented would be more likely to create new future possibilities for themselves, to choose careers in new industries, to relocate to get an interesting job. We speculate that they would be highly attuned to social factors that would affect their individual futures. At the same time, we think that their individualistic initiative would also make them more vulnerable to future social changes.

Considering the third group, it is important to determine why these students are pessimistic. Perhaps these are the students who most identified with their country as a whole. If so, they are particularly sensitive to its problems. Therefore, they might serve future researchers as the "canaries in the mines," a natural early warning system.

Perspectives on Living History

> But fate always combines changes in inner conditions, which are the result of ongoing life stages, and changes in the milieu, the historical situation.
>
> Erikson 1987, p. 676

The topic *Living History* was the most central to our study of sociopolitical identity formation since it focused on adolescents' thoughts and feelings about the recent and ongoing changes in their societies. We were interested in their perceptions of what changes were occurring in their society and the effects of the changes on their own lives, their families, friends, communities, and nation. This topic, like the others, relates to political involvement, defined as political interest, knowledge, affect, and action.

In their responses throughout the interviews, we found that the adolescents in Pécs, Budapest, and Gdańsk consistently indicated that the changes they considered most important were political changes that related to democracy and economic changes related to a free market economy. When discussing what had changed and what had remained the same, students focused on changes at the national level and continuities at the personal level. Most students had limited but generally factual information about these changes. Their understandings were similar to the understandings of the adults around them but were modified by their adolescent perspective. Both students' current age and their age at the time of the major transitions affected their understanding of changes. Gender and type of school were less important variables.

In the following sections we discuss the interplay of factors that influence adolescents' perceptions of their changing societies. We first review several findings from the three studies. For each group of students, the findings related to *Living History* were consistent with findings from *Growing Up in Changing Times*. We then turn to a discussion of the overall patterns that emerged.

Pécs

The Pécs interviews provide contrasts between the perceptions of students in 1991 and students of the same age interviewed in 1993–94. In the 1991 interviews, students were more confused regarding what they thought and felt about the transitions. These interviews occurred soon after the major changes, but when many changes in laws and institutions were still taking place. Indeed, about 35% of the students said that they couldn't decide whether anything had changed or responded that nothing had changed, although most of these students then went on to discuss changes. During this first set of interviews, when students were asked to identify those changes they considered most important, students were generally positive, particularly in their answers relating to the transition to democracy. In contrast, their responses regarding economic changes tended to be mentioned later and were generally negative. These related findings once again underscore students' high expectations for outcome of the transitions and their excitement about living in a democratic society. They also demonstrate that students continued to focus on economic problems that had been issues during the previous regime.

The students interviewed in 1993–94 placed less emphasis on the transition to democracy. Although their responses were still mainly positive, they were less idealistic. Instead, the students in

Pécs emphasized their perceptions of the worsening national economy. During this second set of interviews, a greater proportion of students talked about the financial effects of the changes on themselves or their family, though few considered these major effects. They were usually able to talk about what their parents thought and felt, some even complaining that they were tired of listening to their parents. Overall, their views seemed similar to their interpretations of their parents' views. These findings once again reflect the central role that families played in the lives of these students; they also reflect the ways in which their parents' focus on economic problems influenced students' perceptions.

When students were asked to list the major events of the transitions, they focused on recent happenings. Consequently, there were differences between responses from the 1991 and 1993–94 interviews. After this brief period of two years between the interviews, students talked about the major events and changes of the 1989–91 period in more general terms as those events receded into the past.

Budapest

Budapest interview data portray the same students over time and provide the clearest picture of how processes of development relate to time and place. In 1991, the students talked about the rapid changes at the national as well as municipal levels. Their responses to these items, like the items relating to *Growing Up in Changing Times*, reflected their more complex understanding of society. Like the students in Pécs, most felt that their own lives and the lives of most family members were relatively unchanged. Most expressed a sense of optimism and hope about the political situation, combined with a lesser degree of optimism that the economic situation would improve as quickly.

By the spring of 1993, most students thought that the pace of change at the national level was decreasing, but they saw more changes, though generally minor, in their own lives. Many were discouraged about the political situation, indicating that democracy was not working, that anti-democratic forces were becoming stronger. They also expressed greater hopelessness about the economic situation.

These students frequently voiced their concern for the welfare of other Hungarians. Most of the students in Budapest reported that their own families were doing all right, but that the gap between rich and poor was widening. They frequently analyzed public reaction. Some pointed to people's initial, unrealistic expectations for a quick transition to democracy and a free market economy.

By 1995, the participants, now young adults, spoke about the changed political situation. They appeared less engaged but, at the same time, less concerned about the future of institutionalized democracy. They seemed more secure that democracy was stable, although they were often very critical of particular parties, politicians, and policies. They were still discouraged about the state of the economy, and once again pointed to the growing disparity between rich and poor. Few were hopeful that the economic situation would soon improve for the majority of the population. Some said that they saw people's lives, including their own, as more serious as people focused on earning enough money. A number talked about the introduction of tuition fees that affected them as students; others who had their own apartments talked about rent and heating bills. This illustrates how the 1995 interviews also marked an important transition in some students' responses, reflecting their increased separation between self and family. When we view this series of interviews, we note that students remained concerned about the welfare of others. Although these students were more individually oriented than their peers, they retained a strong sense of the collective, common good.

Gdańsk

The students interviewed in Gdańsk applauded the changed regime and the general directions of the transitions. When asked to talk about the major changes, they focused on the collapse of the old regime and greater national independence. Students interviewed in 1992 were generally more specific about details of the course of the transitions than those interviewed in 1993 or 1994.

When asked to talk about the effects of the changes and their feelings about them, few offered any in-depth analysis of the effects of the changes on Poland or their city. There was little discussion of any effects of the changes on microsystems such as their school, clubs, or groups of friends. Instead, they talked mostly about what their parents thought about the changes and sometimes gave examples of the effects of the changes on their families. Although some talked about their family's general financial situation, and although Polish polls have shown that adolescents are aware of their family's changing financial situation, none of these students mentioned any changes in their financial situation. Instead, most students focused on the continuities of their family's life, e.g., "we are still together."

In contrast to the students in Pécs and Budapest, students in Gdańsk emphasized that ordinary people had played a role in creating the transitions, albeit in a general way: "the people wanted the changes." These students also spoke more critically about politics and the government than their Hungarian peers. Many made strongly negative comments about the politicians and the course of politics, for example, "what's ridiculous—they (the politicians) don't treat themselves seriously . . . and perform like in a cabaret." The students were also outspoken when they emphasized that the adults in power didn't care about the average person or care about youth.

Conceptualizing Historical Processes

These transitions are the most recent of numerous dramatic and often traumatic changes that have occurred in Hungary and Poland during the past century. First, we found that adolescents' intellectual understanding related to the interpretations that were available to them, particularly within important microsystems. Students repeated commonly heard phrases and sometimes referred to specific expressions of their parents. Second, their emotional reactions to the changes were highly dependent upon the ways that important people conveyed their feelings about the changes. Some students spoke of changes. Others, of crisis. Others, of chaos. Third, the characteristics or nature of the transitions also influenced how adolescents conceptualized historical processes.

We found that students focused on aspects of the transitions adult Hungarians or Poles thought were "historic": transitions to democracy and to a market economy. Like the adults around them, students discussed "living history" in relation to "near history" rather than "distant history." None of the students talked about the broader historical context. They talked about their country's experiences during the communist regime and, in a few instances, World War II or the pre-war period, but never discussed the innumerable pre-war transitions or historical power relationships. When discussing democratization, students talked about their country no longer being in the Soviet sphere, but did not discuss the broader international situation. When they talked about free market economy, few students discussed fluctuations in the international markets.

Similarly, students' emotional responses generally reflected the way that their parents felt about the transitions. As we have pointed out, the Polish students voiced their criticism of the previous regime far more strongly than their Hungarian peers. Perhaps their more strident criticism and their view that ordinary people made a difference in bringing about the transitions is explained by recent Polish history. These students were generally uninterested in politics despite the fact that their city was the birthplace of *Solidarity* and that Poland had experienced more than a decade of opposition to the previous regime. Nonetheless, considering this history, we would expect that students' expressions of criticism of the government would be expressed strongly and will continue to be expressed strongly, mirroring what they heard from their parents and others, even among these students who considered themselves largely anti-political.

From these findings, we see that the nature of the historical changes affected how adolescents conceptualized them. The greatest difficulty for students was that though the transitions were processes—multiple processes, students conceptualized and discussed them as events. For example, students in Hungary and Poland had an idealized sense of what democracy would look like and how quickly it would occur. They could point to a date or a timeframe for the end of the last regime. They sought a similar instant transformation for the institution of democracy and a market economy. They talked about democracy as an on-off switch and were disappointed that the light was not shining brightly. The students viewed the transitions as end-points rather than processes. This finding leads us to think that their further political involvement would be reduced by their decreasing political interest—including their interest in obtaining information—and increasing sense of cynicism.

Patterns of Perception: The Macro-Micro Continuum

We found a dramatic split between most students' perceptions of changes at the level of the macrosystem and their perceptions of changes at the level of the microsystem. Overall, the adolescents focused on what had changed at the level of the national macrosystem. In contrast, they focused on continuities at the level of the microsystem, that is, what remained the same in their own lives and the lives of members of their families.

In all three cities, students talked about national problems of unemployment and national hardship, yet they usually said that they and their families were basically unaffected. This was true even for the few students who went on to talk about their parents losing jobs. Conversely, students rarely associated changes within their family with changes at the national level.

Throughout the interviews, students focused upon their family, and talked about themselves in relation to their families. When asked to talk about the effects of the major changes, most spoke very briefly about the effects of the changes on their country. In Pécs and Gdańsk, most said nothing about the effects on their city.

This macro-micro split was less evident in the responses of the students in Budapest. As we have seen, these students emphasized the importance of microsystems other than their families and close friends, such as school and international friends. Their discussions of the changes included more references to macrosystems, exosystems, mesosystems, and microsystems outside their homes. Their responses were characterized by a more international perspective and included more detail about events.

When we consider this split, we note that for the Budapest students the meaning and influence of the media, a critical exosystem, may have been different. Although they personally did not participate in demonstrations or see debates in the Parliament, when they watched television or read newspapers, they could relate more personally to news stories because they involved places in Budapest that were part of their local, personal environment.

What is the meaning of this macro-micro split, pervasive particularly among students in Pécs and Gdańsk, and, to a lesser extent, among those in Budapest? This split mirrors the separation of public and private worlds often considered characteristic of the previous regime but a split with a much longer historical shadow.

When we discuss it as a pattern of perception, we mean that students viewed events through their parents' eyes, thus dividing the world into different spheres, rather than through a lens that simultaneously perceived the broad continuum and connected the micro with the macro. This means that until these students can view the continuum as a whole, it is less likely that they will perceive the full range of changes along it.

Explaining the Salience of Particular Changes

Our finding of a pervasive macro-micro split helps explain why students emphasized certain changes rather than others. First, most students viewed the transitions and their effects through the lens of their key microsystems. In both Hungary and Poland, different changes proceeded at uneven rates through and across levels of the social ecological system. For these students, the salience of a particular change increased as processes of change moved from the level of the macrosystem to affect students' key microsystems more strongly. For example, many students discussed the higher prices of goods in the stores. The students in Pécs who could hear the shelling in Croatia were those who talked the most about the fighting there. Second, some transitions affected the students' microsystems more rapidly than others. For example, in the first sets of interviews students pointed to the new products that had quickly appeared at local stores. Third, the transitions sometimes took different forms in different contexts. For example, students discussed the effects of free speech differently when they talked about the media reporting news, Parliament debating an issue, and their right to disagree with their teachers. Fourth, some changes affected key microsystem differentially for different students, e.g., the change to a free market economy meant that one student's mother started a new, thriving business while another's mother lost her job.

Families as Filters in Times of Social Change

Overwhelmingly, families were students' most important microsystems. Students were close to and trusting of their families. As we have discussed, parents frequently acted to insulate and protect their children from effects of the transitions in a number of ways, for example, in the way that they interpreted threatening information or environmental changes or gave priority to their children's needs when allocating financial resources. When the students in Pécs and Gdańsk talked about discussing the nature of the transitions, it was usually with their parents.

This family filter was a critical factor in maintaining the macro-micro split. When families downplayed or failed to discuss the nature and effects of the changes, their influence on their children's perceptions was strong and their children were less likely to situate their own experiences within the larger social context at the local, national, and global levels. When we examined all 222 interviews, we were struck by the relatively few references to European or global social, political, and economic forces that had and continued to influence the national processes of change. Few students drew connections between the national and global economy, or between issues of trust in their government and trust in other democratic governments. When we consider adolescent development, this macro-micro split becomes a splint that binds further political involvement.

History through the Eyes of Younger vs. Older Adolescents

These data suggest that adolescents' age at the time of the early, major transitions was an important variable. Memories involve a reconstruction of events and ideas. Our data point to four factors related to age that made a difference.

First, the student's age at the time of major transitions affected their memories of the changes. Students interviewed in 1991 were able to talk about the situation prior to and during the major changes in government that occurred when they were already in middle adolescence. The students of the same age who were interviewed in Pécs and Gdańsk at a later time (1993 and 1994) seemed to remember less about the "time before the changes" that had occurred when they were younger. Their memories were the simpler memories of childhood and early adolescence and, likewise, the feelings they associated with that time were the feelings of younger children.

Second, students who were younger in 1988–91, those interviewed in Pécs and Gdańsk in 1993 and 1994, indicated that the current situation seemed more normal to them. These students were becoming adolescents during the changing times and may have experienced the conditions then as "normal." These young people had a more restricted perspective for understanding normal times, since most of their adolescent experiences had taken place during rapid social transitions. Reflecting this greater sense of normalcy, fewer referred to negative feelings associated with the changes, and fewer talked about the transitions leading to a brighter future.

Third, the more limited life experiences of the younger students made them more dependent for information about the transitions upon what they heard from others in their microsystems. In the case of the students in Pécs and Gdańsk, these "others" were probably family members since families were their most important microsystems for learning about recent events.

Fourth, the data from the Budapest sample suggest that as students matured, they began to view contemporaneous changes in more abstract, systemic ways. Memories of the events did not become more simple. When responding to the items related to the topic *Living History*, the Budapest students' ability to think more abstractly was particularly salient. While the students in Budapest forgot details between 1991 and 1995, their recollections of the transitions involved numerous abstract, complex concepts. In 1991 few of the students discussed the systemic nature of the changes. Most listed the changes as distinct "entities." By 1995, however, more discussed the changes in a more complex and systemic way, i.e., noting relationships among the changes. While more participants said that they were less interested in "politics," perhaps these young people were, in fact, more able to make informed political decisions than they perceived themselves to be.

Understanding Political Concepts:
Concepts in the Construction Zone

The nature of political and economic transitions means that certain words are introduced into public discussion, that historical meanings shift and change, and that collisions take place between new institutions and idealized political and economic conceptions. Additionally, in both Hungary and Poland, new political and economic systems were introduced simultaneously, setting the stage for added confusion. Each country was developing its own realization of these abstractions and, therefore, the meaning of concepts such as democracy, and the institutions designed to realize those concepts were in flux. Terms such as "political right" and "political left" were changing and referred to a political landscape that differed, for example, from that in the U.S. And within each country there was great public debate regarding the manner of instituting these changes. The situation was further complicated by the use of old terms in new ways. For example, "democratic people's republic" referred to old regimes at the same time that "democratic" referred to new.

Polish and Hungarian adults were also having difficulties explaining the political concepts that characterized their new government. For example, in the early 1990s a survey of adult factory workers in Poland found that only 41% of the workers had heard about privatization before it was introduced to their factories. Of these, most felt they knew only general facts about privatization. The majority said they got information about privatization by chance (Balawajder and Popiolek 1993). The decisions that resulted in changes in working conditions were made at the national level, the macrosystem, or the municipal level, the workers' exosystem. It is understandable that citizens in any rapidly changing country require a period of relearning before they can make connections between the new political system and their own local mesosystems and microsystems. The changes that were taking place in the political landscape of Poland and Hungary took time to be implemented and more time to be understood.

Constructing New Meanings Takes Time and Active Experience

Given this background, how did these young people we interviewed in Hungary and Poland understand the political and economic concepts that had become part of public discourse? Most students applauded the changes, but stood on the sidelines, watching "politics" at the national level. They did not see themselves as active citizens. Few had people in their lives who could be models. In Hungary and Poland, there were no cultural expectations that, as adolescents, they should be active. But their experience of everyday life made a difference in small ways, even if they were rarely aware of it.

In the first interviews we found that students' definitions of concepts such as government and citizen reflected the way that these terms had been used in Hungary and in Poland throughout much of this century. They understood the role of a government as the active agent and viewed citizens' roles as limited, e.g., obeying the laws.

Students' definitions reflected the state and status of institutional change during the time of the interviews. In Hungary, for example, the new government spent 1991 focused on developing a new legal system and formulating new laws. Therefore, during the 1991 interviews, when the students in Budapest said that the role of the government was to "organize the country," "be responsible for people," and "make laws," they were talking about vital tasks of a new government during a transitional period. In 1995 their answers "maintain democracy," "protect the rights of citizens," and "protect minorities" suggest an expanded concept of democratic government. This concept of a democratic government includes the rights of the minority as well as the majority, and includes government intervention to protect citizens' rights. If this is what the students meant, their definitions illustrate that they may be unaware of the more complete knowledge they have.

The findings from all three studies clearly demonstrate that students' knowledge of concepts reflected their range of experiences. In 1991, when students in Pécs were asked to define nationalism, many did not know this term and others confused it. In 1993–94 a number of students related nationalism to the ethnic conflicts in the neighboring countries of Croatia, Serbia, and Bosnia. In 1993–94 there was also less confusion between a free market economy and democracy, and a somewhat greater discussion of each. By this time, students had spent four to five formative years in a changing economic system.

The Budapest students' understanding of political concepts also changed, reflecting development from middle adolescence to early adulthood, as well as the interplay of time and experience. As we have noted, their answers reflected their international experiences as exchange students in countries with Western-style democracies and free market economies as well as their attendance at a school with strong international influences. At their first interviews in 1991, most students were able to describe two to four attributes of a democracy. By 1995, the students' responses were more detailed and more focused on citizen participation and the government's vital role in serving the people's interests. These young adults also talked more about ideals of democracy. In 1995, they recognized that under the present economic system people would not become equal in financial terms, but some students thought that for democracy to survive, people had to have a "good" basic standard of living. By that time none thought that democracy and a free market economy were necessarily associated. Their responses show that they recognized that people in a democracy could vote on the form of government, and, therefore, if the standard of living did not meet people's minimal expectations, they could vote to change the form of government.

Many students in Gdańsk had difficulty answering the items related to political concepts, such as the purpose of a government, and, for the most part, their responses were vague. The emphasis of their responses was also somewhat different from year to year, and reflected the political and economic situation. In 1992, more students emphasized the role of a government in organizing the country, a key role during that time. In 1993, there was more emphasis on controlling the economic crisis. Their lack of engagement and their cynicism appeared to be a protection against disillusionment. But, at the same time, it was a particularly effective block to their continued development of political knowledge.

Relationships between Political Interest and Political Knowledge

It takes time for people to construct complex political concepts, and their interest must be maintained over time. High levels of interest across microsystems, exosystems, and macrosystems, and high levels of trust in new political and economic structures are necessary to create a synergy that promotes interest at the individual level.

We found that students associated "politics" with national politics, a great distance along the social continuum from themselves and their families. Students' low interest in politics reflected and paralleled their perceptions of the low level of political interest within their central microsystems of families and peers. The level of political interest was lowest in Pécs and Gdańsk where few students reported discussing politics with family members or friends. Few read, watched, or listened to the news. Of note was one small group of students who had low interest in politics and had parents who talked about current issues with others but not with them.

This finding underscores the importance of parents engaging their children actively if they wish their children to become interested, and possibly active, in politics.

Compared to Pécs and Gdańsk, the students in Budapest showed higher levels of political interest in 1991, reflecting their international interests, the political interests of teachers, fellow classmates, and foreign visitors in the microsystem of the school, as well as the political interests of some students' family members. In 1991 the students were excited to be living in Budapest, which they perceived as the heart as well as the capitol of their country, at a time when they felt part of an exciting new generation. Thus several key microsystems acted synergistically to support the development of political interest. However, by 1993, and certainly by 1995, their interest in politics and in the news had diminished. Some explained that they had less time than in the past; others, that the news and politics were less interesting. In addition, our analysis showed that few had support for continued political involvement from friends, family, teachers, or others. Just when these students became old enough to vote, they became less likely to do so.

When we examine students' level of political interest in relation to the social continuum, we find that while politics was written in capital letters at the national level it was writ small in students' everyday lives. This finding points to the effectiveness of the macro-micro split as a barrier to students' further development of knowledge. In Pécs, Budapest, and Gdańsk, students' assessment of their own low political interests and low levels of interest of those in their microsystems explains why their overall political involvement was so fragile.

When Capacity Develops but Interest Wanes

The Budapest study provides a good though unfortunate example of what happens when students become more able to understand abstract concepts but become less interested in political and economic issues. In 1991, when they were younger, the students at this specialized school were fairly knowledgeable and interested in society at large, including politics. As they grew up, however, their general interest in what was happening in their society, including their political and economic interests, waned as their cognitive abilities increased in their own academic fields of study as well as their areas of personal interest. As a result, just as they were becoming more capable of using abstract and systematic reasoning in other areas, they had less opportunity to develop a complex conceptual framework about their national, social system. In 1995 they were attending different faculties at different universities where political and economic issues were rarely discussed outside those particular fields of study. (Note: In this educational model, university students follow a course of study in one area and, unlike their American peers, do not take a wide range of electives.)

Throughout the interviews, although the students in Budapest discussed their support for democratic concepts and governments, they, like their peers in Pécs and Gdańsk, typically portrayed the government as the active agent and citizens as passive agents. The data from 1995 suggest that the students were beginning to view citizens in a more active role, yet they themselves gave almost no examples of their own activities. This was even true of voting. Almost all underscored the importance of voting and identified their own party preference during the 1991 interview but, as young adults in 1995, some had let their parents decide how they should vote or simply had not voted.

This example foregrounds the importance of a high level of interest on the part of people in adolescents' microsystems in supporting the instigation and development of their political involvement. Perhaps low levels of knowledge can still be a sufficient condition for high levels of political interest and participation, but low levels of interest are insufficient to support political behaviors.

Perspectives: Adolescent Development and Social Change

This exploratory research in Hungary and Poland contributes to our general understanding of adolescent development in rapidly changing societies. Adolescents are an integral part of their changing system. To understand their development, we must view it in the context of the entire system, as we illustrated in Chapter One, Figure 1.1. This means describing the complexity of a system, rather than simply characterizing it as "rapidly changing" or "in transition," as we sometimes did. Indeed, we would expect that initial changes would be fragmentary and often superficial, and that it would take time for these changes to deepen and pervade the system. A coherent sense of sociopolitical identity is grounded in a coherent system. Changes move through a system at different rates and take different forms.

We see in the case of these Hungarian and Polish adolescents that they expected that the changes would be instantaneous and transformational rather than incremental, an expectation that frequently lead to their disillusionment. In the same way, we as researchers had also expected more dramatic changes and bolder findings!

The model we developed that included the social and historical continua, based upon Bronfenbrenner's ecological model, provides a broad framework that illuminates numerous dimensions of adolescents' sociopolitical identity formation. In the case of these Hungarian and Polish adolescents, for example, the use of this model helped us understand why they did not see politics as part of their everyday lives, as well as why they perceived changes at the national level but continuities at the personal level. We believe that this model has wide applications for those who study adolescent development.

When we turn to adolescents' age as it relates to development within the changing system, we found that two or three years can make a great difference in the life of an adolescent. The relationship between adolescents' age and the time of the changes made a difference in their memories of the past, their life histories, and their sense of what constituted "normal times."

The Hungarian and Polish Omega-Alpha Generations

> Historical processes in turn seem vitally related to the demand for identity in each new generation; for to remain vital, societies must have at their disposal the energies and loyalties that emerge from the adolescent process.
>
> Erikson 1987, p. 676

Democratization in Hungary and Poland does, indeed, relate to a new identity in these generations. Hungarians and Poles have high hopes for these young people. In the first chapter we also wrote that whether and how these Hungarian and Polish youth develop the knowledge, interests, and activity associated with democratic traditions will help shape the future of their countries. Erikson underscores that vital societies draw from the vitality inherent in adolescent processes. What "energies and loyalties" will emerge from the sociopolitical development of these young people in Hungary and Poland? Based on our findings, we think that the outcome is dependent on the support they receive from their families and the wider society.

In this research, we found that both Hungarian and Polish students' level of political involvement was generally low and did not increase during the ensuing years. They did not see themselves as involved in politics, which they defined as national politics. They were uninterested, had relatively low levels of factual political knowledge, and did not consider themselves politically active.

Low levels of political involvement may have been adaptive in the past. Perhaps among peoples such as the Hungarians and the Poles who have experienced war, financial depressions, dictatorships, and occupations, one finds culturally adaptive mechanisms evolving that protect children physically, psychologically, and economically. In times of stress, families may become more important and protective. Among the students in Pécs and Gdańsk, we found that families acted effectively as filters. These students did not have high hopes that went unrealized, and they were generally sanguine about both their present situation and their future, e.g., "you can get use to living on an iceberg." Thus, the microsystem of the family played a special role in minimizing the effects of changes in the macrosystem. In a democratic society, these disconnections between public and private, which may have been more unambiguously adaptive in the past environment, are maladaptive, negative forces vis-à-vis the further development of democracy.

There are also drawbacks to the individualistic orientation that was more pervasive among students in Budapest. Their public and private spheres were not so separate and they did not exhibit such a pervasive macro-micro split in the way that they viewed their environment. Their outlook for their own future was rooted in their trust in their own competence as well in their connection to family, friends, and school. At the same time that they are more adaptable, more open to change, it is, however, their more individualistic orientation that may make them more vulnerable.

If these Hungarian and Polish young people are to contribute their energies and loyalties to a democratic society, their families will have to protect them without distancing them from the wider world. Similarly, if the adolescents who are more individualistic are to contribute, they will need social support to become resilient to future hardships.

Furthermore, adaptations to changing social conditions require changes in social support. According to Erikson, a mature psychosocial identity is one that includes a consistent and resilient sense of self. But, at the same time, the model of psychosocial identity development includes the challenge of identity confusion. Both qualities have adaptive dimensions. Positive outcomes of historical transitions require new balances between individuals and society. The transition to a democratic society requires that the Hungarian and Polish adolescents of these omega-alpha generations grow into adults who trust in democratic processes and work to create trustworthy governments.

> We're going to finish our growing up in a free country, a totally free country. We're going to have a different way of thinking.

This adolescent's statement reflects the needed enthusiasm and commitment to a changing ideology. Neither Hungarian nor Polish adolescents can draw from a deep cultural wellspring of optimism about the outcome of the historical transitions. Unfortunately, in both countries, the latest upbeat historical moment passed quickly. The initial excitement about transitions was frequently replaced by cynicism that democracy and a market economy were not instant successes.

The challenge for these adolescents, as individuals, and for their society as a whole is a great one. If a vital democracy involves the vitality of its citizens, from the individual level to the social level, then the process of democratization requires adaptations from the individual level to the social level. This involves the possibility of breaking with the past in order to reconfigure and invent—in other words, grappling with identity confusion. This disposition is a necessary part of a transition to democracy for both a country and its citizens.

If these omega-alpha generations are to develop an identity congruent with the need for active citizens within a democracy, the whole social fabric must change. If, as our research indicates, adolescents' sociopolitical identity formation is inseparable from their social context, adults in emerging democracies must hand their young the tools that will foster political involvement. It is not enough for adults to point to young people and expect that the next generation will harness their vitality to create the futures the adults envision. If these young people are to grow up to enable their societies to become more democratic, their families, communities, governments, and nations are likewise challenged to develop a democratic identity.

References

Angvik, M., and B. von Borries, editors, 1997. *Youth and history: A comparative European survey on historical consciousness and political attitudes among adolescents, Vol. B.* Hamburg: Körber-Stiftung.

Ash, T. G. 1992. Budapest: The last funeral. In *Eastern Europe: Transformation and revolution*, edited by L. H. Legers. Lexington: D.C. Health and Co.

Balawajder, K., and K. Popiolek. 1993. Why people dislike the privatization of their work places? *Polish Psychological Bulletin* 24 (1):15–23.

Berg, B. L. 1995. *Qualitative research methods for the social sciences.* 2d ed. Boston: Allyn and Bacon.

Boski, P. 1993. Socio-political value orientations among Poles in presidential '90 and parliamentary '91 elections. *Polish Psychological Bulletin* 24 (2):151–170.

Bronfenbrenner, U. 1979. *The ecology of human development: Experiments by nature and design.* Cambridge, MA: Harvard University Press.

Bronfenbrenner, U. 1988. Interacting systems in human development. Research paradigms: Present and future. In *Persons in context: Development processes*, edited by N. Bolger, A. Caspi, G. Downey, and M. Moorehouse. New York: Cambridge University Press.

Bronfenbrenner, U. 1989. Ecological systems theory. In *Annals of child development, Vol. 6,* edited by R. Vasta. Greenwich, CT: JAI Press.

Bronfenbrenner, U. 1993. The ecology of cognitive development: Research models and fugitive findings. In *Development in context: Acting and thinking in specific environments*, edited by R. Wozniak and K. Fischer. Hillsdale, NJ: Erlbaum.

Bronfenbrenner, U. 1995. Developmental ecology through space and time: A future perspective. In *Examining lives in context: Perspectives on the ecology of human development,* edited by P. Moen, G. H. Elder, Jr., and K. Luscher. Washington, D.C.: American Psychological Association.

Bronfenbrenner, U., and A. C. Crouter. 1993. The evolution of environmental models in developmental research. In *Handbook of child psychology: Vol. I. History, theory, and methods,* edited by P. H. Mussen (Vol. Ed.) and W. Kessen (Series Ed.). New York: Wiley.

Bruszt, L., and J. Simon. 1991. *The change in citizen's political orientations to the transition to the democracy in Hungary.* Budapest: Institute for Political Science of the Hungarian Academy of Sciences.

Bruszt, L., and D. Stark. 1992. Remaking the political field in Hungary: From the politics of confrontation to politics of competition. In *Eastern Europe in Revolution,* edited by I. Banac. Ithaca: Cornell University Press.

CBOS. 1992a. *Poland in adolescents' eyes.* Warsaw: Public Opinion Research Center.

CBOS. 1992b. *Polish adolescents in 1992.* Warsaw: Public Opinion Research Center.

CBOS. 1994a. *Adolescents' views about politics.* Warsaw: Public Opinion Research Center.

CBOS. 1994b. *Adolescents in their eyes: Values, customs, problems.* Warsaw: Public Opinion Research Center.

CBOS. 1994c. *Evaluation of material / financial situation of adolescents.* Warsaw: Public Opinion Research Center.

CBOS. 1994d. *Significant others: Parents or peers.* Warsaw: Public Opinion Research Center.

CBOS. 1996a. *Adolescents and school.* Warsaw: Public Opinion Research Center.

CBOS. 1996b. *Adolescents' plans, goals and aspirations.* Warsaw: Public Opinion Research Center.

CBOS. 1996c. *Evaluation of material / financial situation of adolescents.* Warsaw: Public Opinion Research Center.

Chivian, E., J. P. Robinson, J. R. H. Tudge, N. P. Popov, and V. G. Andreyenkov. 1988. American and Soviet teenagers' concerns about nuclear war and the future. *New England Journal of Medicine* 309:407–413.

Cichowicz, M. 1993. Lyrical Model of Capitalism. In *To be young in 1992*, edited by K. Kosela. Warsaw: Public Opinion Research Center.

Creswell, J. W. 1998. *Qualitative inquiry and research design: Choosing among five traditions.* Thousand Oaks, CA: Sage Publications.

Csepeli, G. 1993. The school of freedom. In *State and citizen: Studies on political socialization in post-communist Eastern Europe,* edited by G. Csepeli, K. László, and I. Stumpf. Budapest: Institute of Political Science, Hungarian Center for Political Education.

Csepeli, G., L. Kéri, and I. Stumpf, editors. *State and citizen: Studies on political socialization in post-communist Eastern Europe.* Budapest: Institute of Political Science, Hungarian Center for Political Education.

Csepeli, G., and A. Örkény. 1993. Conflicting loyalties, citizenship and national identity in Hungary and eastern Europe. In *Reconceptualizing politics, socialization and education,* edited by R. R. Farnen. Oldenburg: Bibliotheks- und Informationssystem der Universität Oldenburg.

Curtis, G. E. (Ed.) 1994. *Poland: A country study.* Washington D.C.: Library of Congress, Federal Research Division.

Czapinski, J. 1994. The anchorage of the Polish soul: Social indicators of psychological well-being in the systematic transformation period. *Polish Psychological Bulletin* 25 (3):163–185.

Davies, N. 1984. *The heart of Europe: A short history of Poland.* Oxford: Clarendon Press.

Dawson, R. E., K. Prewitt, and K. S. Dawson. 1977. *Political socialization, 2d Ed.* Boston: Little, Brown and Company.

Dekker, H. and R. Meyenberg. 1991. *Politics and the European younger generation: Political socialization in Eastern, Central and Western Europe.* Oldenburg: Bibliotheks- und Informationssystem der Universität Oldenburg.

Denzin, Norman K. 1970. *The research act: A theoretical introduction to sociological methods.* Chicago: Aldine Publishing Company.

Derleth, J. 1997. *Politics in East and Central Europe.* New York: Prentice Hall.

Dziewanowski, M. K. 1977. *Poland in the twentieth century.* New York: Columbia University Press.

Easton, D. and J. Dennis. 1969. *Children in the political system: Origins of political legitimacy.* New York: McGraw Hill.

284 *References*

Echikson, W. 1992. Bloc Buster. In *Eastern Europe: Transformation and revolution*, edited by L. Legters. Lexington: D.C Health and Co.

Elder, G. H., J. Modell, and R. D. Parke. 1993. Studying children in a changing world. In *Children in Time and Place: Developmental and Historical Insights*, edited by G. H. Elder, J. Modell, and R. D. Parke. New York: Cambridge University Press.

Erikson, E. 1987. Psychosocial identity. In *Selected papers from 1930 to 1980, Erik Erikson*, edited by S. Schlein. New York: W. W. Hutton.

Erikson, E. H. 1950. *Childhood and society*. New York: W. W. Norton.

Erikson, E. H. 1964. *Insight and responsibility*. New York: W. W. Norton.

Erikson, E. H. 1982. *The life cycle completed: A review*. New York: W. W. Norton Company.

Erikson, E., J. Erikson, and H. Kivnick. 1986. *Vital involvement in old age*. New York: W. W. Norton and Co.

Farnen, R. 1993. Cognitive maps: The implications of internal schemata (structures) versus external factors (content and context) of cross-national political research. In *State and citizen: Studies on political socialization in post-communist Eastern Europe*, edited by G. Csepeli, L. Kéri, and I. Stumpf. Budapest: Institute of Political Science, Hungarian Center for Political Education.

Fatyga, B., G. Fluderska, and J. Wertenstein-Zulawski. 1993. Polish adolescents' everyday life. In *To be young in 1992*, edited by K. Kosela. Warsaw: Public Opinion Research Center.

Fratczak-Rudnicka, B. 1988. Political socialization in Poland. In *European studies: Politics and the European younger generation*, edited by H. Dekker and R. Meyenberg. Oldenburg: Bibliotheks- und Informationsystem der Universitat Odenburg.

French, P., and J. Van Hoorn. 1986. Half a nation saw nuclear war and nobody blinked? *International Journal of Mental Health* 15 (1–3):276–297.

Gallup Hungary Ltd. 1994. *New York Times*.

Gazsó, F. 1993. The processes of political socialization in the school. In *State and citizen: Studies on political socialization in post-communist Eastern Europe*, edited by G. Csepeli, L. Kéri, and I. Stumpf. Budapest: Institute of Political Science, Hungarian Center for Political Education.

Glaser, B. G. and A. L. Strauss. 1967. *The discovery of grounded theory; strategies for qualitative research*. Chicago: Aldine Pub. Co.

Gieysztor, A., S. Kieniewicz, E. Rostworowski, J. Tazbir, and H. Wereszycki. 1979. *History of Poland. 2d Ed.* Warsaw: Polish Scientific Publishers.

Griffin, M. 1994. Hungary. In *Encyclopedia Britanica Yearbook*. Chicago.

Griffin, M. 1996. Hungary. In *Encyclopedia Britanica Yearbook*. Chicago.

Halecki, O. 1957. *Poland.* New York: Frederick A. Praeger.

Hankiss, E., R. Manchin, L. Füstös, and Á. Szakolczai. 1982. *Off track? Changes in the value system of Hungarian society.* Vol. 1–2. Budapest: Szociólogiai Kutató Intézet.

Haste, H., and J. Torney-Purta, eds. 1992. *The development of political understanding: A new perspective.* San Francisco: Jossey-Bass.

Hyman, H. H. 1959. *Political socialization.* Glencoe, IL: The Free Press.

Inhelder, B., and J. Piaget. 1958. *The growth of logical thinking from childhood to adolescence.* New York: Basic Books.

Jansen, G., and A. Peshkin. 1992. Subjectivity in qualitative research. In *The Handbook of qualitative research in education,* edited by M. LeCompte, W. Millroy, and J. Preissle. San Diego, CA: Academic Press.

Jennings, K. M., and R. G. Niemi. 1981. *Generations and politics.* Princeton: Princeton University Press.

Kéri, L. 1993. Facing new challenges: Possible dilemmas of political socialization in Hungary. In *State and citizen: Studies on political socialization in post-communist Eastern Europe,* edited by G. Csepeli, L. Kéri, and I. Stumpf. Budapest: Institute of Political Science, Hungarian Center for Political Education.

Kéri, L., and Z. Békés. 1997. Youth and history—Hungarian peculiarities. In *Youth and history: A comparative European survey on historical consciousness and political attitudes among adolescents, Vol. A,* edited by M. Angvik, and B. von Borries. Hamburg: Körber-Stiftung.

Komlósi, S., ed. 1974. Patterns of parental behavior. Vol. XIV, *Pszichológiai Tulmányok.* Budapest: Akadémiai Kiadó.

Korboński, A. 1992. Poland: 1918–1990. In *The Columbia history of Eastern Europe in the Twentieth Century,* edited by J. Held. New York: Columbia University Press.

Korzeniowski, K. 1993. Is it possible to build a democracy in Poland? A psychological analysis of threats. *Polish Psychological Bulletin* 24 (2):109–119.

Langton, K. P. 1969. *Political socialization.* Glencoe, IL: The Free Press.

Ministry of Foreign Affairs. 1996. *Fact sheets on Hungary: The Hungarian education system.* Author: Budapest.

Najdowski, J. 1993. Lost hopes season. In *To be young in 1992,* edited by K. Kosela. Warsaw: Public Opinion Research Center.

Nelson, H. D. 1983. *Poland: A country study.* Washington, D.C.: American University.

Niemi, R. 1973. G. Political socialization. In *Handbook of political psychology,* edited by J. N. Knutsen. San Fransico: Jossey-Bass Publishers.

Okey, R. 1986. *Eastern Europe: 1740–1985. 2nd ed.* Minneapolis: University of Minnesota Press.

Pataki, F. 1991. Family orientation and parental models of life in secondary school students. In *Children and family structures,* edited by M. Kalliopuska. Lahti, Finland: University of Helsinki.

Pataki, J. 1992. Hungarians dissatisfied with political change. *REF/RL* 44 (6):66–67.

Patton, M. Q. 1990. *Qualitative evaluation and research methods. 2d Ed.* Newbury Park, CA: Sage Publications.

Rady, M. 1992. History of Hungary. In *Eastern Europe and the Commonwealth of Independent States.* Rochester: Europa Publications Limited.

Reykowski, J. and Z. Smolenska. 1993. Collectivism, individualism, and interpretation of social change: Limitations of a simplistic model. *Polish Psychological Bulletin* 24 (2):89–107.

Reykowski, J. 1996. *Psychological factors in functioning of democratic institutions: Final report.* Warsaw: Polish Academy of Science.

Rothschild, J. 1993. *Return to diversity: A political history of East and Central Europe since World War II.* 2d ed. New York: Oxford University Press.

Rubin, H. J., and I. S. Rubin. 1995. *Qualitative interviewing: The art of hearing data.* Thousand Oaks, CA: Sage Publications.

Schöpflin, G. 1992. World Affairs: Hungary. *Encyclopedia Britanica: Book of the Year.* Chicago: Encyclopedia Britanica.

Schöpflin, G. 1993. World Affairs: Hungary. *Encyclopedia Britanica: Book of the Year.* Chicago: Encyclopedia Britanica.

Schöpflin, G. 1994. World Affairs: Hungary. *Encyclopedia Britanica: Book of the Year.* Chicago: Encyclopedia Britanica.

Schöpflin, G. 1996. World Affairs: Hungary. *Encyclopedia Britanica: Book of the Year*. Chicago: Encyclopedia Britanica.

Sigel, R. S., and M. B. Hoskin. 1981. *The political involvement of adolescents*. New Brunswick, NJ: Rutgers University Press.

Simon, T., J. Van Hoorn, L. Chivian, and S. Hollan. 1990. *Hungarian adolescents' hopes and worries: Relationship to health and illness*: Non-published manuscript.

Skarzyńska, K. and K. Chmielewski. 1995. Young people in the world of politics: Associated with the new system or alienated from it? *Polish Psychological Bulletin* 26 (1):57–71.

Smith, M. B. 1973. Political attitudes. In *Handbook of political psychology*, edited by J. N. Knutsen. San Fransisco: Jossey-Bass Publishers.

Solantaus, T. 1990. *Mental health of young people and the threat of nuclear war: Socioepidemiological and activity theoretical studies*. Helsinki, Finland, Department of Public Health, Helsinki University.

Stefanowicz, J. 1996. Poland. In *Perceptions of Security: Public Opinion and Expert Assessment in Europe's New Democracies*, edited by R. Smoke. Manchester: Manchester University Press.

Stumpf, I. 1993. Political socialization of the new generation: Alliance of Young Democrats. In *State and citizen: Studies on political socialization in post-communist Eastern Europe*, edited by G. Csepeli, L. Kéri, and I. Stumpf. Budapest: Institute of Political Science, Hungarian Center for Political Education.

Szabó, M. 1991. Political socialization in Hungary. In *Politics and European younger generation: Political socialization in eastern, central and western Europe*, edited by R. Meyenberg and H. Dekker. Oldenburg: Bibliotheks- und Informationssystem der Universität Oldenburg.

Szabó, M. 1992. Contradictions and dilemmas of European and Hungarian identity. In *Perceptions of Europe in East and West*, edited by R. Meyenberg and H. Dekker. Bibliotheks- und Informationssystem der Universität Oldenburg.

Taras, R. 1986. *Poland: Soviet state, rebellious nation*. Boulder, CO: Westview Press.

The Economist Intelligence Unit. 1996. Annual Survey of Political and Economic Background of Hungary: Country Profile. London.

The Europa World Year Book. 1996. Poland. *Vol. 2. Kazakstan-Zimbabwe:* Europa Publications Limited.

Van Hoorn, J., and P. French. 1986. Facing the nuclear threat: A cross-age comparison. In *Growing up scared? The psychological effects of the nuclear threat on children*, edited by B. Berger-Gould, S. Moon, and J. Van Hoorn. Berkeley: Open Books.

Van Hoorn, J., and P. French. 1988. Different age groups' similar outlook on nuclear war (comment). *American Psychologist* 43 (9):276–279.

Van Hoorn, J., and P. LeVeck. 1990. Adolescents' and young adults' response to horrendous-type death. In *Horrendous death, health, well-being*, edited by D. Leviton. Washington, D. C.: Harper and Row, Hemisphere Press.

Van Hoorn, J., and P. LeVeck. 1992. Young adults' understanding of political issues: A social-ecological analysis. In *The development of political understanding: A new perspective,* edited by H. Haste and J. Torney-Purta. San Francisco: Jossey-Bass.

Van Hoorn, J., P. LeVeck, and P. French. 1989. Transitions in the nuclear age: Late adolescence to early adulthood. *Journal of Adolescence* 12:41–53.

Vári-Szilágyi, I. 1992. Jövö: Vonz vagy taszít? In *Társadalom és Felsöoktatás II,* edited by Z. Solymosi. Budapest: Felsooktatasi Koordinácios Iroda.

Wandycz, P. S. 1974. The lands of partitioned Poland, 1795–1918. *A history of East Central Europe, Vol. 7.* Seattle, WA: University of Washington.

Appendix A

Interview Protocol

Name_____

Age_____ Sex: M F

School_____ Grade_____

City/Town in which you live_____

INSTRUCTIONS: Prior to beginning, discuss issues of confidentiality, fluency.

1. First would you please tell me about yourself.
   a. What are your main interests?
   b. Tell me a little about your life history.
   c. Tell me how you would describe your main personality characteristics, both positive and negative, as you see yourself.
   d. People sometimes describe themselves as part of a group that is important to them: their family, their city, their clubs, their school or school class, their religion, their country, the region in which country is, or the world. When you think about your identity, which of these groups is most important to you? You may name more than one.
   e. When you think about yourself, what are the 3 or 4 most important values in your life?
      1. Are your values similar to or different from those of your mother?
      2. Your father?
      3. Your good friends?

*f. If you had three wishes, what would they be? You can wish for anything, from the personal to the global. (Explain if necessary.)

g. What are your three greatest fears?

‡h. In your opinion, if you have children, will their life be
1. better than yours?
2. the same as yours?
3. worse than yours?
4. or would you say that you don't know?

i. Tell me a little about your parents:
1. Father's education _____
2. Father's occupation and position _____
3. Mother's education _____
4. Mother's occupation and position_____

‡j. 1. Compared to your parents' life, do you think that your life has been
   a. better?
   b. same?
   c. worse?
   d. I can't decide
2. Compared to your father's life, do you think that your life has been
   a. better?
   b. same?
   c. worse?
   d. I can't decide
3. Compared to your mother's life, do you think that your life has been
   a. better?
   b. same?
   c. worse?
   d. I can't decide
4. Comments:

‡k. When you think about the future, do you generally feel
1. very optimistic?
2. fairly optimistic?
3. sometimes optimistic/sometimes pessimistic?
4. fairly pessimistic?
5. very pessimistic?
Comments:

1. News:
   1. How often do you read the news in newspaper?
      Which paper do you read most often?
   2. How often do you listen to the news on the radio?
      Station?
   3. How often do you watch the news on TV?
      Channel?
2. We are interested in what it is like to be a teenager in Hungary/
   Poland at this time. We are interested in your opinions about the
   things that stay the same and the things that have changed in your
   life, in Hungary/Poland, and in the world in the past few years.
3. First I would like to ask you some questions about what things have
   stayed the same (unchanged) in the past few years since you were
   _____ years old.
   a. What in your life has remained unchanged in the past 3–4 years?
   b. When you think about your family, what has remained unchanged
      in the past 3–4 years?
   c. When you think about the area in which you live, what has re-
      mained unchanged in the past 3–4 years?
   d. When you think about Hungary/Poland, what has remained un-
      changed for the past 3–4 years?
   e. When you think about this region in Europe, what has remained
      unchanged for the past 3–4 years?
4. What countries do you consider part of the same region as Hungary/
   Poland?
   a. When you think about Europe, what has remained unchanged for
      the past 3–4 years?
   b. When you think about the world, what has remained unchanged
      for the past 3–4 years?
5. Now I'd like you to tell me what are the most important changes that
   have taken place in Hungary/Poland during the past 4 years (since
   19___)?
   a. Which do you think are the 2–3 most important?
      1.
      2.
      3.
      Comments:

6. Analysis of each of the above 2–3 most important changes
   #1_____ #2_____ #3_____
   (NOTE: The same series of items are repeated for the 2 and 3 most important changes.)
   a. When did this change begin?
   b. Tell me, what were things like before this change?
   c. How are things now?
   d. Did this change happen slowly or quickly?
   e. What were the reasons that this change happened?
   f. (If appropriate) Did ordinary citizens/people have any influence in making this change? _____ How?
      1. Did your parents?
      2. People whom your family knows?
      3. You?
      4. Classmates?
      5. Other young people?
   g. I am interested in your opinions about the effects of this change.
      1. What are the effects on Hungary/Poland?
      2. What are the effects on (your city)?
      3. What are the effects on your neighborhood/the area in which you live?
      4. What are the effects of your family?
      5. What are the effects on you?
   h. Does this change affect everyone equally (for example, people in the cities, people in farm areas, workers, middle class, intelligentsia, minority groups)?
   i. (Explain scale regarding feeling about change)
      Very negative _____ very positive
      | 1   2   3   4   5   6   7|
      1. How do you feel about this change?

         | 1   2   3   4   5   6   7|
      2. How do you think your mother feels?

         | 1   2   3   4   5   6   7|
      3. How do you think your father feels?

         | 1   2   3   4   5   6   7|
      4. How do you think most of your friends feel?

         | 1   2   3   4   5   6   7|

5. How do you think most Hungarians/Polish people feel?

1	2	3	4	5	6	7

6. Who in Hungary/Poland favors this change the most?

1	2	3	4	5	6	7

7. Who in Hungary/Poland favors this change the least?

1	2	3	4	5	6	7

7. Now I'd like to talk to you again about the overall changes and also the events that have taken place in the past 3–4 years. Could you please give me a brief, historical picture of the major events that changed Hungary/Poland in the past 3–4 years? List the important events that you remember. You may put in as many or as few as you wish. If there are some events that occurred at about the same time, or if you are not sure of the order, you may put the events together as a group. Use the line below to draw a time line—like in a history book. (Use time line on separate page.)

§8. Democratization (if not mentioned)
   a. What do you see as the key features that any country has to have to be a democracy?
   b. This is a list of possible features. For each one, please tell me if you think that it is essential/non essential (basic) for a country to be a democracy.
      1. trial by jury
      2. more than one political party
      3. separation of powers
         e.g., legislative, judicial, executive branches
      4. right to hold private property
      5. good standard of living
      6. free elections
      7. right to criticize the government
      8. a written constitution
      9. principles of majority rule
      10. freedom of speech
      11. freedom to travel abroad
      12. freedom to emigrate
      13. the right to have free medicine and education
   c. When you think about freedom, what does it mean to you to have freedom in a country?
      1. Do you think that you have freedom to disagree in school?
         a. Now?
         b. Before?

9. When you think of a "free market economy," what are the basic characteristics or the most important features?
10. Overall, what do you see as the purpose of a government?
11. You have been talking about a lot of changes, how does living in this time of change affect your development as a person? When you are five years older (_____ years), and look back on this time, how do you think you will think that it has affected your development as a person?
12. We have discussed the changes that you think are very important. How do these changes influence how you think about Hungary/Poland and being Hungarian/Polish?
13. Have these changes influenced how you think about political change?
    a. Previous involvement:
       1. Before these changes, were you involved in politics?
       2. Your family?
       3. Your friends?
    b. After these changes, are you more/less likely to be involved in politics at any level (local/national)?
    c. Do you support any political program or party?
       Why?
    d. If you were old enough to vote, would you vote?
    e. How would you vote?
14. In some countries, schools have programs for citizenship education to teach students about the form of government and the role of the citizen.
    a. Was there something like that in your school before these changes? What was taught?
    b. Now? What is taught?
    c. What do you see as the changes in the program?
    d. What do you think it means to be a "good citizen?"
    e. Was it different before the changes?
    f. What should be the role of the school in preparing you and other students to be a citizen? What would you like to learn about citizenship in school?
    g. What does it mean to be "patriotic?"
15. (Models)
    a. Can you name a country where teenagers have the kind of life you think of as a "good life"? Why?
    b. What country do you see as a model for the kind of society you would like to have in Hungary/Poland? Why?
    c. Who are 1–3 people in the world you admire the most? Why?

16. If you imagine Hungary/Poland in ten years as a "good place to live," describe the living style.
17. a. What are the things that make you proud to be Hungarian/Polish?
    b. What are the things that make you not so proud?
18. Hungary/Poland/U.S./U.S.S.R. questions (asked in 1991):
    a. In a few words, tell me about the present relationship between Hungary and the U.S.S.R.?
    b. In a few words, tell me about the present relationship between Hungary/Poland and the U.S.?
    c. In a few words, tell me about the present relationship between the U.S. and the U.S.S.R.?
19. Some people say that there is an increase in nationalism here. Do you agree? Explain? How do you feel about that?
§20. Opinions about self, town, country, Europe, the world.

*Solantaus (1990)
‡Chivian et al. (1988)
§Sigel and Hoskin (1981)

Appendix B

Table B-1
Pécs Students' Perceptions of Groups that Are Important to Them in 1991 and 1993–94

Description	1991	1993–94
Family	84%	88%
Sport team	41%	37%
Social club	33%	12%
Friends	30%	55%
Religion	19%	21%
Nation	17%	6%

Table B-2
Pécs Students' Wishes and Fears 1991 and 1993–94

Wishes	1991	1993–94	Fears	1991	1993–94
Financial welfare	45%	22%	War	38%	34%
Happy family	31%	38%	Own illness	34%	16%
Own health	30%	21%	Own death	31%	21%
Peace	25%	28%	Loneliness	19%	13%
Good job	17%	4%	Poverty	17%	3%
Success at school	17%	19%	Death of family member	11%	13%

Table B-3
Pécs Students' Understandings of Nationalism and Patriotism in 1991 and 1993–94

What is the meaning of "nationalism"?	1991	1993–94
Don't know	42%	30%
Emphasis on national consciousness at the expense of other countries	22%	41%
Racial segregation	11%	41%
National feeling	8%	14%

What is the meaning of "patriot"?	1991	1993–94
Lives for country	23.4%	10.3%
True to country	18.8%	8.8%
Does a lot for his/her country	15.6%	32.4%
Loves his/her country	17.2%	4.4%
Same as citizen	7.8%	11.8%

Appendix C

Table C-1
Major Themes in Budapest Students'
Responses: Identification of the Major Changes in 1991

Theme 1: Systemic changes (11)
freedom of whole system
new way of thinking
our future is in our hands
more free—after 400 years
iron curtain disappears
separate from Soviet Union
open to West
Western influence, mostly bad
more foreign books and culture

Theme 2: Political changes (29)
political way of thinging
good political changes (3)
new government
multi-party system/free elections (5)
Hungary not yet really democratic
think/speak freely (11)
freedom to travel (6) (Note: This
    occurred in 1988 or 1989)
leaders not ready to lead

Theme 3: Economic changes (30)
economic changes
people can make own decisions about work
more job possibilities (2)
new businesses
privatization of factories
economy is getting worse
inflation (11)
decreased standard of living
increased difference between rich and poor
a few people get rich in "not so legal" ways
personal taxation
increased unemployment (2)
no more security
"people are losing control over their greed"
foreign companies
more goods in shops (2)
more western goods

Theme 4: Education (4)
education more open, more choice
may have to pay for education
new education scholarships
don't have to learn Russian in school
    (Note: this occurred in 1989)

Theme 5: Religion (4)
religious freedom (3)
changed role of the church

Theme 6: Other (3)
privatization of health care

Theme 7: Changes are not that significant (7)

299

Appendix D

Table D-1
Gdańsk Students' Perceptions of What
Remained Unchanged

Most Common Responses	1992–94 (n = 59)
Nothing has changed	36%
Living standards are the same	37%
Everything has changed	29%

Table D-2
Gdańsk Students' Perceptions of the
Most Important Changes

Most Common Responses	1992–94 (n = 59)
Wałęsa becomes president	42%
End of communism	36%
Quarrels in government	20%
Criticism of the government	12%
Change of economic system	10%
Increasing influence of the Catholic Church	7%

Index

free market economy, 243–244
political involvement, 246
purpose of a government, 240–241
Gierek, E., 203
Gieysztor, A. S., 200
Golden Bull, 61
Gömbös, G., 63
Gomulka, W., 203
good citizen, 51, 53, 78
good life in twenty years
Budapest study, 160–161
Gorbachev, 66, 204
government, 28, 50. *See also* purpose of
a government
Green Party, Poland, 213
Griffin, M., 70
Grósz, K., 66–67
group identity
Budapest study, 156–157
Pécs study, 88–89
growing up in changing times, 20–24,
88–96, 154–165, 257–262
Budapest study, 154–165
facing the future, 157–159
good life in twenty years, 160–161
group identity, 156–157
perceptions of how changes
influenced development, 161–165
satisfaction with self and society,
159–160
self descriptions, 155–156
conclusions, 257–262
Gdańsk study, 220–230
facing the future, 226–229
group identity, 223–225
national identity, 225
perceptions of how changes
influenced development, 229–230
self descriptions, 221–223
items, development of, 35–41
Pécs study, 88–96
being Hungarian (national
identity), 90–92, 193–194
facing the future, 92–96
group identity, 88–89
self descriptions, 86–90

Halecki, O., 199
Hapsburg Empire, 61–62

historical context of development, 32–33
Hollan, S., 9
Horn, G., 70
Horthy, M., 63
Hoskin, M. B., 6, 27–28, 50, 52, 121–
122, 135, 295
Hungarian Communist Peoples Republic,
64
Hungarian Democratic Forum, 66, 68,
70
Hungary. *See* Budapest study,
demographic information, 59
economy
inflation, 69, 77, 93, 109, 168
elections, 46, 68–70, 167
history, 57–71
Antall, J., 68
Árpád, Chief, 60
Béla III, 60–61
Beszelö, 65
Bokros, L., 70, 168, 171, 175
collectivization, 64
Csurka, I., 173
Déak, F., 62
Eötvös, J., 62
Francis Joseph, Emporer, 62
Gerö, E., 64
Golden Bull, 61
Gömbös, G., 63
Gorbachev, 66
Grósz, K., 66–67
Hapsburg Empire, 61–62
Horn, G., 70
Horthy, M., 63
Hungarian Communist Peoples
Republic, 64
independent republic, 62
Kádár, J., 65–67, 103, 167
Károlyi, M., 62
King Andrew II, 61
King István, 60
Kossoth, L., 62
Kun, B., 63
Magyars, arrival, 60
Nagy, I., 64
NATO, 46
Németh, M., 67
New Economic Mechanism (NEM), 65
Ottoman Empire, 61